CW00811051

(used)
£12 -
ge

LIKE BLACK SWANS

LIKE BLACK SWANS

SOME PEOPLE AND THEMES

Rara avis in terris nigroque simillima cygno:
Juvenal, *Satires vi, 165*

by

BROCARD SEWELL

with an introduction by

COLIN WILSON

Tabb House

First published 1982 by
Tabb House, 11 Church Street, Padstow, Cornwall

Copyright © Brocard Sewell 1982

ISBN 0 907018 13 0

'A rare bird in our world, and very like a black swan.'
Juvenal.

Printed and bound in Great Britain by
T.J. Press (Padstow) Ltd.

To

MARY SILVERTHORNE

ACKNOWLEDGEMENTS

I AM GRATEFUL to Father Godfrey Anstruther, O.P., for kindly allowing me to read his biography of Cardinal Howard, which awaits publication; and to Miss Elizabeth Poyser, archivist of the diocese of Westminster, for allowing me to see the letters of Cardinal Howard, and other relevant papers, in the archives at Archbishop's House, Westminster. The essay on Cardinal Howard was first published by The Royal Stuart Society, as Royal Stuart Paper no. xv, in 1980.

'George Anne Bellamy' first appeared in *The Aylesford Review*, vol. iii, no. 3, Autumn, 1960.

'Baron Corvo at the Scots College' is reprinted from *The Innes Review*, organ of the Scottish Catholic Historical Society, vol. xxvi, no. 1, 1975.

'Thomas Hardy and G. K. Chesterton: A Contrast' is reprinted from *The Chesterton Review* (Saskatoon, Canada), vol. v, no. 1, 1978.

The essay on Father Vincent McNabb incorporates part of an article published in *The Aylesford Review*, new series, vol. 1, 1968, and some excerpts from a lecture to a conference of The Chesterton Society at York University, Toronto, in January 1977. I must thank Father Bede Bailey, O.P., archivist to the English Dominican Province, for allowing me to borrow, and to retain for some considerable time, the opening chapters of Father Bernard Delany's unachieved biography of Father McNabb, together with Father Bernard's notes, and much related material. I am indebted to the same source for access to Father McNabb's letters to Hilary Pepler.

'Olive Custance' was first published, in 1975, in a limited edition of 500 copies, by The Eighteen Nineties Society, as the opening monograph in its series 'Makers of the Nineties'. The poems of Olive Custance cited in this essay are reprinted by kind permission of The Bodley Head.

'Henry Williamson' incorporates part of an article published in the *Journal* of The Eighteen Nineties Society, no. 9, 1978, of which Society Williamson was the first President. For permission to quote from the writings of Henry Williamson my grateful thanks are due to Richard and Anne Williamson.

The study of Robert Stephen Hawker as churchman has not been previously published. I should like to acknowledge the kindness of Mr and Mrs Peter Melville, who have so often extended to me their generous hospitality at The Old Vicarage, Morwenstow, where one catches the authentic Hawker 'atmosphere'.

The memoir of Hilary Pepler was written to mark the thirtieth anniversary of his death on September 20th, 1951, and has not been previously published. I am indebted to Father Conrad Pepler, O.P., for kindly supplying me with a photocopy of an article by his father which appeared in *Blackfriars* for February, 1950.

'Ann Quin: In Memory' is intended as a frame in which to set some of the letters which she wrote to me. It was originally composed for inclusion in a symposium on her life and work, with contributions by some of her friends, among them Carol Burns, Eva Figes, Robert Creeley, Penelope Shuttle, and others. Sadly, the difficulties of the times have so far prevented its publication.

'Montague Summers' is the text of a lecture given to The Ghost Society, of London, on 7th December, 1981. Like all students of the life and work of this remarkable man I am greatly indebted to the late Leslie C. Staples and to Mr Timothy d'Arch Smith, in whose agreeable company I have passed pleasant hours in reminiscence and discussion of 'Montie'.

For the loan of photographs it is a pleasure to thank Major-General His Grace the Duke of Norfolk (Cardinal Howard); The M. R. Keatin Theatre Collection, Houghton Library, Harvard University (George Anne Bellamy); Mr William Waddon-Martyn, of Tonacombe Manor (R. S. Hawker); the BBC Hulton Picture Library (Olive Custance); Father Bede Bailey, O.P. (Father Vincent McNabb); Mrs Margaret Tremlett (Hilary Pepler); Mr Oswald Jones (Henry Williamson); and Mrs Marion Boyars (Ann Quin). The copyright in these photographs rests with the owners.

Finally, I must thank Mr Colin Wilson for consenting to write the Introduction; Miss Sylvia Bruce for reading the proofs; and Mrs Caroline White for help in selecting the book's contents.

BROCARD SEWELL

CONTENTS

	List of Illustrations	xii
	Introduction	xiii
1	The Cardinal of Norfolk	1
2	George Anne Bellamy of the Covent Garden Theatre	32
3	Robert Stephen Hawker: the Pastor of Morwenstow	44
4	Baron Corvo at the Scots College	65
5	Olive Custance	76
6	Thomas Hardy and G. K. Chesterton: A Contrast	97
7	Father Vincent McNabb	112
8	H. D. C. Pepler	126
9	The Mystery of Montague Summers	157
10	Henry Williamson	172
11	Ann Quin: In Memory	183
12	Monastic Life Today	193
13	Catholic Spirituality, Anglican and Roman	217

LIST OF ILLUSTRATIONS

page

1. Cardinal Philip Howard, with members of his family   xx
2. George Anne Bellamy   31
3. The Reverend Robert Stephen Hawker   43
4. Olive Custance   75
5. Father Vincent McNabb, O. P.   111
6. H. D. C. Pepler   125
7. Henry Williamson   171
8. Ann Quin   182

INTRODUCTION

WHEN, SOMETIME in the 21st century, the *Cambridge History of English Literature* gets around to issuing its volumes on the 20th century, I think it highly likely that the name of Father Brocard Sewell will figure in the index. He is, to begin with, the author of a minor classic of autobiography, *My Dear Time's Waste*, beautifully written, and containing an evocative account of the literary scene between the wars, as witnessed at first hand by the young Michael Sewell, who was G. K. Chesterton's assistant on *G. K.'s Weekly*. But he has also, as the editor of *The Aylesford Review*, played his own distinctive part in the history of literature since the mid-1950s. During the thirteen years of its existence, the *Aylesford Review* was, together with Miron Grindea's *Adam*, probably among the best small literary magazines in the whole of Europe; Fr Sewell became a kind of literary liaison man, bringing together writers as different as Henry Williamson, Ann Quin, Bernardine Bishop, Laura Del Rivo, Michael Hastings and myself. The literary movements that captured public attention during that period were the 'Angry Young Men', the kitchen sink school of dramatists and the Beat Generation; but Fr Sewell's friends and protégés constituted in themselves an independent literary movement, united by his enormous and disinterested passion for literature. Complete sets of the *Review* are now well on their way to becoming as valuable as complete sets of *Horizon*.

But it is not, I think, as an editor or 'literary liaison man' that Brocard Sewell will eventually be judged. A glance down the list of essays in the present book reveals that he seems to be fascinated by rather 'off-beat' figures, like Montague Summers, Baron Corvo, R. S. Hawker and Olive Custance. And this is undoubtedly because he feels that they all reflect some aspect of himself. What seems to fascinate him is the problem of the creative individual *of less than major stature*, and the way that such individuals succeed—or fail—in finding their own place in

the world. To say 'of less than major stature' in no way implies
criticism. The Beethovens and Balzacs and Shaws will always
succeed in creating their own place. Shaw once remarked that, in
his early days, before he had succeeded in 'tuning the Shavian
note to harmony', he was the 'complete Outsider'. But Shaw
eventually achieved success—it took him more than fifty
years—and he ceased to be an Outsider. In that sense, Montague
Summers and Baron Corvo never ceased to be Outsiders; nor did
Henry Williamson, in spite of the early success of *Tarka the
Otter*. Fr Sewell has himself been fortunate in finding his own
'place' in the Church. Yet, as all his friends are aware, he himself
remains something of an Outsider, and his literary work shows a
kind of obsession with this problem of the creative individual in a
more-or-less hostile environment. If he has never, as I have,
attempted to generalise about the problems of the Outsider, it is
because he remains aware of them as individuals, each facing his
own destiny in his own unique way. For him they are, in William
James's phrase, 'stubborn, irreducible facts.' And so his own
work is as central to the 'Outsider' tradition of the 20th century
as the work of Camus or Jack Kerouac.

This is something of which I became only gradually aware. I
first met him in 1958, when I was living in a small Elizabethan
cottage on a farm near Mevagissey; Charles Causley arrived one
day with a small, softly-spoken man in a brown monk's habit,
who listened to the conversation with a friendly expression but
said very little. He made me think of Chesterton's Father Brown.
From the beginning, I felt perfectly at home with him; for, unlike
many people, I have never found anything either odd or alarming
in the idea of being a monk. In fact, I had given careful
consideration to the idea myself at the age of eighteen. It was at
about this time that I came across Thomas Merton's *Seven Storey
Mountain*, and, as a result of this, began at one time taking
instruction in the Catholic faith. I have to admit that this was not
because I was strongly drawn to Christianity as such—in many
ways I felt more deeply in tune with Hinduism—but because I felt
that modern life offered me a number of choices that all struck me
as boring and disagreeable. I didn't want to work in offices; I
didn't want to be a labourer; I didn't want to 'get on'. I wanted to
be a writer, but even that was a kind of second best. What I really

wanted was to be allowed to think, to evolve, to allow something inside me to grow at its own pace. And a monastery seemed the only practical solution. Publication of *The Outsider* in 1956 solved the problem on a practical level, but I was still fascinated to meet someone who had taken the plunge, and who seemed to be having no difficulty in combining the religious life with his literary and intellectual interests.

I discovered later that the 'plunge' had been taken with some hesitation—in fact, that an earlier experiment in monasticism had been unsuccessful. This was when he was twenty, and he wrote in his autobiography: 'From the first I had felt insecure in the life, but it would be difficult to say exactly where the trouble lay. I developed a sort of claustrophobia and increasing nervous tension, and after seven months I decided I had had enough.'

Michael Sewell was born in 1912 and brought up by his grandparents in Launceston, Cornwall. His father was a master at a college in Bangkok, and his mother had died there shortly after Michael's birth. At the age of nine, he was sent away to school at Weymouth College. I must admit that to me, with my working class background, all this sounds rather horrifying. Working class families tend to have strong ties, particularly between mother and son, and I have never been able to understand the far more casual attitudes of the middle and upper classes about such things. But perhaps I am over-identifying when I assume that such an upbringing must have produced some degree of loneliness. At Weymouth College, Michael became interested in Catholicism—it was, he says, basically 'a revolt against the aridities of public school religion'. (He was also, I should mention, incredibly bad at mathematics, and was the only pupil to obtain a nil—out of 300—in the maths exam; a sure sign of the artistic or literary temperament.) He read Belloc and Chesterton, and became interested in the ideas of Distributism. I personally would define this as a sentimental, impractical, 'two-acres-and-a-cow' type of socialism, with its roots in William Morris and the Pre-Raphaelites. But at that time, before various Labour governments had demonstrated repeatedly the shortcomings of socialism, it looked a brave and idealistic alternative to the old British party system. Eric Gill and Hilary Pepler attempted to set up a Morrisian community of craftsmen on Ditchling Common, and when Michael went to see Pepler in 1928, he was offered a job as an apprentice in the printing shop. He was sixteen at the time, and financial necessity, as well as lack of mathematical ability, forced him to abandon the idea of a university education. Then *G. K's Weekly* offered him a job, and he accepted eagerly. Understandably, his Catholic inclinations were strengthened, and he made his profession of faith at the age of eighteen. Predictably, he discovered that Fleet Street was not his spiritual home, and in the following year, he commenced his novitiate at the Dominican Priory at Woodchester. When this failed to work out, he took up the job with Hilary Pepler and spent the next five years at the St Dominic's Press. He was eventually ordained in 1954.

So, compared to many of the 'Outsider' figures of the past century, Fr Sewell has been lucky. By temperament, he is a contemplative. And one of the things that fascinates him is this whole struggle of the contemplative to find a place in our increasingly automated civilisation. According to Marxian doctrine, contemplatives are parasites who serve no useful purpose. But there are many good Christians who hold a similar view. T. S. Eliot once gave a talk on the use of cathedrals in England which ends with an impassioned plea for leisure in modern society; he attacks the view that the Dean and Chapter ought to be continually busy with the affairs of the diocese, and says that good theological thinking requires a certain amount of freedom to stand—or sit—and do nothing. He goes on to say that he himself has solved the problem by working for a publisher, so that he has been able to write precisely what he wants to. And Eliot's words remind us that poetry is also essentially a fruit of 'contemplation'. So is most worthwhile intellectual work. A society in which everybody was made to be 'useful' would soon become as barren and decadent as later Roman civilisation.

It is tempting to say: 'So what is to be done?', and then to generalise about the need for government support of the arts, or for monastic communities, or Utopian communes and cooperatives. But that would be to sidestep the real issue. For there are no general solutions. The real problem is that civilisation has evolved to a point where fairly large numbers of individuals experience the need for 'self-actualisation' (the phrase of the psychologist Abraham Maslow.) Most of these are perfectly willing to work for a living and contribute to the community. But they must also be allowed the leisure to think and evolve in their own way. And it is more than a simple question of free time. In *Heartbreak House*, Shotover asks Ellie—sarcastically—how much her soul eats, and Ellie replies: 'Oh, a lot. It eats music and pictures and books and mountains and lakes and beautiful things to wear and nice people to be with. In this country you can't have them without lots of money: that is why our souls are so horribly starved.' In other words, we need far more than leisure; we need a society that is actively interested in these problems of 'self actualisation'. It is not simply a question of writing poetry or starting a commune. Montague Summers did neither; Aleister Crowley did both; yet both of them remained misfits. Henry Williamson and Ann Quin were both successful writers; but again, both remained misfits. This is a complex problem of individuals, and we must be prepared to treat them on that basis.

And here, I feel, I have come close to putting my finger on Brocard Sewell's importance, both as a writer and as a human being. He is fascinated by these 'Outsiders' *as* individuals, and his work for the past quarter of a century has been focused on their problems. When he told me that he was devoting an issue of *The Aylesford Review* to Frederick Rolfe (Corvo), my first reaction was that it was a waste of time. Rolfe was not only a highly unpleasant man, 'his own worst enemy', but a thoroughly unsatisfactory writer; all his work is too personal, too self-obsessed. I could not understand why Fr Sewell wanted to devote space to such a man. Yet slowly, as I got to know him better, I began to understand. It is instructive to watch him talking to someone who is thoroughly out of sympathy with the whole notion of monasticism, and who feels that becoming a monk is a 'cop out'. (The last time this happened was when he was staying with us a few months ago, and some noisy friends arrived from the local pub.) The kindliness and patience are deeper than mere restraint; he can enter into the position of the objectors with total sympathy. His essay on monastic life today in the present volume contains a passage that summarises his attitude:

'From what has been said so far it might seem that the monk's is a self-centred life. But this is not so. He lives in a community precisely in order that he may avoid the dangers of extreme individualism; and he may undertake his work of self-reformation in the hope that he may progressively become less self-centred and more and more God-centred. The God-centred man or woman sees all other beings somewhat as God sees them, that is, with an intensive love and sympathy.'

So while, for me, Rolfe is ultimately an unpleasant little bore, Fr Sewell sees him impartially as a highly creative individual whose good qualities remained submerged by frustration and material hardship. I judge him by his products, Fr Sewell by his whole life. His view is undoubtedly wider, and therefore truer, than my own.

When he told me his title, I assumed that he was referring to Popper's famous argument about induction: that although the existence of a million white swans does not prove that all swans are white, the existence of one black swan *does* disprove it. Brocard Sewell is here speaking about black swans in the sense of rare birds; but the association remains appropriate. All these essays are centred around the problem of black swans in a society that insists that all swans must be white.

Ruskin had the same thing in mind when he remarked to Yeats's father that as he made his daily way to the British Museum, he saw the faces of the people become more and more corrupt. In such a society, black swans become outlaws and outcasts. But Ruskin, like so many late romantics, has proved to be altogether too pessimistic. There seems to be some law of nature that, no matter how hostile the conditions, black swans continue to exist. So, fortunately, do rare birds like Fr Sewell. And while that continues to be true, black swans will remain a protected species.

COLIN WILSON

Gorran Haven
February 1982

Cardinal Philip Howard, with members of his family
(from a contemporary painting—at Arundel Castle)

THE CARDINAL OF NORFOLK

PHILIP HOWARD is a personality of the Restoration who deserves to be better known. It is surprising how many biographers of King Charles II have ignored this prominent member of his court at Whitehall. Pepys, Evelyn, and Burnet have left us their impressions of him; they all found him good company. But none of them was in a position to assess his achievements as a quiet, wise, and resolute upholder of the Old Religion in the dark days of the seventeenth century, and as a counsellor whose advice, had it been heeded, might have saved James II the loss of his kingdoms. Anthony à Wood notices Howard kindly—Wood always treated Jacobites and Papists better than he did Protestant sectaries and dissenters—in his *Athenae Oxonienses*. Although Howard was not an Oxford man, Wood gives him a very substantial notice as part of his entry on a previous English cardinal, William Allen, who had been a Fellow of Oriel College. 'The next Card. that the English Nation hath been honoured with', Wood says, 'is *Philip Howard* . . . ; who at this day is living at *Rome*. He was born in *Arundel* House, in the parish of *St Clement Danes* without *Temple-Bar* near London, an. 1629.' He was born on 21st September of that year; at the time the painter Rubens was living in the house, working on a portrait of his grandfather, Thomas 24th Earl of Arundel. Philip was the third son of Lord Frederick Howard and Elizabeth Stuart, daughter of the Duke of Lennox. The dukedom of Norfolk had been forfeited by attainder in 1572, when the fourth duke was convicted of conspiracy in the cause of Mary Queen of Scots; the head of the house of Howard at the time of Philip's birth was his grandfather, the 24th Earl; but in 1661 the dukedom was restored to Philip's eldest brother, Thomas. Through his Stuart mother Philip inherited royal blood, and was related to the sovereigns whom he was to serve so well, Charles II and James II.

Philip's great-grandfather, Philip the 23rd Earl, had died in the Tower of London in 1595, and was venerated by Catholics as a

1

martyr. (He was canonised in 1970.) But in spite of this example
of sufferings borne for conscience' sake, Philip's grandfather had
conformed to the Established church, in which his grandchildren
were brought up; but their grandmother, Alethea Talbot,
remained a firm Catholic, and under her influence they were
reconciled to the old religion at Antwerp, where she had taken
refuge from the troubles of the times. Philip and his brothers had
been sent overseas at the outbreak of the Civil War. Their
education was continued at Utrecht. When he was thirteen years
old, while at Antwerp, Philip felt a call to the religious life, and
wished to enter the Carmelite Order; but he was dissuaded by his
grandfather, whom he held in great respect. Three years later,
while travelling in Italy, he again felt drawn to the Carmelites.
But once more he abandoned the idea, this time because he found
that there were in Italy no Carmelites of the Flemish observance,
which followed the constitutions of the Reform of Touraine. It
seems that he was not attracted by the Discalced Reform, initiated
in Spain by St Teresa and St John of the Cross, which did have
houses in Italy.

At this point Philip Howard met an Irish Dominican, Father
John-Baptist Hackett, who was prior and regent of studies at the
convent of San' Eustorgio in Milan. He was greatly impressed by
this religious, and decided to join the Order of Preachers
(Dominicans). This time nothing was to turn him from his
purpose. Immediately, he encountered strong opposition from his
family. Notwithstanding, he entered the novitiate at Cremona,
without their permission. The family reacted at once, and
presented a memorial to the Congregation of Propaganda, in
Rome, seeking to get the errant youth debarred from entering the
Dominican or any other religious order without the sanction of
his family and of the Pope. The family thought it beneath the
dignity of a Howard to join an order of mendicant friars; they also
feared, and with some reason, that if Philip did enter a religious
order, even beyond the seas, the Parliament might declare the
Earl's property forfeit. The whole affair is not a little reminiscent
of the family opposition that another friar of noble birth, Thomas,
son of the Count of Aquino, encountered when he sought to join
the Dominicans in the thirteenth century. A letter from Philip's
grandmother the Countess to her husband the Earl, written from

Antwerp on 29th July, 1645, begins: 'My deerest harte, I receaved yesterday your letter with the saddest news . . . of Philip.' On Easter Monday, 1646 John Evelyn recorded in his Diary that he had breakfasted that day at the Earl of Arundel's. 'I tooke my leave of him', he says, 'in his bed, where I left that greate and excellent man in teares on some private discourse of crosses that had befall'n his illustrious family, particularly the Undutifullnesse of his Grandson Philip's turning Dominican frier.' In the previous January Philip had written to his grandfather, expressing sorrow that 'your Excellence taketh it so ille that I have made myselfe a friare, for God Almighty knoweth very well that I would never have done any such thing, if hee had not inspired and caled mee unto such a holy Religion'. He says that he believes God will give him perseverance, and that he prays daily for all his family; 'therefore most humbly craving your pardon . . . and humbly desiring your blessing', he remains, 'your Excellence's most dutiful & obedient grandchild, freyer Thomas Howard, of the Order of the Preachers.' It will be noticed that on being admitted to the Order he had taken, very appropriately in the circumstances, the name of Thomas, after St Thomas Aquinas.

In the meantime the Papal Nuncio at Brussels had intervened with the Roman authorities on the family's behalf. Philip stood his ground, respectfully but firmly. His superiors had moved him from Cremona to the convent of SS. Domenico e Sisto in Rome; then, on papal instructions, he was sent to complete his novitiate with the Oratorians at the Chiesa Nuova: an odd arrangement, clearly intended to satisfy his family that the Dominicans were not subjecting him to any pressure. Next, Philip himself sent an eloquent memorial to the Holy See, in which he affirmed that his decision to enter the order had been come to with perfect freedom. Finally, he was received in audience by the Pope, Innocent X, who approved his course of action, and authorised him to make his profession.

When Philip Howard was given the habit of the Dominican Order at Cremona he was admitted as a member of the English Province, attached to the convent of the Blackfriars in London. This, of course, was a kind of legal fiction, for the Order no longer had any corporate existence in England, the titular office of Prior

Provincial being held by a member of the Master-General's council in Rome. While he was still studying for the priesthood Philip addressed a General Chapter of the Order on the subject of the reconversion of England, and made this moving plea: 'O my fathers, give me leave to go back to my home—to England—give me leave to go back amongst my brethren—not me alone, but all of my nation who are yet abiding with you, and all that I may gather round me, so that we may at least pour out our heart's blood for the land from which we have sprung; for those, that is, who are our brothers, bone of our bone, and flesh of our flesh.' The Chapter decreed that the provincials and priors of all provinces should be ready to receive English novices, who would be made available for missionary work in England after their ordination.

Under Queen Mary a Dominican community had been established in London at St Bartholomew's, Smithfield, originally a house of Austin Canons; and the Dominican nunnery at Dartford, in Kent, had been reopened; but with the coming of Queen Elizabeth both these foundations were closed. Some of the brethren and sisters departed to the Low Countries, where they maintained an uncertain existence in foreign convents, but managed to send a few missionary priests back to England in secret. It was not until the coming of Father Thomas (Philip) Howard that English Dominicans were able to resume conventual life in houses of their own, albeit on foreign soil.

Philip spent the last two years of his studies at Rennes, in Brittany, a town in which many English Catholics had settled. Rennes was also the focal point of the Carmelite Reform of Touraine, which Philip had so much admired in Flanders. Two of the Reform's principal promoters, the Venerable Dominic of St Albert and the blind laybrother musician and mystic the Venerable John of St Samson, had belonged to the Carmelite community at Rennes; Howard must certainly have heard of them. But by now he was totally dedicated to the Dominican Order. He was ordained priest at Rennes in 1652, by dispensation, since he was a year below the canonical age. But he did not return to England until 1657, when he came to confer with the little 'underground' band of Dominican fathers who were working there. How many they were we do not know; in 1634 there had been twenty Dominican missioners in the country; but during the Commonwealth there were only six who were actually English. To his assembled brethren Father Howard proposed the foundation in Flanders of a convent for English friars only; this would provide a nursery for the training of young friars for the English mission, and a step towards the re-establishing of the Order's English province as a normally functioning body. This was a bold project for so young a priest to put before his seniors, most of whom he had not met before. The Vicar-General of the English Dominicans, who depended directly on the Master-General in Rome, was Father Thomas Catchmay, who was fifty-nine, and had taken over the office of Vicar-General from Father Thomas Middleton. Middleton had been Vicar-General for the past thirty years, and was now aged about seventy. The immediate acceptance of Howard's proposal is evidence of his attractive personality; but neither that nor his noble rank and influential background would have been enough to carry the day. It is clear that he must have impressed the brethren as being a thoroughly practical man of affairs. To get things moving he promised to contribute from his patrimony a considerable sum of money. Father Middleton contributed £200, and the others agreed to raise what money they could.

On 15th December, 1657 the English Dominicans took possession of a property at Bornhem, a village in East Flanders, between Antwerp and Aalst, four miles north-west of Mechelen (Malines). The buildings, which included a church, had been intended for a Franciscan community which never occupied them. Here the new English Dominican community was set up, with Father Howard as the first prior and novice-master, and normal conventual observance was begun. The convent was at the same time a novitiate house and a house of ecclesiastical studies. In 1660 a school for the sons of English gentlefolk was added, in the hope of attracting from it recruits for the Order. (In 1825 this school was transferred to England, where, as the Cardinal Howard School, it flourished, successively, at Carshalton, Hinckley, Hawkesyard, and Laxton, surviving down to the nineteen-fifties.) As a result of all these activities it was not long before the buildings had to be enlarged. An old print of 'the English Dominican College at Bornhem in Flanders' shows a large and rather elegant three-storey building, whose style of architecture might be described as 'Graeco-Flemish', with well-laid-out gardens in front. Also in 1660 Howard established a community of English Dominican nuns at Vilvoorde, near Brussels. At first they were few in number, so that three Flemish nuns assisted in the foundation. Among the founding sisters was Father Howard's niece, Lady Antonia Howard (Sister Catharine Howard, O.P.), who died only a few months later.

In 1650, after the battle of Worcester, the exiled King Charles II had set up his court in Paris. At that time Philip Howard was still studying at Rennes. Trying to discover houses of his Order where the old traditions and observances were well kept up, he visited Paris and Brussels. In Paris he presented himself at the court of King Charles (which soon afterwards was transferred to Brussels). Here he paid his respects to his royal kinsman, who quickly recognised his abilities and began to employ him on matters of diplomatic business. In May 1659 the King sent him on a secret mission to England. Cromwell had died a few months before, and Howard's task was to explore the possibility of a restoration of the monarchy, and to rally support for the royal cause. But on arrival in England he was betrayed by his companion in this dangerous mission, one Richard Rookwood, an ex-Carthusian and ex-Jesuit. He had to seek refuge with the Polish ambassador in London, in whose suite he made his way back to Flanders.

In March 1660 Father Howard admitted to the Dominican Order his brother Francis (Father Dominic Howard), the seventh of Henry Howard's nine sons. 1660 was the year of the Restoration. Philip Howard followed his royal kinsman to England, and for the next two years he was engaged in negotiations for the King's marriage. These involved him in lengthy absences from Bornhem; but in November he was reappointed Prior by letters-patent of the Master-General, the day to day running of the house being left in the hands of the Subprior: an arrangement that did not work well. In 1661 Father Catchmay resigned as Vicar-General of the English province, and the Master-General appointed Father Howard to succeed him, while continuing him in office as Prior at Bornhem until his term of office ran out. In his letter conferring the appointment the

7

Master-General, after paying tribute to Father Catchmay's long and zealous service in that office, says that: 'Fortunately for our purpose we find in yourself that union of youthful strength with the prudence of mature years, and gifts both natural and acquired, that seem to point you out as eminently fitted, in these troublous times, to replace the reverend father in the arduous and exhausting labours of the mission field.'

At Bornhem, where he was now allowed to delegate any of his powers that he chose to, Howard had established a good pattern of regular observance. The normal daily programme of the house was:

5.00 a.m.	Rise. Matins: followed by meditation and first mass.
7.00 a.m.	Schools of humanities.
9.00 a.m.	Schools of philosphy and theology.
10.00 a.m.	Conventual Mass (usually sung).
12.30 p.m.	Dinner. Followed by an hour's recreation.
2.00 p.m.	Schools.
4.00 p.m.	Schools close. Vespers and Compline (said), with sung *Salve regina* and *O lumen ecclesiae* (antiphons to the Blessed Virgin and St Dominic).
6.00 p.m.	Supper.
8.00 p.m.	*De Profundis* and other suffrages, followed by Solemn Silence.
8.45 p.m.	Lights out.

In March 1662 Father Howard was awarded the degree of Master of Sacred Theology. Later in the year he played a principal part in negotiating the marriage of the Duke of York with the Princess Mary of Modena. The marriage, which took place at Modena, in the ducal palace, was solemnised somewhat quietly owing to the non-arrival of the expected papal dispensation. This dispensation had been thought necessary since although the Duke of York's religious sentiments were well known, he was not yet formally a Catholic. Later, in Whitehall, a second marriage ceremony took place, presided over by Howard's ecclesiastic uncle, Louis Stuart, Lord Aubigny, son of the Duke of Lennox.

Some time previously, Howard had been appointed principal

chaplain to the Queen, Catharine of Braganza. In November, 1663 the Queen wrote to the Dominican Master-General to thank him for Father Howard's zeal and care in her service. By this time his term of office as prior at Bornhem had run out, but the community declined to elect anyone to replace him, so he was allowed to retain the office, though clearly this must have been an awkward arrangement. One of the most striking things in the story of Philip Howard is the unfailingly high esteem in which he was held by his religious brethren; there seems to be no record of any dissenting note.

In 1665 the Queen's Grand Almoner, Louis Stuart, died, and Howard was appointed to succeed his uncle in that office. The Grand Almoner was responsible for the supervision of the Queen's chapel at Whitehall, and its college of chaplains. He had a salary of £500, with a further £500 allotted for his mensal fund, to allow him to exercise hospitality on a becoming scale. The Grand Almoner had his own state apartment in the palace of Whitehall, and was addressed, and spoken of, even by the King, as 'My Lord Almoner'. He was the only ecclesiastic of the Roman communion who was allowed to appear at court in his canonical habit, and even in the streets of London. To avoid offending Protestant susceptibilities Howard did not wear the picturesque white and black garb of the Friars Preachers, but the black cassock, bands, and cincture, with silver-buckled shoes, of a continental abbé.

It was in January, 1667 that Samuel Pepys, in company with his friend Lord Brouncker, the first President of the Royal Society, 'he being acquainted with my Lord Almoner, Mr Howard, brother to the Duke of Norfolk', met Father Howard in the palace, where they sat and talked for a while in the Almoner's suite. Pepys formed the impression that he was 'a good-natured gentleman'. He noticed that Howard had attached to an arm of his chair a movable 'deske', or bookstand. This seems to have struck the diarist as something of a novelty. The Almoner, he recorded, 'discoursed much of the goodness of the Musique in Rome', and of the new buildings that the Pope ('whom in mirth to us he calls Anti-Christ') was erecting there.

Later in the day Pepys and his friend returned to the palace, where the Lord Almoner showed them the Queen's chapel and the 'new Monastery'; that is, the chaplains' quarters, where they saw the library, the refectory, and the kitchen, 'where a good neck of Mutton at the fire', and the cells of the Capuchin friars whom the Queen had brought over from Portugal. 'In so good company, living with care, I thought it a very good life,' says Pepys. 'So away with the Almoner in his coach,' he concludes, 'talking merrily about the differences in our religions.'

By 1665 the community of Bornhem, perhaps through the absence of its efficient prior, had got into financial difficulties, and Howard began subsidising it with money raised from his patrimony and from his income as Almoner. He was no less generous in London, where he became known as 'the common father of the poor'.

He regulated carefully the rites observed in the Queen's chapel. In view of present-day liturgical troubles in the papal communion it is interesting to find Howard obtaining from the Master-General of his Order permission for all Dominicans in England to substitute the Roman liturgical use for their own. Perhaps he thought that the Catholic laity might find an unfamiliar rite confusing. Only a few of the Dominicans refused to make the change, which, tactfully, was not insisted on, except in the Queen's chapel, where Howard banned the Dominican rite absolutely, notwithstanding the presence among the chaplains of two or three Portuguese Dominicans. Why he should have done this is not clear.

By the terms of the Royal Marriage Settlement the Queen's Grand Almoner was supposed to be a bishop, and it was a source of annoyance to Howard that the matter of his episcopal consecration was continually being shelved. That he was being treated unfairly was not his prime consideration; for him it was the Queen's dignity, and the rights that had been solemnly guaranteed to her, that were the real issue. Another important consideration was that as a bishop he would have a firmer control over the Queen's chaplains and other foreign priests about the court, and also over the swarms of Irish and other alien priests who took refuge in London after having got themselves into various kinds of trouble at home. The Grand Almoner had, in fact, been nominated to a titular bishopric; but the briefs from Rome authorising his consecration were held up, and never reached England. By these briefs he had been appointed Vicar-Apostolic of All England; but the King demurred at this. He would have been happy to see his wife's rights in this matter respected; but he wanted a bishop with the full 'ordinary' powers of a diocesan bishop, and not a vicar-apostolic, who had only limited and delegated authority, which could be revoked by Rome at any time. The King felt that a bishop who was a mere vicar of the Pope would be more obnoxious to Protestants than a bishop of the normal kind. In this he was probably right.

Howard was always concerned for the good of the oppressed and struggling English Catholics. At Whitehall a bishop would have enjoyed diplomatic immunity from the penal laws against Catholic priests, and with tact and discretion an episcopal Grand Almoner would have been able to do much to help the poorly tended flock beyond the palace walls. There had been no bishop in England since Dr Richard Smith, bishop of Chalcedon and vicar-apostolic, had resigned in 1631 and left the country. This meant that there was no one to administer the sacrament of Confirmation, and that there was no clear and firm discipline over the clergy.

In a letter of 26th June, 1662 to Cardinal Rospigliosi, the internuncio at Brussels, Howard says: 'I may mention . . . my anxiety at not having received the faculties of Ordinary required by my position, as not only the spiritual welfare of Her Majesty's household, but many other matters of importance are affected by the delay, as will appear by the Articles of Matrimony.' He assured the Cardinal that he was not anxious or ambitious to interfere in other people's concerns, having his hands already full enough with the Queen's affairs and his own.

Five years later, on 18th November, 1667, he wrote to Cardinal Barberini, in Rome, saying that for lack of a bishop 'we are worse off not only than our neighbour Holland, but than other nations and missions where there are fewer Catholics than here. Thus the sacrament of Confirmation cannot be administered; and there are many other reasons why a bishop should be granted.' In a letter of the year following, written to William Leslie, the Roman agent for the English and Scots clergy, he puts the blame for the hold-up, and the inconveniences it causes, on bad information received at Rome from 'impertinent and stupid people'. 'We marvelled very much', he says, 'that after having waited so long our mistress the Queen should have been so little considered at the Court of Rome that she has not even received an answer, if it had only been out of courtesy . . .'

In the same letter he tells how he has been able to help an Irish Dominican who, through tactless behaviour, had been put in prison in Dublin by the Viceroy. 'Notwithstanding my great efforts,' he says, 'he still remains in prison, and had I not sent him some succour from here, he might have perished.' Commenting on the inept Roman handling of Irish church affairs, he says that 'if they continue like this they will make those unhappy discords even worse, while His Holiness employs various people who all act against each other, erecting altar against altar, while those in Rome make use of fools (and very often scoundrels), so that if our Most Holy Lord knew all he would see that what is sent by one man is contradicted by another; and if we send from here what is true and wise information, it all ends in sending and re-sending, waiting and more waiting, and hardly anything is accomplished, in fact nothing.' He begs to be excused for his freedom of speech, 'but if you could see and know all that I know, you would not blame me.'

Apparently about to conclude what is already a very long letter, he warns Leslie that when he passes on the information to Cardinals Rospigliosi and Barberini he must not translate it verbatim, but should put it into the proper form, 'quia non omnia omnibus'. He then adds several more pages about abuses which he cannot control so long as he lacks episcopal authority; such as the recent arrival in London, from the Continent, of two English abbesses, with some of their nuns, whose visit seems to have no serious purpose. The Queen is much scandalised that such persons can so easily leave their cloisters, to which some of them seem unlikely ever to return. The King, he says, had complained to him two or three years ago about a similar case, and asked him to deal with it as it was a scandal to see nuns 'gadding about' (the King's own words). 'I replied to His Majesty that I would do my best with regard to the matter, but that having no jurisdiction over them I could not answer for my success.'

On 30th April, 1669 Howard wrote again to Barberini: 'I am compelled with much regret to make known to you the sadness of heart caused me by the confusion and misunderstandings that reveal themselves daily not only without but within the Palace, in the Royal Household itself.' No little harm has been done to religion here through the lack of episcopal authority. 'I suppose there is no nation in all Europe that has a King and Queen as gracious and indulgent as our own, nor have our Catholics ever lived in such prosperity since the orthodox faith perished as they do now. And yet we are as lost sheep as long as the concordat in our favour . . . remains unconfirmed by his Holiness.' And in a letter to Barberini written on 23rd June, 1671, from Windsor Castle, where the court was staying, Howard, writing about the uncontrollable foreign priests harbouring in the capital, says: 'I cannot, without indescribable indignation, witness the abuse of the Sacraments administered by such persons as these, while I have no certain grounds to act upon.'

At court Howard was held in great esteem; but as time went on his presence there became increasingly resented by elements determined on the repression, and if possible the extinction, of the old faith, and complaints began to be laid against him. These grew stronger after it became known that he had had some part in the preparation of the royal Declaration of Indulgence, mitigating the penal laws against catholics and sectaries. His known assiduity in receiving converts from the Established church brought him further unpopularity. In 1673 the Dean and Chapter of St George's, Windsor, denounced him to the King for having reconciled one of their minor canons; and there was trouble over a manual of rosary devotions that he had compiled and published. He had included in this little book the text of some papal bulls listing the indulgences attached to the recitation of the rosary. The publishing of papal bulls was a statutory offence. When the Capuchin chaplains of Charles I's queen, Henrietta Maria, had printed and published the rosary indulgences no one had complained; but now such a storm was raised that it was thought best that Howard should leave the country for a time. He was never to return.

In September, 1674 Father Howard was back at Bornhem, and resumed his duties as prior. In spite of the difficulties and vexations that he had experienced during his twelve years at Whitehall, his devotion to duty and his services to religion and to the Catholic Queen had not gone unnoticed in Rome. Once he had left England there could be no further bar to his promotion. There was now no especial reason to make him a bishop; but on 9th June, 1675, Trinity Sunday, he received notice that the Pope, Clement X, had created him a cardinal of the Holy Roman Church, in the grade of cardinal-priest. It seems that the appointment was made largely on the recommendation of Howard's old friend and confrère Father Hackett, now a member of the papal household. On receiving the news the Prior retired to his cell, where he spent some hours in prayer and reflection. The next day he went to consult the bishop of Antwerp, who advised him to accept the promotion. In a letter to his friend William Leslie he said:

I have lately received yours of May 28 which congratulates a promotion that was no lesse unexpected by me, than it was by you and my other friends. There having been so little of human interest engaged to procure the charge, I may with you look upon it as coming from the hand of God in a particular manner. I hope the same hande will always guide me so, that the dignitie conferred upon mee may be instrumentall toward procuring some advantage to the distracted condition of our poore countries.

At the time of his elevation Howard was much exercised as to how he could hope financially to support the dignity of a Prince of the Church. To a friend he observed: 'I am afraid that my promotion will prove more hurtful than beneficial to the convent of Bornhem, as I have not the means to keep up a Cardinal's dignity.' Someone suggested that the King of Spain would be happy to support him; but this he refused to consider, saying that 'if a man attaches himself to a prince by receiving a favour he is always at the prince's beck, even against his conscience.' He returned a gift of a hundred gold crowns from the Grand Duke of Tuscany, Cosimo de Medici; but allowed himself to accept a similar gift from a fellow-cardinal. The Pope eventually saw to it that he had a sufficient income; but immediately the news of his elevation reached England his family came forward handsomely to acknowledge the honour done to it. On 14th June his brother Henry, earl of Norwich, wrote to him at great length. At the beginning of his letter Henry says that he has had some difficulty in finding a safe means of corresponding with him, 'for fear of offending our masters here', and that in future they had better write under pseudonyms: "Mr Grane' for the cardinal, 'Mr Hay' for the earl: a course which they followed thenceforward. The Earl says that he is going that very night 'to supp with his Ma.ty and the duke [of York]', where 'I will make your compliments and ask if they desire you should write or not.' Time will show that the Earl himself is 'sensibillisimo del honore'. 'I desire your Em. to reckon upon it, that I will ever be a true friend, as well as a kind brother, to one who has ever bin so kind and sincere to me in all my concernes. And I reckon up on it also, that one in your Em. condition now and ever will be as just and kind to me, and the concerns of our family, as all other persons in their posture.'

By the next post, Henry tells his brother, he is sending a bill for one thousand pounds sterling, payable at sight at Antwerp, or in Italy if that is more convenient. This sum the Cardinal may repay, if he should find that he can do so without hardship, either after his death or earlier; but should there be any difficulty the Earl freely remits the sum. He asks the Cardinal 'to add to your traine your nephew Tom', and to allow him 'at my cost' to keep a man-servant, a coach and two horses, and two footmen, 'all in your livery, and to pass as if it were at your cost, though I pay under-hand for it.' He adds that he likes extremely the suggestion that Philip should adopt the style of 'Cardinal of Norfolk'. He has sent to a friend in Padua 'a good store of silver plate, and some very good moveables'. These the Cardinal can have forwarded to Rome for his present service, over the next two or three years, until his condition may be better. 'And do consent, if you please, to put out the armes, if any were now graven upon such plate, and put yours in the place, the which, at your return of it hereafter, may again be altered, and no hurt neither if it remaine.'

The Cardinal left Flanders for Rome accompanied by his uncle William Viscount Stafford,—who was to be one of the victims in 1680 of Titus Oates' Popish Plot scare—the Viscount's son the Hon. John Howard, the Cardinal's nephew Lord Thomas Howard, Monsignore Patrick Con (Cardinal Barberini's agent for English affairs), and Dr John Leyburn, President of the English College at Douai, who acted as the Cardinal's secretary. Anthony à Wood records that on their way the party halted at 'Doway', putting up at the English College, where the Cardinal was received with great solemnity. 'The next day he designing to visit the college of *English Benedictines* at that place, he was received by the whole Convent in their Church, in a solemn procession with Copes, a *Te Deum*, and other Ceremonies, as appointed in the Ritual, for such receptions. From the Church he was conducted into the Cloyster, and entertained with a banquet, and a Panigyrick spoken to him by a Student of that college. All of which was so well performed, that Visc. *Stafford* was pleased to say, that it was the only fit reception his Eminence had met with in all his journey.'

In Rome Howard received his red hat from the Pope. As his titular church he was given Santa Cecilia *trans Tiberim*; this was later changed to the Dominican church of Santa Maria *sopra Minerva*. He was appointed to serve on four of the Roman Congregations: those of Bishops and Regulars, Propaganda Fide, Sacred Rites, and the Council of Trent, the last being charged with the task of implementing the decrees of that council. In addition, the next Pope, Innocent XI, a Dominican, appointed him to the oddly named Congregation of Relics. In Rome he was known variously as the Cardinal of Norfolk—by which style he always signed himself—or as the Cardinal of England. In 1676 he obtained for the English Dominicans the Roman church of SS. John and Paul—an arrangement which did not last very long—and repaired its fabric at a cost to himself of £3000. In the same year he was appointed Archpriest of the basilica of Santa Maria Maggiore.

Among the English Catholics who frequented his *palazzo* the Cardinal valued especially the three sons of John Dryden, the Poet Laureate. The youngest, Erasmus, entered the Dominican Order at SS. John and Paul's, taking the name—perhaps in part as a compliment to the Cardinal?—of Thomas. Father Thomas Dryden was ordained in 1694, and until 1700 acted as Subprior, and then Prior, at Bornhem. In 1700 he succeeded to the family baronetcy, and went to live, as Sir Erasmus Dryden, at the family seat at Canons Ashby, in Northamptonshire; but the penal laws deprived him of the actual ownership of the property. He died there later in the same year, after having been visited on his deathbed by the Dominican provincial, Father Thomas Worthington, who was very kindly received by Father Dryden's

Protestant relatives.

The time of 'prosperity' for the English Catholics, of which Howard had written in his letter of April, 1669 to Cardinal Barberini, did not last very long. It had depended almost entirely on the good will of the King, who was not strong enough to maintain it indefinitely. When Titus Oates produced his fabricated plot, nine Dominicans were implicated. On 7th April the House of Commons impeached all those named by Oates; Howard was among them, but fortunately he was in Rome. Six other Dominicans were arrested, and narrowly escaped the extreme penalty, after suffering longer or shorter periods of imprisonment. Father Alexander Lumsden, being a Scotsman by birth, was found not to come under the statute. Father Dominic Maguire was released when it was shown that he had been born in Spain and could claim Spanish citizenship. He lived to succeed the martyred Oliver Plunkett as archbishop of Armagh. Father Peter Atwood was reprieved, to his visible sorrow, at the very moment when he was mounting the hurdle on which he was to be dragged to Tyburn.

After he became a cardinal *in curia* Howard never again saw any member of the Royal Family; but with some of them he continued to correspond. England and English church affairs remained the centre of his interest. In 1680 he was appointed Protector of the English College in Rome, and in 1684 he was named Cardinal Protector of England and Scotland. On 13th January of that year he wrote an interesting letter to the Dean of the English Chapter, Dr John Barnesley, *alias* Perrott. The Chapter was a body of twenty canons which had been set up by Dr William Bishop, the first bishop of Chalcedon and vicar-apostolic, as an advisory body to himself. When his successor, Dr Richard Smith, resigned, in 1631, it was to be fifty or more years before there would next be a bishop in the country. Throughout this time the Chapter claimed jurisdiction over all English church affairs, in the absence of episcopal government. Its foundations were perhaps juridically uncertain or insecure, but that did not deter it, later, from contesting the authority of the vicars-apostolic when they tried to introduce some measure of canonical order into the confusion of the English mission field. Dr Smith's departure had been the result of these conflicts. Later, Philip Ellis (in religion Dom Michael Ellis, O.S.B.), bishop of Aureliopolis and vicar-apostolic of the Western District, had similar difficulties with the Chapter. Ellis, whose nickname of 'Jolly Phil' at Westminster School, followed him through life, gained the notice of the Duke of York, who appointed him one of his chaplains. When the Duke came to the throne as James II he secured Ellis's nomination as one of the three new bishops (vicars-apostolic) of 1688. The King's downfall followed almost at once, and the new vicar-apostolic never saw his Western district. He followed his sovereign to St Germain-en-Laye, outside Paris, and later went to Rome, where he became friendly with Cardinal Howard, who employed him as his secretary. In 1708, long after the Cardinal's death, he was appointed bishop of Segni. He ruled this diocese, where he was popular and successful, for eighteen years, and died in 1726.

Towards the end of 1683 Dean Perrott (as Barnesley was more commonly known) had written a personal letter to Howard, with which he enclosed a formal letter from the Chapter, inviting him to return to England as vicar-apostolic. This must be reckoned a considerable compliment to Howard, considering the prevailing hostility in England between the secular and the regular clergy. But he had never shown any inclination to favour regulars above seculars; the Chapter could be confident that in Rome he would not use his influence to favour one side over the other. The chaptermen knew that it was not very likely that the Pope would allow the Cardinal to leave Rome, so they submitted to Howard the names of six English priests, from whom they asked him to choose one whom he would recommend for their bishop, or who might act as his suffragan or coadjutor if he could not come himself.

In reply to the Dean's letter and petition Howard wrote:

I must render you thanks for the expressions of yr affection & for the confidence you professe in my readiness to doe you all good offices within my power. As I am fullie persuaded of yr sincerities in the former so shall I never give occasion to any diminution of the latter I am no less convinced than yr-selves of the necessitie there is to have Episcopal government restored & settled in our country it is what I have ever desired & what apon yr present application to me, I shall endeavour to procure. Yr desire of having the authoritie and character placed in my person is an obligeing mark of the kindness & confidence which I have alreadie acknowledged with my thankfullness for them but upon mature consideration I do not perceive the consequences or advantages that might be expected from a compliance with yr desire to be such as may sufficientlie induce me to it or merit yr farther insisting upon it. I should esteeme myself happy (if circumstances were happy for it) not onely to co-operate with you att this distance but to be fellow labourer amongst you & beare my part of the burden wch is so cheerfullie and profitabely undergone by you.

As to the six alternative names submitted, he says that he wishes it were within his power to serve every one of them, but since this is impossible he will endeavour to make choice of one.

In this letter the Cardinal deals at some length with the Chapter's difficulties, and the lack of confidence felt in it by the authorities in Rome. For his own part, he had always believed in the usefulness of a Chapter, in the existing state of things, and he would be very willing to help them as far as he was able. But in Rome the Chapter is generally thought to be an illegal body, lacking proper canonical foundation. However, this could be remedied by a new erection, '& with some few limitations & reservations is a thing peradventure might be obtained without much difficultie.'

In January, 1684 the Cardinal wrote to a senior English priest, Mr Winster, to recommend that there should be, if possible, a yearly meeting of all the clergy, or at least the greater part of them. By this means it would be known what progress was being made in cultivating the 'Spirituall vinyard'; the progress and problems of each priest could be assessed, and the condition of the laity reported on. The missioners would get to know each other better; union and charity would be promoted among them. In April he sent a pastoral letter to the clergy, both secular and regular, urging them to adopt, as far as might be possible, the 'common life'. The dangers to the spiritual life of priests living singly in hired lodgings, disguised as laymen, and lacking both the companionship of fellow priests and ready access to their superiors, was obvious. Even two priests living together and sharing common devotions and a common table would have been a help to each other.

As we have seen, Howard was always careful to act impartially in his dealings with the seculars and the regulars. As a member of the latter body himself he was in a delicate position. Among the

'Records Miscellaneous' in volume three of Dodd's *The Church History of England* (Brussels, 1737-42) is a letter from the Cardinal to Alexander Holt, an English secular priest, whom he must have known well since the letter is subscribed as from 'Your most affectionate friend'. In this letter he declares: 'I have ever considered the secular clergy as a principal part of the spiritual *militia*, which God has employed to uphold his cause in our own country, since it's rebellion against him by a revolt from his church.' After paying tribute to the zeal of the clergy, he says that 'The respect I bear to your persons, and to your whole body, will not permit me to dissemble certain complaints, which have been sent up hither against some of your brethren, not without an odious reflexion upon the rest in general.' These complaints concerned the two oaths the Government wished to exact from Catholics, in return for some possible relaxation of the penal laws against them. With the first, the Oath of Supremacy, none of the clergy would have anything to do; but there were some priests who were willing to take the Oath of Allegiance, arguing that there was now no hope of a second restoration of the Stuart monarchy, so that it was only realistic to acknowledge the new political order of things as having a claim to the loyalty of all subjects. The Holy See, however, had ruled against the Oath of Allegiance equally with the Oath of Supremacy. Finally, Howard says that he is now in a position to give more effective proofs than hitherto of his goodwill towards the clergy, but that difficulties of this kind may frustrate his best intentions and render his endeavours unsuccessful; which would be a great disappointment to him.

His respectful and sympathetic attitude to the clergy was by no means congenial to all the regulars. Dodd prints a letter (undated) strongly hostile to Howard from the Prior of the English Benedictines at Douai to an unnamed confrère who had recently arrived in Rome as their agent. The President of the English Benedictines had arranged for this emissary of the Anglo-Benedictine Congregation to be accommodated in the Cardinal's lodgings, 'that so you may seem to have his countenance, and also be in better circumstances to observe the motions of him, and such as are about him.' The Prior thinks it would not be amiss to let people in Rome know how much the Cardinal is 'of his uncle

Aubigny's spirit, a sufficient Jansenist, and in his practice a sworn enemy to all regulars'. The agent of the monks is told to make it his business also to try to get the Holy See's annual grant to the English College stopped, as that 'would certainly bring the clergy upon their knees'. He is also urged to intimate in the right quarters that 'those whom they call chaptermen' are all Blackloists or Jansenists, 'and consequently *Hereticks*'. (Thomas Blacklow was a priest of unorthodox views, whose treatise on *Obedience and Government*, and other writings, had been censured by the university of Douai.)

The writer of this letter, 'your most obedient servant and brother, F.W.H.', wisely concludes by urging his correspondent: 'I beseech you, burn this when perused.' However, he failed to do so. The writer was Dom William Hitchcock, alias Nedam, who was professed a Benedictine *c*. 1659. He was a prior of St Gregory's, Douai, from 1667—1673, and from 1685—1693. Father Hitchcock was secretary to the 14th General Chapter of the English Black Monks, which was held in London, at the Old Bailey in 1666. He was secretary also to the 19th Chapter, 1685, which was addressed by King James II, who spoke to persuade the Brethren to love and charity. In 1701 Hitchcock became prior of the English Benedictine house in Paris, where he died in 1711.

The accusation against Howard of Jansenism was especially unscrupulous. In the seventeenth century suspicion of Jansenism could blast a churchman's career as effectively as could a charge of Modernism in the early years of the present century. In Howard's case the accusation was patently absurd, and would have harmed only the man who brought it. It was probably based on Howard's courteous personal relations with one or two known Jansenists, and his disapproval of the Holy See's condemnation of the writings of his fellow Dominican Natalis Alexander, suspected of Jansenism.

The affairs of the English Dominicans remained the Cardinal's special concern, not least the convent of nuns he had founded at Vilvoorde. In 1669 the community, which today is at Carisbrooke, Isle of Wight, moved from Vilvoorde to a property in Brussels known as Spellekens. In the archives at Carisbrooke is a long letter, of 20th December, 1687, from Cardinal Howard to the Prioress, Mother Barbara Boyle. This remarkable woman took the habit in 1661, but was kept a novice for three years owing to the opposition of the local bishop and the civil authorities to the establishment of a specifically English religious house. Eventually Father Howard overcame this opposition, and she was allowed to make her profession in July, 1664. Sister Barbara was appointed Prioress by Howard in 1667; she was elected for a second term in 1700, and for a third in 1706. She lived on until 1717, and died at the age of 94, in the fifty-seventh year of her religious profession. In this letter to her the Cardinal is concerned to mitigate some aspects of the rather severe régime prescribed for the nuns by the last provincial, Father Vincent Torre, who was the first to hold that office with full powers since the Dissolution. Howard says that he has consulted the Pope on the matter, although there was no necessity for him to do so, and that he has decided to 'take away the last Provl's and others unnecessary zeale'. Accordingly, he gives the nuns permission to eat meat three times a week, and allows the 'pensioners' (children boarding with the nuns) to 'go abroade' sometimes, on suitable days, at the Prioress's discretion.

A list of obligations of the Community, approved by the Provincial, Father Thomas Worthington, in 1726, records that the Founder, Cardinal Howard, established for the nuns the practice of reciting daily, after the Conventual Mass, the psalm *Exaudiat te Dominus* (Psalm 19) 'for his Britannick Majesty, our Lawfull Soverain, then Raigning, Charles the 2nd and for the happy conversion of England: which hath ever since been performed by this our Community'.

In 1685 Charles II died, and was succeeded, as James II, by his brother the Duke of York, now an openly professed Catholic. The Cardinal found the new King, whom, of course, he had known at Whitehall, difficult to deal with. Before long he had to suffer the annoyance of James's efforts to get the Pope to nominate the Queen's uncle, Rinaldo d'Este, as Protector of England and Scotland (instead of Howard himself), and to bestow on him the red hat as well. The trouble was that d'Este had no qualifications whatever for the supervision of English and Scots church affairs. In these matters the Cardinal's advice was always for moderation; but such advice was not acceptable to the obstinate monarch. Gilbert Burnet, who met Howard during a visit to Rome, says in his *History of our own Times*: 'The Cardinal told me that all the advice writ over from thence were for slow, calm, and moderate courses. But he saw violent courses were more acceptable and would probably be followed. And he added that these were the production of England, far different from the counsels of Rome.' Howard was dismayed by the new King's policies; in the hope of influencing James to wiser measures he secured the appointment as Vicar-Apostolic of All England of Dr John Leyburn, President of the English College at Douai. It must have been quite a triumph for Howard, after his years of battle on this front, to have at last secured a bishop for the Catholics of England; but the triumph, such as it was, was short-lived. Leyburn duly arrived at court, where he was instructed to appear in his episcopal habit: a typical piece of Jamesian tactlessness, guaranteed to upset almost everyone. Dr Leyburn was able to make little impression on his sovereign, whom he followed into exile in 1688.

In June of that year, to celebrate the birth of James Francis Edward, Prince of Wales, the Cardinal gave a feast in Rome at which an ox roasted whole and stuffed with lambs and fowls was enjoyed by a multitude of the common people. In December he sent a letter of Christmas greeting to the Queen, which presumably reached her in exile:

Madame,
The happiness which I wish your Majesty in the approaching holy dayes of Christ-Masse is the same for which I pray his devine Majesty for all the yeare whilst the approaching of these times gives me an occasion of renewing and redoubling more earnestly the same wishes and prayers which will never be wanting whilst it pleaseth God to graunte me the honour of being
      Madame
                          your Majesty's
                Most humble and Obedient Servant
                      CARD^L OF NORFOLKE

Soon after Christmas, on 18th January, 1689, the Cardinal wrote to the Principal of the Scots College at Paris to give him the latest news of the King.

Heare came yesterday an expresse dispatched from ye Post-master of Lions, with a long relation of his Ma.ty's escape and safe arrivall at St Germains where he is with her Ma.ty and our Prince, for all whch miraculous escapes God almighty be ever thanked, as I yett firmly hope he will at last comfort and help them against all theyr barbarous enemys and restore them after theyr so great sufferings for his cause only!

Writing again to the Principal, Monsignor Louis Innes, on 27th November, 1690, he encloses two letters to be delivered to the King, and says that he will probably be asked to forward others, 'it being the usual way heare at this time of the yeare, to send theyr Boni festi, as they cale them, which is to wish theyr Ma.tys a good Christmas and new yeare, of whch Ceremony they are very free heare, and expect exact answers, as they receave from all other Kings, Queenes, and great Princes.' The Cardinal adds that all his endeavours are chiefly for the King's service; but he fears that his good words outrun his deeds. The Holy Father has said that he will do all he can for the King, but complains with truth that he has so many expenses that he is now very poor.

After the fall of James II Howard increasingly lost touch with England; but he kept up his interest in the training of priests, especially Dominicans, for the English mission. In Rome, although he had his own *palazzo*, he lived mostly at the Dominican convent of Santa Sabina, the residence of the Master of the Order, on the Aventine. He took part in three conclaves, those which elected Innocent XI (1676), Alexander VIII (1689), and Innocent XII (1691). After his creation as cardinal he refused all other proffered dignities.

Once King James had gone into exile there was nothing to cause further difficulties between himself and the Cardinal. In the archives of the Historic Manuscripts Commission there are many letters that attest to Howard's continuing devotion to the Royal Family and to their cause.

In the summer of 1694 the Cardinal was suffering from the aristocratic complaint of the gout, and also from the gravel. His eyes also were giving him trouble. Among the Carte manuscripts in the Bodleian Library is a letter, written on 1st June of that year, from the Cardinal's secretary, Bishop Ellis, to the King. The bishop says that he has discovered certain things that he dare not impart to his master while he continues in this weak condition; 'for he lays yr Ma.ties concerns so much to heart that what I have already talked to him of them, afflicts him more than his distemper, whch is very great and not without danger.' The allusion to these 'concerns' is obscure; but it seems that there was hostility to the exiled King in some Roman circles. Earlier in the same letter there is mention of several ministers and ambassadors who are trying to 'dissemble' their real sentiments; and of some plots that are being hatched, and of negotiations with the 'Usurper' (William of Orange).

Two weeks later Ellis was writing again to the King, this time to report the Cardinal's death. He says:

It is certain grief was ye principal cause of his death, and he had no other cause for it besides what relates to yr Ma.tie. From ye time he had heard how forward some proposals and negotiations went that seem'd to want a due regard to yr Ma.tie he never held up his head: he suffer'd much from ye gout and stone, but had got ye better of them, and there remained no indications on his Body that either of them has taken away his life; for all the noble parts were perfectly sound.

Allowing for a little pious exaggeration here, it is evident that the Cardinal's thoughts were with his King and Queen to the last moments of his life.

He had made his will on 9th June, being 'Sound by the grace of God in mind, sense, hearing, & sight, & understanding . . . tho' weak of Body, & for that cause lying sick a Bed.' He directed that the eight thousand Roman crowns lent him so many years ago by his brother Henry, now Duke of Norfolk, should be repaid to the Duke's eldest son, Lord George Howard, to be shared among the Duke's children by his second wife. To his old friend Cardinal Altieri he left the best of his English clocks. After various miscellaneous bequests the residue of his estates is to be used to found a new college for English Dominicans in the Low Countries; failing this, it is to go to the convent of Bornhem. By a codicil small sums of money were left to a number of English friends, among them John Dryden, who received fifty crowns. Dryden survived the Cardinal by six years. The remainder of his goods were left to Father Thomas White, the Provincial, for the benefit of the English Dominican Province. By a further codicil his coach, horses, and their harness were left to Bishop Ellis.

Two days after making his will the Cardinal wrote a short note to the Pope, Innocent XI:

Most Holy Father,
I hope that the Mercy of God will give me Grace to pass from this to a

better life. The only regret that troubles me is to have to leave affairs in England in so doubtful and so uncertain a state, for which reason I warmly beseech your Holiness with this my last breath with your usual goodness to constitute a Congregation of Cardinals before whom may be heard every thing that regards that poor King and the Catholic religion in such Kingdoms, when there is question of that peace which I trust will soon come now.

He asks also that the Pope will retain the services of 'our English bishop', Philip Ellis, 'for the service of his Country and his Monarch', since he is a discreet man, and likely to be more useful than anyone else where these matters are concerned.

Philip Thomas Howard, of the Order of Preachers, Cardinal-Priest of the title of *Santa Maria sopra Minerva*, died at Rome on 17th June, 1694, in the sixty-fifth year of his age, the forty-eighth of his religious profession, and in his twentieth year as cardinal. In his will he had asked to be buried 'with as little Pompe and charges as possible, in the Church of the Minerva, with a little stone, a very Ordinary One, with the sole Inscription of my Name.' He is buried in that church, but the inscription on his tomb is rather more elaborate than he would have liked. It describes him, very justly, as 'the Father both of his country and of the poor, the Parent and Restorer of the English Province of his Order'.

*　　*　　*　　*

We have followed Philip Howard through the varied phases and vicissitudes of his life; his words and actions seem to disclose certain aspects of his personality. What his words and actions reveal is confirmed by the various portraits of him that exist; especially, perhaps, by the one in the English College at Rome. This is a head and shoulders study, by an unknown artist. It shows him wearing a black cassock, bands, and a scarlet biretta. He has a fairly full, though less than round, face; and is of a dark complexion. His hair is dark, and almost curly, worn just less than shoulder length; he has dark eyes, and a rather long nose. His expression is one of shrewd alertness, with a hint of humour.

He was a man of clear mind and firm purpose, with a marked capacity for affairs. His piety was as undemonstrative as it was evident. Of easy disposition and pleasant manners, he could speak and act forcibly when occasion required. For instance, in 1686 James II sent Lord Castlemaine—scarcely a happy choice in view of his wife's association with the former monarch, Charles II—as his special emissary to the court of Rome, to press the King's petitions for a bishopric for his Jesuit adviser Father Petre and a red hat for the Queen's uncle Rinaldo d'Este. The ambassador was accommodated in the English College, where Cardinal Howard happened to be staying at the time. While he was there Castlemaine spent a good deal of time conferring with the rector of the college, Father Morgan, S.J. One evening the Cardinal, who wished to see the ambassador, was kept waiting while Father Morgan was with Lord Castlemaine in his apartment. When the rector at last emerged, Howard was further irritated by seeing that the good *padre* was in his night attire, and roundly told him that 'if for the future he should see him there, he with his own hands should break his neck over the stairs. Which expression from so meek a gentleman and clothed with the purple was not without great provocation.' The outcome of this incident was that the Pope had Father Morgan sent back to England for good.

Howard was always a friend to learning, and he was especially concerned for the education of the clergy. He revised the rules of the English College at Douai, which had been framed largely by foreigners, and were unsuitable for English students. The rebuilding of the Venerable English College in Rome was begun in 1680, and was continued under his direction. Here too he was responsible for a revision of the régime. He was conscious of the unsatisfactoriness of having the future priests of the English mission trained abroad, according to foreign ideas. He told Burnet that these future priests 'came over young and retained all the English that they brought over with them, which was only the language of boys. But their education being among strangers they had formed themselves so upon that model that really they preached as Frenchmen or Italians in English words.'

Pepys had been amused when Howard had jokingly spoken of the Pope as 'Anti-Christ'. As a cardinal Howard could still enjoy a joke of this kind, even if it was made by Protestants. In 1685 Gilbert Burnet, not yet bishop of Sarum, was on a visit to Rome. Calling on the Cardinal one day, he found him giving some relics to two French gentlemen. Burnet whispered to him that it was odd that a priest of the Church of England should be 'helping them off with the wares of Babylon'. Howard was so pleased with this that he repeated it to the others in French, saying that they should tell their countrymen 'how bold the heretics, and how mild the cardinals, were at Rome'.

Burnet thought highly of Howard, as can be seen from this passage from a letter of his written from Rome in December 1683. 'Cardinal Howard', he says, 'is too well known in England to need any character from me. The Elevation of his present condition hath not the least changed him, he hath all the sweetness & gentleness of Temper that we saw in him in England & he retains the unaffected simplicity & humility of a Friar amidst all the dignity of the Purple, and as he sheweth all the generous care and concern for his countrymen that they can expect from him; so I met with so much of it in so many obliging marks of his goodness for myself, as went far beyond a common civility, that I cannot enough acknowledge it.' (*Some letters containing an Account of what seemed most remarkable in Switzerland, Italy, &c*: Amsterdam, 1686.)

An earlier testimony to his character is that of his brother Henry, the future Duke of Norfolk, in a letter written from London, to William Leslie, in Rome, in November 1667. Henry says that 'The King will, I am sure, like him much better than any other, nay, knows his gentle temper so well, as that where he will let him enter and meddle, I am sure another . . . unknown or of a fiercer and more dangerous temper would be put by and not suffered. And truly, though he is my brother I must in conscience say he is a man of a most unspotted life and reputation, and so fortunately beloved as I vow to God I never could yet hear of envy itself to detract from him in the least, and has no enemies but is loved of all here.' (Blairs Papers: cited in M.V. Hay, *The Jesuits and the Popish Plot*: London, 1934.)

Philip Howard's devotion to the house of Stuart seems to have been shared by all the English Dominicans of those times. Among other Dominicans attached to Catharine of Braganza's chapel at Whitehall was a Portuguese father, Dominic de la Fuente, who at one point was proposed for the office of Vicar-Apostolic. Father Ambrose Grymes (later baronet by succession), sometime Provincial, was preacher-in-ordinary to Catharine when she was queen-dowager. Father Cornelius O'Heyn, from Limerick, was *socius* to Father Christopher Daly, confessor to Queen Catharine. Father Thomas White, later Provincial, was present at the marriage by proxy at Modena of the Duke of York and the Princess Mary of Modena; he is said to have been the priest who solemnised the marriage. Brother Henry Packe, a laybrother, was steward to Father Howard when he was Lord Almoner, and followed him to Rome. Father Albert Anderson was a friend of Charles II, who commuted his sentence of death to banishment for life. He was granted a free pardon by James II.

Somewhat later Father Patrick Bradley, chaplain to the Sardinian ambassador, was named bishop of Derry by James III (as Dominican documents of the time always call the Old Pretender), and was consecrated in 1751. And it was through James III that Father Dominic Williams, whom Bede Jarrett describes, in *The English Dominicans*, as 'a rather effective Jacobite agent', was appointed Vicar-Apostolic of the Northern District in 1725. In 1745 Father Joseph Hansbie, ex-Provincial, was arrested in the excitement of the Young Pretender's march south. He was imprisoned for a time, but was released. In 1748 he was re-elected Provincial, at the age of eighty-five.

It was the same with the nuns. One of the sisters at Spellekens was sought in marriage by Bonnie Prince Charlie. Rome was willing to dispense her vows, but she would not consent. Cardinal Howard had two nieces in the community, Sister Dominica Howard and Sister Mary Rose Howard. Sister Mary Rose had strong Jacobite sympathies. She was a friend of the Pretender, and acted as a kind of agent for transmitting his correspondence to his friends in England. The Prioress and community were worried in case these activities should get them all into trouble, but the Master of the Order was sympathetic to 'His Royal Majesty of Great Britain', and ruled that letters of His Majesty received by Sister Mary Rose Howard for onward transmission should be exempt from inspection by the Prioress. The Cardinal had donated the dowry for his two nieces, £600, which was invested at 4½% in 'a great Taverne in Bruxelles at the sign of the Ellefan'.

The House of Stuart certainly had no more loyal and affectionate servant than the Cardinal of Norfolk. He deserves the gratitude of Catholics for his untiring efforts to keep the faith alive in England when it was reaching its lowest ebb. Professor J.P. Kenyon, in *The Stuarts: A Study in English Kingship*, blames the Jesuit party at the court of James II for Howard's permanent exclusion from England. This group was led by Father Edward Petre, S.J., and had the support of such influential 'Celtic adventurers' as Lords Castlemaine and Tyrconnell. The Chapter of the clergy had actually invited Howard to return; but the opposition of the Jesuits and Benedictines, and divisions within the laity, would have made his position extremely difficult if not impossible. It must have saddened Howard that the last twenty years of his life had to be spent in exile; but his position made his return impossible—as the chaptermen seemed to recognise when they suggested that he might be represented by a coadjutor. There was no need for the Jesuit faction to conspire to keep him out. A cardinal would never have been allowed to reside in England. Hence the absurdity of King James's attempt to secure the red hat for Father Petre.

Howard's greatest achievement, as his first biographer, Father Raymund Palmer, has said, was to restore the English Dominican province as a means of forwarding the spiritual welfare of his country. For about 190 years after he had made the foundation at Bornhem the province continued a precarious and more or less 'underground' existence; but he had laid the foundations well. The brilliant revival that was to follow dates from the opening of Woodchester Priory, in Gloucestershire, in 1846, and seems to have reached its zenith with the opening of the priory of the Holy Ghost ('Blackfriars') in Oxford in 1921. Among the alumni of the English province in the present century are such distinguished names as Father Bertrand Wilberforce (a grandson of the liberator of the slaves), Father Bede Jarrett, Father Vincent McNabb, Father Gervase Mathew (historian and Byzantine scholar), and Father Victor White (author of *God and the Unconscious* and *Soul and Psyche*, the product of twenty years of exploration on the frontiers of theology and Jungian psychology).

After the second Vatican Council the Dominicans, like most other Orders, went through a period of disorientation, during which there were many defections from its ranks; it liturgy (the Dominican rite) was jettisoned, and a number of other ill-judged 'innovations' were made. However, this period seems to have ended, and there now is every sign that the English Dominicans will contribute effectively to the life of the church in the completely new age on which it is now entering. Truly Philip Howard was, as the inscription on his tomb proclaims, 'the Parent and Restorer of the English Province of his Order'.

George Anne Bellamy
(the Van Haeken portrait)

GEORGE ANNE BELLAMY OF THE COVENT GARDEN THEATRE

The smile of peace—the wildness of despair—
The soft'ning sigh—the soul-dissolving tear;
Each magic charm the boasted Oldfield knew,
Enchanting Bellamy! revives in you.

SO WROTE the eighteenth-century Scots poet John Cunningham in his Ode to Mrs Bellamy of the Covent Garden Theatre, whom Boswell refers to in his life of Johnson as 'the celebrated Mrs Bellamy'. Enchanting and celebrated she was; but her fame has not endured outside the annals of the stage and the pages of the *Dictionary of National Biography* and the *Oxford Companion to the Theatre*. Or so it was until 1958, when Mr Cyril Hughes Hartmann published his biography, *Enchanting Bellamy*. His main source is her own autobiography, *An Apology for the Life of George Anne Bellamy, late of Covent Garden Theatre, Written by Herself*, whose narrative his researches have enabled him to supplement from other sources.

When it appeared in 1785 the *Apology* became an instant best-seller, going through three editions in its year of publication, and a fourth in 1786. The book is now forgotten, and copies are not easily found. Chronologically it is a most confused and confusing book. There is hardly a single date in it from beginning to end. Written in the form of letters to a woman friend, it runs to nearly twelve hundred crown octavo pages, and has much the same urgent fascination as Richardson's *Pamela*. Its author was a Catholic; and in the course of her narrative she gives the reader many glimpses of Catholic life in eighteenth century London and elsewhere. For the most part these are not included in Mr Hartmann's narrative; understandably, since he was writing for a general public, and had to try to make a long book not over-long. But the incidents that she records in relation to her practice of her religion are of considerable interest.

32

Georgiane Bellamy was born at Finglas, near Dublin on 23rd April, 1728; by some blunder her name was entered in the baptismal register as George Anne, and as such she was always known. Her mother was a Quakeress from near Maidstone who had taken to the stage; her father, to whom her mother was not married, was James O'Hara, Baron Kilmaine and 2nd Lord Tyrawley (1690-1773), field-marshal and diplomat, ambassador in Portugal and Russia. Lord Tyrawley's private life was considered 'singularly licentious even for the courts of Russia and Portugal'; but he evidently had great charm, and some feeling for the arts and for letters; he had been on terms of friendship with the poet Alexander Pope. He was not a Catholic; but he had George Anne brought up and educated by the Ursuline nuns at Boulogne. She remained true to the faith which they taught her, and often looked back nostalgically to her happy childhood days in the convent.

Her mother, who had been deserted by Captain Bellamy, the husband she had married just before George Anne's birth, settled in London, where she obtained minor parts in the theatre and got to know most of the actors and actresses of the day. In 1743 she was invited by Mrs Woffington to bring her young daughter, then aged about eleven, to take part in some amateur theatricals to be held at Mrs Woffington's house at Teddington. George Anne was a great success as Andromache in Ambrose Philips's play *The Distressed Mother*, and Garrick, who was playing Orestes in the same play, saw at once that she had talent. So in due course George Anne made her début at Covent Garden as Monimia in Otway's tragedy *The Orphan*. The leading man, James Quin, resented the introduction of this inexperienced child-actress in so exacting a rôle; the other players also objected strongly. But the manager, Rich, ignored their protests. On the first night George Anne was so nervous that her appearance was nearly a fiasco. But in the fourth act, she tells us, 'I felt myself suddenly inspired. I blazed out at once with meridian splendour . . . Mr Quin was so *fascinated* at this unexpected intervention that he waited behind the scenes till the conclusion of the act; when lifting me up from the ground in a transport he exclaimed, "Thou art a divine creature, and the true spirit is in thee."'

Not long after this auspicious opening of her career George

Anne was travelling in Essex, and stopped one evening for dinner at an inn at Ingatestone, near which town was the mansion of the prominent recusant family of Petre.

During dinner [she says]the landlady informed me that Lord Petre had a noble house and estate adjoining that town; adding that his Lordship's family was one of the worthiest in the world, although they were *Roman Catholics*. I could not help smiling at this reservation; which she observing, begged my pardon; saying, 'I fear, Madam, you are one.' As I spoke, the starting tear glistened in my eye, at the recollection of my remissness in the duties of the religion I professed. I however smothered the upbraidings of my mind, and inquired who lived at the farmhouse which was so pleasantly situated at some distance from the town. She informed me that it belonged to a rich farmer, but they were *Papishes*. I then desired she would instruct me in the distinction between Roman-Catholics and Papishes, as she termed them. 'Lord, Miss', answered she, 'sure you know the difference between a Hind and a Lord?'

George Anne was able to arrange to stay for a while with this family, and permission was obtained for her to attend Lord Petre's domestic chapel at Ingatestone Hall. Roman Catholic churches were still prohibited by law; the diplomatically-privileged embassy chapels were the only places of worship in London to which Catholics had regular access.

George Anne's regret for her neglect of her religious duties was sincere. She soon came to know all too well the dangers to which life as an actress on the London stage could expose her, and against which her religious principles were perhaps her only protection. Her good nature and imprudence were to involve her in a series of compromising situations; compromising also in the sense that she really did try to strike a kind of balance between her own inclinations, her desire to please, and her conscience. The remarkable thing is that, with a dissolute father and a worldly mother, she remained for the whole of her life faithful to the religion in which she had been brought up.

George Anne was hardly beautiful, it would seem; perhaps she was handsome rather than pretty; but she was certainly attractive. The delightful full-length portrait of her by Lindo in the Garrick Club shows us a small, dark-haired young woman of considerable dignity, yet with strong hints in her expression of liveliness and intelligence. Because of contemporary references to 'the fair Bellamy' it has often been assumed that she was blonde; but she tells us that she had dark hair and blue eyes. The Van Haeken portrait of 1735, which shows her seated, wearing a voluminously-skirted silk dress and holding on her lap a book of songs with musical notation, is extremely appealing, and seems to express every aspect of her personality.[1]

Soon after her début at Covent Garden she began to receive attentions from Lord Byron, 'a nobleman who had little to boast of but a title and an agreeable face', and from a well-to-do Mr Montgomery Metham. In 1749 Metham renewed his addresses, which he had allowed to lapse for a time. He was a Catholic, and during the Lent of that year he and George Anne met regularly at the Bavarian embassy chapel in Golden Square. This chapel, now the church of Our Lady of the Assumption and St Gregory in Warwick Street, W1, has a history going back to soon after the Restoration of 1660.

Originally the Portuguese embassy, the property of Golden Square was taken over by the Bavarian ambassador in 1736, when the Portuguese removed to South Street, Mayfair. As a result of her attendance at the chapel Mrs Bellamy, as she was now known,[2] became acquainted with the Bavarian ambassador, Count Franz von Haslang, who was to become one of her closest friends, and one of her most faithful supporters during her times of stress and need. The Count was a good, warm-hearted man. For a time he employed George Anne as his housekeeper—she had a gift for household management; the post was no sinecure—in order to give her the protection of diplomatic immunity when she was being hounded by her creditors and would otherwise have been liable to imprisonment.

In 1780 the Bavarian chapel was wrecked by the Gordon rioters. It is usually assumed to have been totally destroyed, but Bellamy's evidence seems to show that this was not so. She was present at the requiem for Count Haslang held there in 1783, and the actual restoration of the chapel did not begin until c. 1787. Probably the furniture and appointments were destroyed in the riots, and the fabric badly damaged; but not so badly that public worship, at least on special occasions, could not continue.

If this is so, then Warwick Street church can presumably claim the longest continuity of public worship of any Catholic church in England today, other than certain chapels belonging to religious communities or to ancient recusant families. Such is Mr Hartmann's opinion, and he may well be right.

Among the clergy at Golden Square whom Mrs Bellamy knew was the Reverend John Darcy, who was attached to the embassy from 1748-1758, and seems to have been her confessor and spiritual director as well as her friend. She also knew Dr James Archer, who had begun life as a potboy at The Ship Tavern, near the Sardinian chapel in Holborn. Archer's published volumes of sermons were very popular, and were read by Protestants as well as by Catholics. Another of her friends was Father Arthur O'Leary, the Irish Franciscan who founded the mission which is now the parish of St Patrick, Soho Square.

At the Bavarian chapel there was an impressive schedule of services. Mass and Vespers were sung on Sundays and on nineteen other days in the year. During Lent there was sung Compline every Wednesday at four o'clock. The Holy Week rites were carried out each year with full solemnity. During the greater part of the year there were six Low Masses on Sunday mornings, the first at 6.00 a.m., and a High Mass at 11 o'clock, the last Low Mass being celebrated at 12.30. Things seem to have been much the same on weekdays, the High Mass excepted, the last Mass being said at mid-day. The chapel received an annual subsidy from the Elector of Bavaria; this must have been badly needed in order to maintain chaplains and services on this scale for the benefit of the harassed Catholics of London.

George Anne became virtually engaged to Mr Metham; but Lord Tyrawley forbade the match and strongly supported her mother's efforts to get her to marry a wealthy linen-draper named Crump. No doubt her father, who took a strong interest in all his children, both legitimate and otherwise, was anxious to get her married off to a respectable man of sufficient means. He was adamant in his opposition to George Anne's own wishes. One night Metham, driven to desperation, abducted her from the theatre in Covent Garden, still dressed in the costume for her part as Lady Fanciful in Vanbrugh's *The Provok'd Wife*. He carried her off to York, and by promising marriage as soon as his family circumstances would allow he prevailed on her to remain with him. Unfortunately, owing to Metham's financial and other problems, delay dragged on until, eventually, George Anne broke with him after a foolish quarrel. This was a disastrous move, for Metham certainly loved her, and would have married her in time. He still remained her friend, even after their union had become impossible.

The house which Metham had rented for her in York belonged to a gentleman of the old recusant family of Strickland. 'The garden wall of our house', she says in the *Apology*, 'joined to a monastery . . . I therefore esteemed myself exceedingly fortunate in commencing an acquaintance with the chaplain of the adjacent seminary. This gentleman I found to be an honour to the sacerdotal function. For learning and good sense there were very few who exceeded him.' The ladies of the convent were at first doubtful as to the propriety of their receiving Mrs Bellamy, because of her equivocal status; but the chaplain, Mr Blunt,[3] who seems to have been a kind-hearted and sensible man, assured the nuns of Metham's honourable intentions. George Anne was given a key to the garden-door between her own house and the convent, and was allowed to come and go as she pleased.

The ladies of this 'seminary'—who of course did not wear their religious habits—were nuns of the Institute of the Blessed Virgin Mary, founded a hundred or so years earlier by a Yorkshire woman, Mary Ward. The chief work of the 'Mary Ward nuns', as they are usually called, is education. Their convent in York, the famous Bar Convent, has been on its present site, outside Micklegate Bar, since 1680. George Anne Bellamy's house will therefore have been in Blossom Street, then known as Plowson (originally Plowswain) Street.

Bellamy seems to have arrived in York in 1749 or 1750. From 1746-1759 the superior of the community at Micklegate Bar was Mother Mary Hodshon. Father Mannock, S.J., who had been chaplain to the nuns for many years, had died in 1748, and was succeeded by Father John Hawker, S.J. Father Hawker was succeeded by Father Thomas Talbot, and he by Father Thomas Evans, both of the Society of Jesus, which supplied the nuns with their chaplains. There is no record in the convent archives of any Father Blunt; but this name may well have been an alias for one of the foregoing priests, the use of aliases still being not uncommon with the recusant clergy in the eighteenth century.

At this period the nuns' school had among its pupils members of the Constable family from Everingham Park, and of the Burton Constable family, as well as Gerards, Salvins, and Vavasours; in fact, all the notable Catholic families of the north and midlands were represented.[4]

After a time Metham brought George Anne back to London, and it was there that their fateful quarrel took place. As a result of this quarrel she had the bad luck to be caught on the rebound by Metham's treacherous and dishonourable acquaintance John Calcraft, secretary to Henry Fox (later Lord Holland), the Secretary-at-War. Within a few years Calcraft was to become a wealthy financier and army-contractor, and a member of Parliament. This man tricked George Anne with a legally-drawn-up promise of marriage within a specified period, under pain of his forfeiting to her a very large sum of money. His pretext for not marrying her at once was that marriage with an actress would displease his employer and patron, Henry Fox. This was a downright lie, and Fox, who became a very good friend of George Anne's, was horrified when he learned later of this dishonest conduct.

In 1756, after the birth of her son Henry Fox Calcraft, Mrs Bellamy had a long and serious illness during which she received the last sacraments from her friend Mr Darcy. This took place at Calcraft's country seat, Holwood Park, near Bromley, in Kent. The circumstances are sufficiently remarkable to deserve retelling, in her own words.

After suffering, for several weeks, more than human nature could be supposed able to sustain . . . my death warrant was concluded to be signed for one o'clock the next morning. An hour that I ardently wished for; but which, at the same time, made me anxious to see a gentleman from London before its arrival. The gentleman came down the moment he received notice of my danger. And the business being settled for which he came, I was wholly resigned, and waited my visitation with the longing of a bride.

My mind was now perfectly tranquil. The world was lost to me, as well as the recollection of the injuries I had received. In this state, I fell into a sweet sleep, which was attended with a most singular dream. And as I have reason to consider it a sure presage of the calamities I have since suffered, I will here relate it. I imagined I was released from all my cares, and an inhabitant of Heaven. My destined appointment, when I got there, was to light fifty lamps. I entered upon my employment, and executed it with ease, till I came to the last lamp, which I broke in the attempt. The uneasiness this occasioned put an end at once to my dream and sleep, and I awoke in the greatest agitations.

In the morning my visitant of the day before came to take, as he thought, a last farewell. I informed him of my dream. He heard it with manifest pain, mingled with pity. 'My dear child,' said he, 'you are destined to suffer a long life of misery and disappointment. I wish you may be as resigned when your hour of visitation shall come as you now are. I own I could have wished it had been passed.' The holy seer was inspired with the gift of prophecy, as the sequel of my story will too fatally evince.

At dinner the previous evening a clergyman friend of Calcraft's, Dr Philip Francis,[5] who was something of a sponger and was a more or less permanent member of the household, endeavoured to engage the priest, who was George Anne's friend Mr Darcy, in religious controversy. Dr Francis, Bellamy says, thought that Mr Darcy was one of those Irish priests who had acquired a little Latin at colleges abroad and then thought themselves qualified 'to dispense absolutions, without scarcely knowing what the word means'. Mr Darcy, however, was 'a profound theologist, and united to great learning a gentleness of manners and a natural politeness that would have graced a court'. The reverend doctor was reduced to silence; and as a result of the discussion 'two ladies who were present, convinced of the superiority of Mr Darcy's arguments, were in a very short time introduced to the bosom of the mother Church'.

During the penal times, owing to the confused state of church government, and the lack of bishops with normal jurisdiction, there was always a certain number of more or less disreputable semi-freelance priests in the capital, some of whom came from the neighbouring island. But Mrs Bellamy is at pains to make it clear that by no means all the Irish priests in London were of that kind. 'To my own knowledge', she says, 'the late Mr Archer and Mr Richardson were ornaments to the world, and to the religion they professed; as is the present Mr O'Leary, who, with unaffected piety, is blest with that innocent cheerfulness which, joined to his brilliant wit and sound understanding, makes him the admired darling of all who have the happiness of knowing him'.

We cannot here follow George Anne in her dazzling career as an actress, and as a fashionable hostess whose gatherings were attended by all the quality. Nor shall I attempt to recount her many financial and matrimonial involvements. As an actress she did not, perhaps, attain a rank of quite the first eminence, although for some years she was constantly employed in capital parts, as leading rôles were then called. But she was certainly a very brilliant player. Her recorded parts amount to no fewer than eighty-three, as set down by Genest in his *Some Account of the English Stage*, published in 1823. She played Juliet to Garrick's Romeo, and seems to have been at the height of her powers as Monimia in *The Orphan*, as Belvidera in *Venice Preserv'd*, and as Almeria in Congreve's tragedy *The Mourning Bride*. On seeing her in *Venice Preserv'd* Mr Murray, later Lord Mansfield, exclaimed to his neighbour Mr Fox: 'I came to admire Garrick, but go away enchanted with Bellamy!' In Dublin she had a great success as Portia, in *The Merchant of Venice*, and as Cleopatra in Dryden's *All For Love*. She was not so successful in comedy; her best comedy parts were Harriet in Etherege's *The Man of Mode, or Sir Fopling Flutter*, Lady Froth in Congreve's *The Double-Dealer*, and Lady Fanciful in Vanbrugh's *The Provok'd Wife*.

After her eventual separation from the faithless Calcraft, who, needless to say, did not honour his bond, illness and poverty became her lot. The one man whom she would really have wished to marry, Lord Downe, was killed in tragic circumstances while on active service abroad with the Army. He was accidentally shot by one of his own sentries. Her favourite son, Captain George Metham, died in Jamaica; and the munificent legacy left her by her devoted friend and admirer the actor Henry Woodward was only one among several bequests of which she was defrauded or otherwise deprived. Her last days were spent in very reduced circumstances; but except for a period of depression, when she seems to have contemplated suicide, she managed to keep up her spirits. Although neglected and cast off by many of her fashionable friends and acquaintances, she was not entirely deserted. One or two small pensions from noble benefactors or benefactresses were still paid to her; but they were at once swallowed up in the ocean of her debts. Father O'Leary would dine with her from time to time, however humble her abode. In 1780 she was given a benefit at Covent Garden, and was persuaded to appear in her old part of Alicia in Rowe's *Jane Shore*: her performance, she admits, was but indifferent. Boswell prints a letter written by her to her friend Dr Johnson in 1783, requesting his attendance at another benefit on her behalf. Her last benefit took place at Drury Lane on 24th May, 1785, the play being Jephson's *Braganza*. After the performance Mrs Bellamy appeared on the stage, but could utter only a few broken words.

Her last days are obscure. She died on 16th February, 1788, apparently confined to a mean lodging within the Rules of the King's Bench prison—an area in Southwark which included the district of St George's Fields. Her place of burial is unknown.

'Pop', as George Anne was called by her family and intimates, was a vivacious and gifted woman of great charm. Her only real fault—and it proved her undoing—was a quite extraordinary lack of prudence: a virtue which neither her rakish father nor her worldly mother could give her or help her to acquire. During almost the whole of her life she seems to have been the victim of consistent and unusual bad luck.

George Anne was well read; she had a private library of about four hundred books. Her favourite author was Sterne; she was also fond of Dryden's *Aeneid* and Pope's *Iliad*. For a time she made a study of 'natural philosophy'; and she used sometimes to go with her friend Lady Anson to study astronomy at the observatory at Greenwich. But zoology and natural history she gave up after seeing a cat—'an animal I have the greatest dislike to'—tortured in an air-pump during some experiment. After this, she says, 'I left the Pursuit of Philosophy and turned my thoughts to Politics.'

She was generous in everything—especially in money matters—and her recklessness in this respect was in great part the cause of her troubles. She always spoke well of her rivals on the stage; the divine Susanna Cibber, Dr Arne's daughter, she loved, while envying in Mrs Cibber gifts which were greater than her own. Peg Woffington she could not abide, yet in her autobiography she pays generous tribute to Mrs Woffington's beauty and her wonderful powers as an actress.

Her religion was sincere; and so were her regrets at not in all respects living up to it. The fact that exemplary priests such as Mr Darcy and Father O'Leary were among her trusted friends speaks for itself as to her merits. Often, on looking back over her agitated life, she used to wish that she had never left the convent of the Ursulines at Boulogne—which she more than once revisited in after years—and she greatly admired the example of her friend the French actress Madame Brillant, who, like Dryden's friend Anne Reeve, left the stage and took the veil, thus showing, as Bellamy says, 'that she had the resolution to prefer fasting and a breviary to all the elegance and splendor of Paris. This, in my idea, is *real virtue*.'

NOTES

1. The portrait of George Anne Bellamy by J. van Haeken is in the M.R. Keatin Theatre Collection of the Houghton Library, Harvard University, USA.

2. Actresses at this time, once they had ceased to be juvenile, were generally styled Mrs, irrespectively of whether they were married or single.

3. Down to and until 1899 secular priests in England, as everywhere else, were known as Mr (unless doctors of divinity), or by their national equivalent; as, for example, Don Abbondio in Manzoni's *I Promessi Sposi.* In France one speaks of Monsieur l'Abbé, in Germany Herr Pastor, etc. 'Father' is by origin a monastic title, and was aggregated to the diocesan clergy by Cardinal Manning. During the penal times most priests, whether secular or regular, were called Mr.

4. For details concerning the history of the Bar Convent, York, I am indebted to Mother Margaret Mary, I.B.V.M., of the same.

5. Philip Francis (? 1708-1773): B.A., Trin. Coll., Dublin. Miscellaneous writer. Private chaplain to Lady Caroline Fox and tutor to Charles James Fox. Chaplain at Chelsea Hospital 1764-8; crown pension, 1764. Author of a once popular translation of Horace.

The Reverend Robert Stephen Hawker
(1873)

ROBERT STEPHEN HAWKER: THE PASTOR OF MORWENSTOW

I BELIEVE that the first book of poetry I ever owned was a copy of the 1869 edition, published by Parker of Oxford, of Robert Stephen Hawker's *Cornish Ballads and Other Poems*. This book had belonged to my mother, Ethel Dorothy Grylls, of the Gryllses of Helston, whose father, a lawyer, had settled in Launceston, the ancient capital of Cornwall, and had there builded himself a fine house which he named Trenuth, The New Home. At Trenuth Hawker's name was a household word. As a child I was sometimes taken in the summer to spend a few days at Bude, only six miles from Hawker's parish of Morwenstow; but it was not until 1930 or thereabouts that I made my first visit to Morwenstow. Since then, the fascination of the place has often drawn me back. It never ceases to attract, as J. C. Trewin has said, for its isolation, its wealth of tradition, and the splendour of its coast; but also for its association with Hawker, 'a beyond man in a beyond place', as Lord Ramsey of Canterbury described him in a sermon in Morwenstow church on the occasion of the centenary of Hawker's death, in 1975.

Below the cross over Hawker's tomb in a Plymouth cemetery are his words 'I would not be forgotten in this land.' Nor has he been, either in Plymouth, where he was born in 1803, nor in Cornwall, where he passed most of his life. Nor, indeed, in this realm of England, where his name was well known in his own day. His name may no longer be a household word, but it is remembered by poets and readers of poetry, by those who know the story of the Catholic Revival in the Church of England, and, of course, in a special way, by the people of Cornwall and Devon. He has benefited from the services of four biographers, the latest biography being that by Piers Brendon, which appeared in 1975. His *Cornish Ballads and Other Poems*, and his volume of prose pieces, *Footprints of Former Men in Far Cornwall*, have seldom

44

been out for print for long; while at the present time, 1981, two selections of his poems are currently in print. But his master-piece, the long, unfinished poem *The Quest of the Sangraal*, has not yet received the dignity of a separate edition, with the typography it deserves.

The best of Hawker's biographies is that by his son-in-law Charles Byles, which can never be superseded. I knew Charles Byles, and his wife, Hawker's daughter Pauline, and often visited them at their home in Beaconsfield in the 1930s. The worst of the biographies was the first to be written, Sabine Baring-Gould's *The Vicar of Morwenstow*, full of fiction and inaccuracies. Nevertheless, it is a very readable book and conveys an effective impression of Hawker's personality. His religious position is the principal theme of *Memorials of the late Reverend Robert Stephen Hawker, M.A.* by his friend Dr Frederick George Lee. Lee's is something of a partisan book; Baring-Gould's is even more so—from an opposite direction. Lee's aim was to uphold Hawker's religious position, as he understood and interpreted it; but Baring-Gould's view of Hawker's churchmanship was unsympathetic. As a pastor Hawker is perhaps remembered principally for his good deeds; foremost among them, perhaps, his scrupulous care in securing the Christian burial of the remains of shipwrecked sailors cast up by the sea on the rocks at the foot of the steep Morwenstow cliffs. Other aspect of his cure of souls are less well remembered.

Hawker's great-grandfather, Jacob, was Mayor of Exeter in 1744. His grandfather, the well known Calvinistic divine Dr Robert Hawker, was for forty-three years vicar of Charles Church, Plymouth. His father, Jacob Stephen Hawker, a physician, took orders soon after the birth of his eldest son, Robert Stephen, and from 1833 until his death in 1845 was vicar of Stratton, near Bude. Robert was born on 3rd December 1803, and was baptised by his uncle, the Reverend John Hawker, at Stoke Damerel, on 29th December of the same year. Since the family had such a strong clerical tradition, presumably few of their friends were surprised when, after an abortive apprenticeship to the law, Robert Stephen went up to Oxford in 1823 to study for Holy Orders. In 1834 he was appointed vicar of the remote country parish which he served until his death in 1875. His sermons were much appreciated by his parishioners, whether rich or poor—and they were mostly poor; and his reputation as a preacher spread. But it was very rarely that he preached outside his own church.

Hawker's sermons, although substantial quotations from a few of them occur in Byles's biography, have received little attention; in fact, they remain virtually unknown. This is surprising, for in those more believing days the sermon was still an integral part of the Sunday observance in parish church, popish chapel, or dissenting conventicle, and collections of sermons were widely read. But only two of Hawker's sermons appeared in print during his lifetime; and only one, I think, has been reprinted since. The two that Hawker saw in print were his Address to the Clergy on the subject of Rural Synods, and his Visitation sermon 'The Field of Rephidim'. These two discourses were published in 1844 and 1845 respectively. Presumably the editions were quite small and went out of print fairly quickly. In a letter to a friend written in 1871 Hawker says: 'I do very much wish that you could get for me a copy of my "Rural Synods". I want in these days of fuss to recall the fact that the first Ruridecanal Synod held in England was mine."

In 1844 Hawker, as well as being Vicar of Morwenstow, was Rural Dean of the deanery of Trigg Major, in the diocese of Exeter. (The Cornish see of Truro was not established until 1877.) Early in February 1844 each incumbent in the deanery received a printed copy of the following citation.

REVEREND SIR,
In obedience to the desire of many of the Clergy, and with the full sanction of our Right Reverend Father in God the Lord Bishop of this diocese, I propose, in these anxious days of the Ecclesiate, to restore the ancient usage of Rural Synods in the Deanery of Trigg-Major. I accordingly convene you to appear, in your surplice, in my church of Morwenstow, on the fifth of March next ensuing, at Eleven o'clock in the Forenoon, then and there, after Divine Service, to deliberate with your Brethren in chapter assembled.
    I remain,
       Reverend Sir,
          Your faithful Servant,

          R. S. HAWKER
             The Dean Rural

February 1844

On the morning appointed, those of the clergy who had chosen to comply with the citation met at the vicarage of Morwenstow, that remarkable vicarage built by Hawker himself, with its chimneys built in the form of the towers of churches and colleges with which he had been associated. (The absentees, probably there were only one or two, are likely to have been Low Church clergymen who objected to the recent ordinance of the Bishop of Exeter, Dr Henry Phillpotts, enjoining the use of the surplice at divine service, in place of the Genevan gown.) The clergy walked in procession from the vicarage to the church, which was already filled with parishioners. The Vicar of Poundstock, as junior incumbent, read morning service, after which the congregation withdrew. By then it was noon. The clergy moved down into the nave, and the synod, or chapter, was opened by Hawker, who read his address, in which he gave his hearers a careful account of the history and nature of the office of rural dean. He emphasised that his citation to attend the synod had enjoyed the general sanction of the Bishop, but that he himself, and not the Bishop, was responsible for the technical details of the citation; and he announced that he had drawn up, and would submit for the clergy's approval or correction, seven rules for the conduct of their future meetings. In the course of the address Hawker gives interesting and convincing reasons for his request to them to appear in their surplices. Typically, he cites not only ecclesiastical canons and precedent, but expounds the mystical significance of this vestment.

The 'Field of Rephidim' sermon, written for the Bishop of Exeter's visitation at St Mary Magdalene's, Launceston, on 27th June, 1845, was not delivered by Hawker, because his father had died on the previous day. It was read for him by the curate of Stratton, the Reverend T. N. Harper, in later years a priest of the Society of Jesus. The text was taken from Exodus xvii, verses 11 and 12: describing the battle of Rephidim, between Israel and the Amalekites: 'And it came to pass, when Moses held up his hand, that Israel prevailed: and when he let down his hand, Amalek prevailed. But Moses' hands were heavy; and they took a stone, and put it under him, and he sat thereon; and Aaron and Hur stayed up his hands, the one on the one side, and the other on the other side; and his hands were steady until the going down of the

sun.' Hawker called upon the clergy and laity of the diocese to
support their bishop, as Aaron and Hur had stayed up the hands
of Moses. The sermon is an eloquent defence of the episcopal
office and of the national church. Thinking, no doubt, of the
agitations stirred up by the Bishop's injunctions concerning the
wearing of the surplice, Hawker urged the clergy to be loyal, 'in
questions of law, in matters doubtful and dim', to their ordination
promise of canonical obedience. Hawker himself was
scrupulously careful in such matters. For example, when
celebrating the holy communion he had always used the ancient
eucharistic vestments; but when in 1869 a new bishop of Exeter,
Frederick Temple, forbade the use of vestments, Hawker at once
complied. He did not hold, as did many of the pioneers of the
Anglo-Catholic revival, that vestments, the 'mixed' chalice, the
'eastward position', stone altars, incense, etc. were so symbolic of
correct Catholic belief that their use could not be abandoned
without betrayal of the Faith. For him such things were the
proper and desirable adjuncts of public worship; but he believed
that it belonged to the bishop to regulate their use, and the bishop
was entitled to be obeyed. This had been very much Newman's
attitude in his Anglican days, as evidenced in the first chapter of
the *Apologia*, where he says: 'I considered myself simply as
the servant and instrument of my Bishop. I did not much care for
the Bench of Bishops . . . , but what to me was *jure divino* was the
voice of my Bishop in his own person. My own Bishop was my
Pope; I knew no other; the successor of the Apostles, the Vicar of
Christ.'

In 1874 Hawker said to a friend in Exeter: 'Much as I disapproved and was shocked at the nomination of the present Bishop
of Exeter [Temple]; yet, when he was appointed to the episcopal
bench I was bound by my ordination vow to obey him, and I have
obeyed him by discontinuing to wear vestments of which he disapproved. My conscience is my own.' About the same time he
wrote to Dr Frederick George Lee, vicar of All Saints, Lambeth:
'The open disobedience of the Ritualistic party is to myself a
problem and a puzzle. I obey [in the question of vestments];
bowing my head before circumstances and throwing the whole
responsibility on my Father in God. What else can a Christian
priest do?'

Further on in 'The Field of Rephidim' sermon Hawker appeals to the laity to show loyalty and affection to their Bishop, assailed by so many opponents 'in the mental conflicts of the day'. He warns them to be on their guard against all 'attempted return' on the part of the see and bishop of Rome: for, he declares, 'we were not, we are not, we will not be of Rome.' As to the past, and the origins of the *Ecclesia Anglicana*, his sense of history seems here a little defective; but he was highly sensitive to the claim of the national church to be 'the Catholic church of this land'; he disapproved of Dissenters, Roman Catholics included. His parish teemed with Methodists; but he seems to have had no Catholic parishioners. However, after 1850 he had as his neighbour at Bude the liturgiologist and antiquarian William Maskell, who had been the Bishop of Exeter's examining chaplain at the time of the Gorham Judgement. In 1847 Maskell had examined the Reverend G. C. Gorham, then suspect of heresy, for fifty hours before reporting to the Bishop that Mr Gorham was radically unsound in his theology of baptism; whereupon Dr Phillpotts had declined to institute him to the living of Brampton Speke, to which the patron had nominated him. On appeal to the Judicial Committee of the Privy Council Gorham was vindicated; Mr Maskell then seceded to the Church of Rome, as did Dr Manning, the Archdeacon of Chichester. Maskell was married and had a family, and so could not be admitted to Orders in the Roman communion, which demanded celibacy of its clergy, so he bought and restored Bude Castle, where he settled, to become a Justice of the Peace, and eventually Deputy-Lieutenant of Cornwall. Maskell and Hawker, who of course had known each other previously, became very friendly; and whenever Maskell was visited, as he often was, by members of the Roman Catholic clergy, he always included an excursion to Morwenstow, to meet Hawker, in his plans for their entertainment. In this way Hawker got to know Dr Charles Meynell, the professor of theology at Oscott College, and a number of other Roman priests.

Gradually Hawker became more sympathetic towards Roman Catholics and their church. As early as 1845 the idea had been mooted in Roman Catholic circles of setting up diocesan bishoprics in England and Wales, thus restoring normal episcopal government to a body which had for long been under the authority of vicars apostolic, bishops indeed, but without the jurisdiction proper to diocesan bishops. It looks as if rumours of this project had reached Hawker and occasioned the warning given in his visitation sermon. The pope gave his approval in 1847, but nothing was done until 1850. In that year the new dioceses were erected by papal brief, and Dr Wiseman's tactless handling of the matter provoked an outbreak of No Popery demonstrations all over the country, in protest against this act of 'Papal aggression'. But Hawker said that it was all a foolish excitement about nothing. In a letter to a friend he said that the Methodists had been allowed to invade every parish in the land, and in a hundred years no official protest had been made, nor any action taken against them. Compared to the activities and pretensions of the Wesleyans he could not see that the assumption of territorial titles by a handful of popish bishops was any cause for alarm.

In the same letter Hawker deprecated any 'unnecessary conflict' with brethren outside the fold. The Methodists in his parish knew well that his bark was worse than his bite, and that there was no malice in his caustic witticisms at their expense. For a long time he had actually had a Methodist as his churchwarden. This man once said that the Vicar had been one of his best and dearest friends for forty years. In his generosity to the poor Hawker made no distinction between church folk and nonconformists. He once gave a party at the vicarage for ministers of different denominations. When someone expressed surprise, he could not resist making the comment: 'They are the clean and unclean beasts feeding together in the Ark'.

His visitation sermon at Launceston was delivered only four months before John Henry Newman left the Church of England. Some of the 'Oxford men'—but none of the first rank—had already left. Towards the end of the sermon there is a moving reference to these events and apprehensions. Hawker had known some of the Tractarians: among them John Rouse Bloxham, and, though perhaps less well, Newman, Keble, Pusey (whom he did not much care for), Ward, and Marriott. But he had not been of their councils, and had always kept to his own independent line. (In or about 1845 Keble paid Hawker a visit at Morwenstow, and had praised Hawker's ballad 'The Poor Man and his Parish

Church'.)

Hawker's ballads tell us a good deal about his relations with his humble parishioners, and his own line of conduct as a pastor of souls. Further light on Hawker's notions on pastoral theology may be gleaned from his sermons; but, as has been said, only two were published in his lifetime, only one has been published since. Yet there is a large collection of Hawker's manuscript sermons and sermon notes in the Bodleian Library. Some of these are written in Hawker's own hand, others in that of his niece Emma Kingdon. Until a selection of these sermons is published, any attempt to assess Hawker's powers and achievements as a prose writer must be incomplete. When first ordained, and for a good many years afterwards, he wrote out his sermons in full, or at least in the form of copious notes, and read out the text from his manuscript. When a large quantity of these manuscripts had accumulated, he one day burned them. A neighbouring clergyman protested, and told him that if he had had them printed they would have done good to many. Hawker replied that he doubted it, because he had spread the ashes of his sermons over a turnip field on his glebe, and no more turnips had come up in that field than in any other on his land. From that time onwards he always preached extempore. His sermons were carefully prepared, but he could improvise very effectively if there were need.

What kind of preacher was he? Fortunately, there is ample testimony from which to answer this question. Moreover, he has left on record some of his own ideas on the subject of preaching, and some of the principles that he followed in composing and delivering his sermons. Hawker was a tall, well-built man, somewhat robust, with silver hair, and must have been quite a striking figure in the pulpit, which at Morwenstow was of a slightly higher elevation than is usual, until some curate took it upon himself to have it lowered. Hawker thought that the teaching authority of the priest should be emphasised by his speaking from a position well above the level of the congregation. Sometimes, however, he would speak from the step outside the chancel screen; perhaps when speaking to his flock less formally. His voice was strong and clear, his manner slow and solemn. In a letter of 24th October, 1863, to his friend the publisher J. G. Godwin, he says that his friend and neighbour the Reverend William Valentine, a

Yorkshire clergyman who had bought a property in
Morwenstow, 'is regular at Church—a simple-minded Man, as
you will see when I tell you that he thinks it a treat! to hear me
preach! Thank God I never was a popular preacher and never
shall be.' But ten years later, writing to his friend and benefactress
Mrs Watson, he somewhat modified this self-estimate. 'You must
remember', he says, 'that for many years I have had but one
companion. So entirely have I lived alone that except in my
Father's lifetime and in his Church I have never preached in any
other pulpit but my own. Yet Strangers and those who seek to
flatter me say that in a Town I should be a very popular preacher
and have hundreds to listen instead of this small flock.' The truth
of this judgement was proved when, in 1874, the year before his
death, Hawker preached on the evening of Easter Sunday at All
Saints, Lambeth, and made an appeal for offerings to help him
repair the church at Morwenstow. Of this occasion the vicar of
All Saints, Dr Lee, said: 'His Sermon I shall never forget. He
spoke most eloquently of the certainty of the Resurrection, of the
Faith and the Hope and the Joy of the Mother of God, and of the
blessed, and of our own enduring warfare here. His voice,
melodious and of a wide compass, was as clear as a bell; his
manner simple, dignified and loving; his oratory perfect. The
congregation listened with breathless attention, and were deeply
struck by his remarkable powers.'

Another of the rare occasions when he preached outside his
own two churches—he served also the neighbouring church of
Welcombe, in Devon, a mile or two from Morwenstow, though it
was never officially annexed to his cure—was on the evening of
5th January, 1868, when he preached an appeal sermon at
Stratton, near Bude, on behalf of the parish schools. He had often
been asked to preach this annual sermon, but had always refused,
since he was sure he would break down, as so many of his friends
and kindred were buried in and around the church, of which his
father had been vicar. And so it happened. As his son-in-law,
Charles Byles, recorded: 'He suddenly interrupted the thread of
his discourse, and with a faltering voice exclaimed: "I stand amid
the dust of those near and dear to me."'

Hawker was accustomed to record his thoughts—inspirations
or reflections—in manuscript books of a special paper, prepared

and bound to his specifications. These fascinating *Thought Books*, as he called them, are now lodged in the Bodleian Library. They contain many references to preaching, of which a few may be cited here.

Even the language of persuasion seems misplaced in the enforcement of Holy Truth. It is like recommending wares for sale. A mere enunciation of sacred facts, without anticipation of the possibility of disbelief, appears to me the most adapted to the Words of God. A simple oracular communication is best.

*   *   *   *

My style is lowly. May he who made the water wine render my speech acceptable to the taste of my people.

*   *   *   *

Have some mystic sentence in your sermon hard to be understood; themes for future thought.

*   *   *   *

In the pulpit a clergyman should not stoop. He is a pillar. He should stand as if an arch of the roof rested on each shoulder.

His sermons were simple and orthodox, mostly on biblical themes; he usually took the words of Scripture in their literal meaning. He did not trouble his hearers with abstruse points of divinity, or with controversial matters. After the Bible, the book that he consulted most was the *Summa Theologica* of St Thomas Aquinas. Writing to another clergyman in 1855 he says: 'I have used ever since 1835 as my daily manual the Noble work of St T. Aquinas.' He was also fond of a curious old work, Gretser *De Sancta Cruce*, from which he drew much of his symbolic interpretation of Scripture and of liturgy and iconography.

A harvest festival sermon, whose text is preserved in the Bodleian, is a good example of his simple, pastoral manner. This sermon is undated, and was fairly certainly preached at Morwenstow. It would have been understood by every man, woman, and child of the labouring class in the congregation as fully as by the more educated and prosperous parishioners, such as the Waddon-Martyn family, of Tonacombe Manor.

Another contemporary, the Reverend W. Haslam, vicar of

Baldhu, has left us a good account, quoted by Byles, of Hawker's homiletic style.

His preaching struck me very much; he used to select the subject of his sermon from the Gospel of the day all through the year. This happened to be 'Good Samaritan Sunday', so we had a discourse upon the 'certain man who went down from Jerusalem to Jericho', in which he told us that the poor wounded man was Adam's race; the priest who went by was the Patriarchal dispensation; the Levite, the Mosaic; and the Good Samaritan represented Christ; the inn was the Church; and the two pence the Sacraments.

He held up his manuscript before his face, and read it out boldly, because he 'hated', he said, 'those fellows who read their sermons and all the time pretended to preach them'; and he especially abhorred those who secreted notes in their Bibles: 'Either have a book, sir, or none!'

The harvest festival sermon referred to was on the text: 'And they of Bethshemesh were reaping their wheat-harvest in the valley, and they lifted up their eyes and saw the ark, and they rejoiced to see it.' (I Samuel vi, verse 13.) An extract must suffice here.

The Israelites had rebelled against God—in Church and State—and the Lord had sold them into the hands of the Philistines, and they that hated them were lords over them. The Prophets were silent, and the Priests were mute; and there was no King in Israel at that time. The People went up from their cities to battle, and were beaten in the war. So on a day they thought fit to take with them into the field of fight the Ark of the Lord. This was, so to speak, the altar of their church. It held their sacred vessels and their holiest things. The two tables of their law were in that sacred chest—the Books of their Religion, as we should call our Bible, and our Liturgy or Public Prayer. There was a silver cup too, filled with some of the Manna which came down from Heaven—when men did eat angels' food—the staff of Aaron which showed by its blossoms who should be Priest—this was therein. So the ark was the wooden altar or shrine of the Hebrew people. And this they had borne forth upon the shoulders of men—to set in the fore-part of the battle array in order that their enemies might flee. But because the nation had transgressed, God did not think fit to interfere even to save the Ark of His own Church. He suffered the Philistines to take it as a prey for a little while. At the time of the text the Lord thought fit to restore this Altar to the Hebrew land. Peradventure there were fifty righteous in Israel left—and so the guilty cities were favoured for the fifty's sake—be this as it may. The Philistines took a new cart and chose out two milch kine, on which there had never come yoke; and they took their calves away and shut them up at home. They carried out then the Ark of the Lord, and set it in the cart—and let the Ark alone. Now the nature of the kine would have been to have

stood still at the door where their young were shut up. Instead of which
they were constrained (although no man smote them, or was their guide)
to depart; and the kine took the straight way to Bethshemesh, a strange
and distant place to them. And they went along the road, lowing as they
went. They turned not aside to the right hand or to the left. What a
wonderful sight! The mower stood up to see, and his scythe fell forgotten
on the ground. The gleaner ceased from her task, where the ears were
thick and full. They that had bound the sheaves forgot their former
haste, and the men of Bethshemesh who were reaping their wheat
harvest in the valley lifted up their eyes and saw the Ark of God, and
they rejoiced to see it. My brethren, it was a great and solemn memorial
of the Lord which moved their minds in the midst of their summer toil.
God so loved the world that he mingled Himself as it were with all the
simple labours of the ancient men. His first law was not given in cities
made with hands, but it was delivered unto Moses beneath the bright
blue roof of heaven—and it was filled with statutes and ordinances and
customs for men who should sow and reap. The husbandry of the
Hebrews was a religious thing—the common matters of the field and its
daily toil—the pious Jew might if he would behold God. The promise to
the Israelites and their reward was the blessings of the Basket and of their
store—the corn and wine and oil. When the harvest was ripe the sickle
could not be put in until a sheaf of the firstfruits had been reaped and
carried unto the Altar, to wave it there on high to acknowledge that the
earth was the Lord's and the fulness thereof. And when the corn was
carried in, a great part of it was used many a day in the worship of the
Jews. All night, and again at dawn, a meat offering (which was a cake of
unleavened bread) was baked on the coals of the great altar and eaten
before it in memory of Him who first created wheat before it grew. Every
sabbath day the priest set twelve loaves—one for every tribe—on a table
of gold before the vail, to be the shew-bread of the public oblation of all
the people.

And when the harvest was over the feast of Ingathering was held in
memory of Him who had spread out the earth and watered it from above
with the former and the latter rain. All things therefore in the Hebrew
fields testified concerning God. The people themselves were not so much
a nation as they were a Church. Their native soil was to them holy
ground. The fields of their fathers were filled with many memorials of
God, and the Ark of the Lord was that for which the faithful Israelites
lived and laboured, and fought and died. Well might the men of
Bethshemesh rejoice when they saw the Ark once more. That was the
good old Hebrew time—the sects of the Sadducees and Pharisees were
then unknown. In deep and strong simplicity they served their God.

But again let us search the field for memorials of the Christian. How
beautiful are the instructions of Harvest time to us—how thankful ought
we to be that our Blessed Saviour did not leave His Gospel to be delivered
by word of mouth. When men talk of persons as inspired to teach, they
seem to forget the Bible at home, or what a Scripture it is. I am sure that

more good would come if we were to remember and repeat the Parables of Harvest or Harvest time than from any sermon which mere man could preach. Only call to mind who and what manner of person he was who walked with his disciples through the cornfields on the Sabbath day. What a good and solemn thought for us that at such a season as this the Redeemer of man went forth to meditate among the fields, and looked with kind and thoughtful eyes on the homes and harvests of the husbandmen. So again, how striking it is to reflect that he, even Jesus, who could have taught us the same truth in other words yet chose the parable of the Wheat and the Tares to teach us how good and evil grow together till the end of the world: and then will be divided for evermore. Think again how Jesus hath shewn us in a field the way men grow in soul for God—first the blade, then the ear, then the full corn in the ear. Even thus the plants of wheat lift up their voices to us and say: Increase as we do until thou come to thy grave in a full age, like as a shock of corn cometh in his season.

In Stratton in 1834, at Whitestone in 1836, and at Morwenstow in 1837, Hawker preached a sermon on the text 'How Dreadful is this Place,' which was an appeal for contributions towards the restoration of old churches and chapels, and the building of new ones, in England and Wales. This sermon is interesting for its references to the early Church and to the doctrine of the Apostolic Succession; and it seems to set out a way of life for ministers of the Gospel similar to that which Hawker himself followed. A sermon of 1831 on behalf of the sufferers in the Irish famine was presumably preached at North Tamerton, where Hawker was curate from 1829 until he went to Morwenstow in 1834. It survives, but in condensed form only, in the pages of Byles's *Life and Letters*.

As time went on, and the strong tide of biblical criticism gave rise to new, and apparently unorthodox, interpretations of the ancient faith, Hawker, like many others then and since, came to feel that Rome was the only strong bulwark against infidelity. In later years he corresponded, at least sporadically, with a number of prominent Roman Catholic divines, among them Newman, Wiseman, the Bishop of Southwark (Dr Grant), and Dr Meynell. Meynell he knew personally. But in what he taught his flock he never went beyond what he held to be sound doctrine according to the High Anglican tradition.

In his *The Victorian Church* (vol. I, p. 570) Dr Owen Chadwick says that in the Victorian era 'Every denomination

worried over its reason for existence, its doctrine and authority
and government . . . In every church the need for authority con-
flicted with the heritage of freedom and generated tension or
schism. In their different ways Wiseman the Roman Catholic and
Phillpotts the Anglican bishop . . . and Chalmers the Pres-
byterian . . . stood for the independent authority of a religious
society to rule its life and teaching; . . . The early Victorians
witnessed a schism or two among the Methodists, schism among
the Quakers, schism on the grand scale among Scottish
Presbyterians, secession from the Church of England, . . . a
Roman Catholic body divided over everything but the necessity
for not being divided. Because the armies not seldom wheeled
into battle under the generalship of bigots or fools, we may forget
that in some form the battle was necessary to health, an
unavoidable pace in the march towards free churches in a free
state.'

This battle may have been necessary to the health of the
church, or churches; but like all battles it was a dangerous and
nasty affair for those taking part in it. From Hawker's ordination
in 1831 until his death in 1875 one crisis after another disturbed
the peace of mind of churchmen. In 1836 there was the Hampden
affair, when Newman and others raised an agitation against the
proposed appointment of the Reverend R. D. Hampden to the
Regius Professorship of Divinity at Oxford, on the grounds of his
supposed unorthodoxy. Hawker's bishop, Phillpotts of Exeter,
had supported this unsuccessful protest, and had said that he
would dispense Exeter College undergraduates from attendance at
Hampden's lectures.

Then in 1847 Phillpotts and twelve other bishops attempted,
again unsuccessfully, to get Hampden's nomination to the
bishopric of Hereford annulled. The year following came the
Gorham affair, on account of which William Maskell seceded. A
period of relative quiet then followed, until 1850, when Dr
Wiseman's mishandling of the restoration of the Roman Catholic
hierarchy in England and Wales had the effect of forcing the
'papal claims' on the attention of Anglicans, most of whom found
them disturbing.

In 1859 Darwin published *The Origin of Species*, which to
begin with caused comparatively little excitement; in the first

instance the scientific attack on the traditional and biblically-based notions of cosmology and cosmogony came from German higher critics rather than from biologists. In 1860 some of the disturbing findings and theories of the new science of biblical criticism were placed before the British public in a book entitled *Essays and Reviews*. Today the best-known contributors to this symposium are Mark Pattison, Benjamin Jowett, and Frederick Temple (later archbishop of Canterbury). For the first time a widely-read book exposed the gap between Christian belief as traditionally held and the 'secular' beliefs of 19th century men of education. The writers make it clear that a great part of the Bible's contents is made up of poetry, myth, legend, allegory, parable, etc., so that it was impossible any longer to understand everything in Scripture in a literal sense. Today this may seem obvious; but it must be remembered that in the Roman Catholic church it was not until the publication in 1943 of Pope Pius XII's encyclical *Divino afflante Spiritu* that complete freedom of critical research was accepted as both legitimate and necessary in the field of biblical studies.

The writers in *Essays and Reviews* also maintain that the truth of Christianity could not be proved by miracles and prophecy. Statements of this kind came as a great shock to most church people, and there was an instant outcry against the book. In 1862 a prosecution was brought in the Court of Arches, and the book's editor, H. B. Wilson, and one of the contributors, Rowland Williams, were suspended from their benefices for a year. The sentence was overturned on appeal to the Judicial Committee of the Privy Council, which ruled that the ideas advanced by Wilson and Williams could be lawfully held and maintained by Anglican clergymen. The two Archbishops declared that they could not accept this decision.

Hawker had no time for *Essays and Reviews*, which he considered an infidel production; but his own faith was not disturbed by it. As he explained to his friend Godwin in a letter of 30th March, 1862: 'When I was an Undergrad. the Head of a House recommended to my Soul a Book—Hey's Lectures on the Articles. It was a Granary of "Essays and Reviews". I read, and I doubted the total Revelation. My Notes contain at this day each an embryon of modern infidelity. The Book was a Seedplot of

Schism and Disbelief. A friend referred me to the Summa of St Thos. Aquinas. I read and I was rescued. I found therein every question in Theology that can enter into the imagination of a Man discussed *pro* and *con* with the inference laid down and the authorities. Since then I have made it my solitary Book . . . When a theme of controversy brattles in the air, while hostile language throngs the voice and mind, I unclose my ancient page, and there I read the doubt of Ages solved. A few still small words and there is no more to be said.'

There was, too, a vein of mysticism, or poetic imagination, in Hawker that brought him light, a light sufficient at least for him, on many a problem in Scripture that had perplexed his mind. Meditating in the chancel of his church he would often receive illuminations that he regarded as having a heavenly source. He believed that these thoughts came sometimes from his Guardian Angel, sometimes from the Angel of the Altar.

Another worry was the affair of the Bishop of Natal, John William Colenso, a Cornishman from St Austell, who had questioned the traditional authorship and the historical accuracy of the Pentateuch and the Book of Joshua. Colenso also denied the doctrine of eternal punishment, and accepted the criticisms made by Darwin and the geologist Sir Charles Lyell of the chronology and cosmology of the Book of Genesis. Writing to Mrs Watson on 29th May, 1864 Hawker says:

On Thursday the Archdeacon held his Visitation at Bude . . . There was no Sermon but a long charge from the Archdeacon and not in my own private opinion a judicious one. He brought before us and the Church-wardens laymen and Farmers all the topics of the day—about Colenso and Darwin and Sir C. Lyell who had impugned the Bible records of Creation and the Origin of Man and the Flood. What I condemn is his introducing subjects of infidelity and doubt in order to refute them of which the auditors had never before heard. Many of the Farmers, so Cann [Hawker's churchwarden] informed me, would remember the objections to the Bible who would not understand the Archdeacon's reply. You know I daresay from the Papers that Colenso attacks the chronology of Holy Writ, whereas my little children at the School would teach him that whereas in Heaven Time does not exist there could be no such thing regarded in inspiration as Dates or Periods or Years.

Hawker's faith in the Christian revelation as he had received it was impervious to infidel publications, and was quite unaffected

by the views of scientists of whatever eminence; but the attitude
of divines such as Hampden and Colenso, and of the contributors
to *Essays and Reviews*, and the fact that such men could not be
silenced by ecclesiastical authority, nor deprived of their
benefices, lessened his confidence in the Church of England as a
guardian of revelation. What sort of church could it be that
accepted men like Hampden and Colenso among its authorised
teachers, and allowed men like Gorham to exercise the cure of
souls? Hawker loved the Church of his baptism, and to the end of
his life would speak of 'our dear old church'; but there were times
when he wondered if perhaps something had not gone so
seriously wrong at the time of the Reformation changes that the
apostolic succession of the church's ministry had been, if not lost,
at least rendered uncertain. In March, 1874 he consulted Dr
Frederick George Lee, on this question. Lee, who was an
authority on Elizabethan church history, did his best to reassure
Hawker. Lee was a persuasive writer on the Anglican side in the
'Roman' controversy; but from time to time he had doubts
himself. In the end, shortly before his death in 1902, he joined
the Roman communion. Lee was able to some extent to reassure
Hawker; but not entirely. As he put it in his *Memorials of the
late Rev. Robert Stephen Hawker M.A.*, published in 1876:
'Want of sympathy, isolation; a perusal of indigested statements
resulting from a prolonged inquiry into the character and motives
of the "Reformers", entirely overthrowing ordinary and old-
fashioned Anglican traditions, came upon him like a shock; while
doubts about the validity of our English Ordinations, coupled
with the discussion which arose concerning the validity of Archbishop Tait's baptism, added efficiently to his difficulties. Moreover, he saw, or thought he saw, in the future the certain triumph
of an already too-triumphant and ever-encroaching Erastianism,
disestablishment, disendowment, disruption, and confusion. And
so his soul was low.'
    Hawker's health and spirits had begun to fail before the death
of his first wife, Charlotte, in 1863. Even then he was struggling
with an increasing burden of debt. The value of his stipend had
decreased; bad summers and bad harvests had reduced his income
from his glebe. Opium, taken originally, as by so many at that
time, as a medicine, became for him a necessary habit, and added

to his depression. After his wife's death he roused himself to begin his intended masterpiece, the long blank-verse poem *The Quest of the Sangraal*; but he was unable to complete it. To it he prefixed the words:

TO
A VACANT CHAIR
AND
AN ADDED STONE
I CHANT
THESE SOLITARY SOUNDS

But in 1864, at the age of sixty, he married again. His first wife, Charlotte Ians, had been much older than himself; his second, Pauline Kuczynski, was much younger. The first marriage was childless; the second gave him three daughters: Morwenna Pauline, Rosalind, and Juliot. Pauline Kuczynski, the daughter of a Polish father and an English mother, was twenty when she married Robert Stephen Hawker. Naturally, her parents were at first not enthusiastic; but Pauline affirmed that she would rather have ten years with Robert Stephen Hawker than a lifetime with any other man. In the event, neither of them had any regrets.

In 1869, in addition to increasing ill-health, came a new blow. Frederick William Temple, one of the contributors to *Essays and Reviews*, was elected to succeed Henry Phillpotts as Bishop of Exeter. However, Hawker bore up. At an Archdeacon's Visitation at which he was present the clergy were discussing what should be their attitude to their new bishop. Hawker gave it as his opinion that it was their duty, like the sons of Noah, to hide their new prelate's theological nakedness. He ended a witty speech by saying in a grave tone: 'My brethren, we must cover Noah!' (cf. Genesis ix, 20-24.) Yet when all the clergy were avoiding the new bishop at one of his first visitations, Hawker, who was the senior incumbent present, at once came forward to help the Bishop put on his vestments. (Twenty years previously Mr Gorham had called on Hawker at Morwenstow, and had been kindly received. They discovered a common interest in botany!)

In May, 1875 a new curate arrived at Morwenstow, and Hawker, who was unwell, was able to get away for a short visit to his brother Claud at Boscastle. Hawker seems to have sensed that his end was near, and on the previous Sunday he had preached a sermon that was interpreted by his parishioners as a farewell. Would that we had its text; but it was preached extempore and went unrecorded. When the Vicar and Pauline reached Boscastle they found that Claud Hawker was unwell too; so after a few days, and because the new curate and his family were temporarily installed in the vicarage at Morwenstow, Pauline Hawker decided to take her husband to Plymouth, for further medical advice. Before leaving Boscastle, Hawker sent for his churchwarden from Morwenstow and told him that he did not expect to come back alive, and gave him directions as to where he wished to be buried. The move to Plymouth took place at the end of June, rooms having been engaged at no. 9, Lockyer Street. On 26th July Hawker wrote to his curate, Mr Comber, telling him to be sure to attend the Bishop's forthcoming visitation at Welcombe and to present to the Archdeacon the offertory-book and all other necessary information. During these weeks in Plymouth Hawker became increasingly feeble. At times his mind gave way, and he became confused. Pauline knew that he was not likely to recover; wishing for a last photograph of her husband to be taken she sent to Morwenstow for his surplice, his replica of St Cuthbert's stole, and his biretta. The last photograph of him, taken by Hawke of Plymouth, is reproduced in Charles Byles's *Life and Letters of Robert Stephen Hawker*. It is similar in pose, and identical as to dress, with one taken earlier that forms the frontispiece of Lee's *Memorials*. There is a difference in the features, however; the picture in Lee's book shows a handsome old priest, seemingly in good health; the final picture is unmistakably that of a dying man. A few days after this photograph had been taken Hawker became more seriously ill; the physician who was caring for him, Dr Square, diagnosed a clot of blood in the artery of his left arm. There could now be no hope of his recovery.

In spite of her half-Polish parentage, Pauline Hawker was still at this time a member of the Church of England, in which she had been brought up. But she knew her husband's mind as did no one else, and on her own initiative she now asked for a Catholic priest from Plymouth Cathedral to visit him. When she told her husband what she had done, he understood perfectly. He raised himself in his bed, as if all pain were forgotten, and burst out into exclamations of joy and praise. This is the testimony of the Hawker children's governess, Miss Savage, who was present. Like Mrs Hawker, she was not a Roman Catholic.

In the evening Canon Mansfield arrived. Hawker was conscious, and welcomed the priest, kissing his hand. The last rites were then administered. Robert Stephen Hawker, Vicar of Morwenstow, died at 8.20 a.m. on Sunday 15th August, 1875, the Feast of the Assumption of the Blessed Virgin. The funeral took place in what is now Plymouth Old Cemetery, off Ford Park Road, on Wednesday, 18th August. As far as possible, purple was worn by the mourners instead of black, which Hawker greatly disliked. He was buried in cassock, surplice, and stole, and on his coffin was a plate bearing the words:

ROBERT STEPHEN HAWKER
For 41 years Vicar of Morwenstow,
who died in the Catholic Faith,
On the Feast of the Assumption of our Blessed Lady,
1875
Aged 71
Requiescat in Pace

Eighteen years later Pauline Hawker was laid to rest in the same grave.

Hawker's deathbed reception into the Catholic church was the occasion for the outbreak, in the press and elsewhere, of a bitter controversy, which rumbled on for years, and of which echoes may still, now and then, be heard. (See the inscription which is still suffered to remain underneath the photograph of Hawker which hangs on the west wall of Morwenstow church.) But today it is hard to see why these simple facts should ever have been made a matter of such bitter controversy, or why charges of bad faith should have been levelled at Hawker after his death. It is obvious, as his son-in-law and principal biographer has said, that to the very last Hawker cherished a deep affection for the church of his baptism and ordination; equally, it cannot be questioned that over a long period of time he had been gravely disturbed by trends and tendencies towards unorthodoxy in that church.

At the close of his life Pauline Hawker acted on what she knew

to be her husband's deepest wishes; but she told a friend to whom
she wrote soon after his death that he would never have made the
move himself, because, she believed, he had a prevision of all the
trouble it would bring on herself and the children.

Hawker's forebodings concerning the future of the Church of
England have not been altogether fulfilled. On the other hand, the
Roman Catholic church is undergoing today a phase of tension
and disturbance not unlike that which the Church of England was
experiencing in Hawker's day. During the present century the
ecumenical movement has led to better understanding and
friendlier relations between the two churches. Theological discourse has shifted to new areas; the old controversies concerning
apostolic succession and the validity of orders seem to have faded
out.

When the centenary of Hawker's death was celebrated in
Morwenstow church on Sunday morning 10th August 1975
three bishops of the Church of England were present, the first
lesson was read by a Carmelite friar, and Methodists as well as
Anglicans and Roman Catholics were present in the three-
hundred-strong congregation. All were united in thanking God
and honouring the memory of a true shepherd of souls and fine
poet. As Bishop Michael Ramsey said in his centenary sermon,
Robert Stephen Hawker was 'a beyond man in a beyond place'.
His light shines still.

BARON CORVO AT THE SCOTS COLLEGE

FREDERICK WILLIAM ROLFE, also known as Baron Corvo, the author of *Hadrian the Seventh*, *Chronicles of the House of Borgia*, *The Desire and Pursuit of the Whole*, and other remarkable books, was expelled from the Scots College in Rome, in 1890, after only five months' residence as a student for the priesthood. Rolfe was permanently embittered by this experience; but it did nothing to weaken his conviction that he was called to the priesthood; and he always maintained that he had never been given any clear and sufficient reason for his expulsion, which he regarded as unjust.

Apart from an article by Shane Leslie in the *London Mercury* of September 1923, Rolfe's life-story was told for the first time by A. J. A. Symons in his book *The Quest for Corvo*, which was published in 1934. This brilliant book inevitably set the tone for all subsequent writing about Rolfe down to 1961, when three of the contributors to a symposium of essays written for Rolfe's centenary in 1960[1] drew attention to some of the defects of Symons's pioneer biography. Symons believed that the supreme purpose of biography is 'not to record but to reveal'.[2] Mr Julian Symons has said, in his biography of his brother,[3] that *The Quest for Corvo* 'in its balance and fine sensitiveness, in its careful omission of material, however rich, which would have destroyed the Corvine figure in the carpet, . . . is a work of art.' True; but as Dom Sylvester Houédard has said:[4] 'The great (and perhaps only) fault of *The Quest* is that we are mesmerised into believing it to be a real investigation, whereas in fact we are being taken on a carefully conducted tour . . .'

1890 was a crucial year in Rolfe's life; in relation to his biography it is a year of gaps and puzzles. Among these puzzles until recently has been the matter of Rolfe's departure from the *Collegio Scozzese*. *Why* was he turned out? In his autobiographical novel *Hadrian the Seventh* George Arthur Rose (that is, F. W. Rolfe) says: 'After four months in college I was expelled suddenly and brutally. No reason has ever been given me: and I have never been aware of a reason which could justify so atrocious an outrage . . . If my legitimate superiors had grounds for their action, grounds which they durst expose to the daylight; and, if they frankly had stated the same to me, I believe I should have given very little trouble.' The late Canon Carmont and other contemporaries of Rolfe at the college had little of substance to say to A. J. A. Symons about this except that, as they remembered him, Rolfe had struck his fellow-students as eccentric, as not 'fitting in', as not taking his studies seriously, and as getting the college a bad name by getting into debt with Roman tradesmen. Apart from this, Symons was unable to obtain any precise statement of the reasons for Rolfe's dismissal.

In October, 1969, Canon Alexander MacWilliam, of the diocese of Aberdeen, himself an alumnus of the Scots College, was so kind as to inform me of the discovery at the college of some documents relating to Rolfe's expulsion. These papers were duly printed by Canon MacWilliam in an article 'Fr. Rolfe and the Scots College, Rome', which was published in the *Innes Review*'s[5] autumn number for 1970. This article appeared in time for Mr Donald Weeks to be able to mention it in his biography *Corvo*, which was published in the following year.

Mr Weeks's book runs to over four hundred pages, and gives a much fuller account of Corvo's life than A. J. A. Symons had been able to. That was to be expected. Symons was a pioneer in this field. Mr Weeks was writing thirty-six years later, after many years of arduous and enthusiastic research. The quantity of new information about Rolfe that he had discovered, and the number of lacunae in his life story that he had been able to fill, at once placed all Corvinists in his debt. One of his discoveries was the novel *Frank Baylis* by John Crane (the pseudonym of Charles McVarish), published in 1903, while Rolfe was still working on *Hadrian the Seventh.* Like *Hadrian,* Crane's novel deals with the Scots College in Rome, and the picture of it that he gives is not dissimilar to Rolfe's. Mr Weeks says that there is no evidence that Rolfe ever read *Frank Baylis,* or even knew of it, or who the author was. They had known each other in Rome, of course.

Crane left the college of his own volition two months after Rolfe's dismissal, and was ordained in the Anglican communion in 1895.

It must be said that Donald Weeks's *Corvo* is not written with the grace of Symons's *Quest;* but that one could hardly have expected. Symons was a writer of unusual grace and artistry. In fact, Mr Weeks's style would have caused Rolfe agonies. It is hard to understand why his publishers did not submit his text to a thorough overhaul; as it is, the stylistic infelicities are so many and so jarring that the reader's pleasure in an extremely interesting book is diminished.

Another defect in this book comes from its author's lack of knowledge and understanding of Roman Catholic belief and practice, and of ecclesiastical usage and terminology. Symons suffered from the same shortcoming, though in a less marked degree.

Since the publication of *Corvo* a third biography of Rolfe has appeared, by the American scholar Miriam Benkovitz. This book must be considered the best biography so far, in spite of its poor style. One can be grateful to the authors of all three books, while at the same time waiting impatiently for Mr Cecil Woolf's expected biography, which will probably be recognized as definitive: in so far, that is, as any biography can be definitive.

Canon MacWilliam's article on Rolfe at the Scots College is mentioned by Mr Weeks and Dr Benkovitz; but I am not sure that they have understood all the implications of the material that it contains. Indeed, I am not entirely sure that Canon MacWilliam himself did so. Rolfe would certainly have appreciated the article's literary and scholarly qualities, but he would surely have contested the writer's view of his character and personality. At any rate, the documents published by Canon MacWilliam seem to me capable of a rather different interpretation from the one he gives them.

The papers in question are: (1) a letter, in Italian, from Signor Luigi Giomini, a tailor, to the rector of the Scots College, seeking the rector's intervention in the matter of 513.50 lire owed to Giomini by Il Signore Rolfe. This letter is dated 10th April, 1890, and a postscript records that on 3rd March Rolfe had made a payment of 25 lire towards settlement of the debt. (2) An undated letter, of about the same time, written in English, from Mr J. Y. B. Evans, a pharmacist in the Via Condotti, concerning the sum of 156 lire which he is owed by Rolfe. (3) Two letters from Rolfe to Monsignor Campbell, the rector of the college. (4) A report by Monsignor Campbell concerning Rolfe's expulsion. (5) A letter from Father Peter Paul Mackey, O.P.[6], to the rector explaining that his having given some assistance to Rolfe in his difficulties does not imply any approval of Rolfe or his behaviour.

On 23rd March, 1890, Rolfe was told by the rector that he must leave the college. On the same day he wrote to the rector as follows:

Monsignore,
Please allow me to adopt the somewhat unusual course of addressing you on paper, as I find it more easy to express myself in writing than in any other way, and also because, I imagine, it will be more convenient to you if I place my thoughts on this morning's interview in this fashion.

I understood you to say that you were on the point of writing to the Lord Archbishop of St Andrews and Edinburgh, my diocesan, to the effect that I was in the habit of breaking the rules of the house by spending the hours of recreation in private pursuits (literary work), that you could not, under the circumstances, permit me to remain a member of this College, nor would you allow the three months 16 days I have already spent here to count towards my Ordination.

Until you spoke to me this morning, I had not the remotest idea that I was laying myself open to the charge of infringing any rule by using my own discretion as to my occupation in recreation hours and during vacations. Indeed, I have frankly written to Dr Smith[7] telling him how I intended to spend, and have spent, what I considered was my spare time, both before and after I left England. There was no disguise about it on my part and as other members of this house have spent and do spend the time allotted to recreation on their own affairs, I have never had, as I said before, any reason to think that I was meriting such a serious punishment as that with which you are about to visit me.

With regard to vacations, I had no idea I was doing anything unusual in asking leave to do what other members of this house do, viz., to spend them away from the rest of the community. I am not a child who requires careful supervision, but a man, well able to take and with every intention of taking care of myself, both for my own sake and for the sake of that ecclesiastical habit, which, having once put on, I shall never put off.

I understood you to say also, that you have inferred that my theological studies suffered on account of my private occupations. I have already had the honour of assuring you most emphatically that this is not the case, and I must beg to be allowed to repeat that assurance. If my word is not enough, I can offer you the inspection of the MS. work I have done since 7th Dec., which alone will prove that my study hours have been exceedingly well spent.

In conclusion, I repeat my apologies for having given you the trouble of reading this, and I have written to give you a clearer insight into the peculiar motives and circumstances which govern my conduct. Knowing this, I trust you will understand and approve of them, as I feel sure that I shall receive every consideration at your hands.

I am,
Monsignore,
Your faithful son in Xto,
FREDERICK WILLIAM ROLFE

As a result of this letter Rolfe was given a second chance; but in the rector's eyes his conduct showed no improvement, and on 16th April Rolfe was informed that he must leave the college on or before the 21st of the month. He then wrote this second letter to Monsignor Campbell.

Monsignore,
On the point of leaving yr. house, I beg you to notice the following facts:

You have expelled me for a breach of the rules, knowing that it was not in my power to observe them.

You have prevented me, by forbidding me to use my recreation hours for literary work, from acquiring funds to pay my necessary debts.

I have no money at all at present and no friends in Rome who are able to offer me hospitality.

Even supposing I had the means to return to Scotland, I still have no home to go to, nor shall I be able to make any further arrangements by Monday morning.

Having made you aware of these facts, I have nothing to do but leave my effects at the College, to obey your injunctions to the letter, and to turn out into the streets.

I am,
Your obedient Servant,
FREDERICK WILLIAM ROLFE

He was then allowed a fortnight in which to make his arrangements; but, since he was penniless, what arrangements, one may reasonably ask, could he make or even hope to make?

On 23rd April, the rector being absent from the college, Rolfe was forcibly ejected from his bed by some of the students, who left him on his mattress in the college porch. Canon MacWilliam cites an eye-witness as authority for this, which confirms Rolfe's statement in *Hadrian the Seventh* that he was expelled 'suddenly and brutally'. (The rector, of course, cannot be held responsible for the action of the students during his absence; however, Canon Carmont states in his recollections, quoted by Symons in *The Quest for Corvo*, that a number of the senior students had *asked* the rector to expel Rolfe.)

Among these papers found in Rome in 1969 is the report on Rolfe written by Monsignor Campbell after Rolfe's expulsion. It is uncertain whether or no a copy of this report was forwarded to the archbishop of St Andrews and Edinburgh. There is no such document in the diocesan archives, nor is there any trace of Rolfe's letters to the archbishop. The report records the circumstances of Rolfe's acceptance by the archbishop as a candidate for orders. It emphasises that Rolfe's residence in college was to be 'a period of trial as well as of preparation', and states that 'he failed egregiously in his trial'. Mention is made of his 'breaches of discipline and his disregard of the duties required of a divinity student'; but no specific instances are given of these alleged failings. His debts, 'to the ascertained amount of £40', are the only specific offence recorded; the rector adds that Rolfe well knew that he had neither means nor prospect of paying them.

But forty pounds sterling does not seem such a very great sum, even when allowance is made for the much greater value of the pound in 1890 as compared with today. Rolfe's plea that the rector's insistence on his keeping the rule of community recreation—from which others, nevertheless, were dispensed— had prevented him from earning money seems not unreasonable. Knowing that Rolfe's only way of earning money for his support was by his painting and writing, why did the rector refuse him this permission? Presumably it was because Monsignor Campbell simply had no belief in Rolfe's talents as an artist and writer. Perhaps he should not be blamed for this. Prior to 1890 Rolfe had had published only a poem in his school magazine, his privately printed poem *Tarcissus*, and his *Sestina yn Honvr of Lytel Seynt Hew*, which appeared in the *Universal Review* of 15th December, 1888. The seven stanzas of this poem each begin with a large decorated initial letter designed by Rolfe; these water-colour initials were his first published works of art.

Obviously Rolfe was no community man; but there seems to

have been nothing contumacious about his absence from the common recreations. In fact, Canon Carmont (*Quest,* Penguin edition, page 83) says that in the beginning he tried to mix with his fellow-students a great deal. These efforts were not a success, but, given Rolfe's temperament, there is perhaps something to admire in them.

Had Rolfe been allowed to spend his 'free' time in his own way he should have been able, after a while, to pay his debts. For one thing, early in 1890 Elkin Mathews, the London publisher, had announced as forthcoming *The Story of S. William: the Boy Martyr of Norwich*, by the Rev. Frederick William Rolfe. This book never appeared; perhaps because Rolfe did not have time to write it before his troubles came upon him, and more urgent tasks engaged his attention.

Rather strangely, Monsignor Campbell's report on Rolfe makes no mention of his alleged failure to prosecute his studies with sufficient zeal. The late Dom F. M. McClyment said in a letter to Symons (*Quest*, Penguin edition, page 70) that in his earlier period as a church student, at Oscott College, near Birmingham, Rolfe 'kept much to himself and seemed more interested in art than in theology'. But appearances can deceive. Rolfe was older, cleverer, and considerably better educated than most of his fellow-students at Oscott; it cannot have taken him much time or effort to master the courses in philosophy or theology; and the same would have been true of him in Rome.

In his first letter to Monsignor Campbell he repeats the verbal assurances he has already given in this matter, and offers to produce for inspection his written work of the past four months. In the Walpole Collection in the Bodleian Library there is the typescript fragment of the exordium to an essay of Rolfe's on the book of Daniel, written while he was at the Scots College.[8] In this fragment Rolfe says that he intends 'to compare the terms of the prophecy with historical facts' by considering it under four heads. The first three—the remainder of the text is lacking—are: (1) The interpretation of the words '70 weeks'; (2) Whether the title 'Sanctus Sanctorum' relates to the Lord Jesus Christ or to another; (3) Whether what is prophesied of this 'Sanctus Sanctorum' relates to the Lord Jesus Christ alone or to another. This is the beginning of what appears to have been an orderly, well thought out piece of scriptural exegesis. Slight though this fragment is, it gives no support whatever to the idea that Rolfe was negligent over his studies.

That he was a trial both to the rector and to many, perhaps most, of his fellow-students is clear. He always said that he had been victimised by the authorities; but it would probably be nearer the truth to say that he fell a victim to the *system*. The Tridentine system on which seminaries were conducted until recently was authoritarian; it could not possibly have been anything else, and on the whole it worked well. But the fact that the rector or president of a seminary could dismiss a student by mere fiat, without any possibility of an inquiry or an appeal, inevitably produced from time to time a dismissal that was unjust. Rolfe's letters to his rector seem to me courteous and sincere. He was on fairly strong ground in the matter of his use of his free time and vacations; the accusation that he neglected his studies seems to have had no real foundation. There remains only the matter of his debts. This was serious, certainly; but surely not so serious as to justify expulsion?

Canon MacWilliam quotes a contemporary's description of Monsignor Campbell as 'rather choleric, though a generous little man and the soul of honour'. He acted generously, and perhaps against his instincts, in giving Rolfe a second chance, after his first notice of dismissal: but the rector and the baron (as Rolfe was shortly to proclaim himself)[9] were not made to understand each other. Given the system of ecclesiastical training that was then the norm, some such disruptive end to their relationship was probably inevitable. But one cannot help regretting that there was apparently no priest at the Scots College able to recognise this strangely exotic student's fundamental devotion to priestly ideals, and his literary and artistic talents. And surely it is significant that the vice-rector Mr Rooney (later Provost Rooney) said of Rolfe that 'he was most amiable despite all his eccentricities'.

Canon MacWilliam considered that there is today a tendency to 'sentimentalise' over Rolfe. In proof of this he instances some of the contributions to *New Quests for Corvo*. Perhaps there is some truth in this. However, the writers alluded to do at least give specific reasons in support of their more sympathetic attitude to one who has had a fairly consistently 'bad press' since the publication of Symons's *Quest*. May it not also be true that a 'sentimental' view of Corvo has been propagated by some of the writers who have accepted A. J. A. Symons's contrived sketch of Rolfe as an authentic portrait? The sentiments behind *this* view are sentiments of dislike and hostility.

Perhaps we may allow Rolfe himself to have the last word, taken from a passage in his *Chronicles of the House of Borgia*.

Why should good hours of sunlight be wasted on the judgement seat by those who, presently, will take their turn in the dock?

NOTES

1. *Corvo: 1860-1960*, edited by Cecil Woolf and Brocard Sewell: Aylesford, St Albert's Press, 1961. Paperback edition, with new title: *New Quests for Corvo*: London, Icon Books, 1965.

2. A. J. A. Symons, 'Tradition in Biography', in *Tradition and Experiment in Present-Day Literature* by A. J. A. Symons: Oxford, 1929.

3. *A. J. A. Symons: His Life and Speculations* by Julian Symons: London, 1950.

4. In *Corvo: 1860-1960 (New Quests for Corvo)*.

5. *The Innes Review*: organ of The Scottish Catholic Historical Society; published by John S. Burns and Co., Glasgow.

6. Peter Paul (Daniel) Mackey, O.P., S.T.M.: 1851-1935. Professor of archaeology at the Collegio Angelico, Rome. Honorary president of the commission for the Leonine edition of the works of St Thomas Aquinas. His surname is mis-spelled in all editions of Symons's *Quest*.

7. Augustine Smith, archbishop of St Andrews and Edinburgh.

8. The text of this fragment was first published in a symposium of essays by various hands, *Frederick Rolfe and Others*: Aylesford, St Albert's Press, 1961. Recently it has been reprinted, as 'Daniel on the Coming of the Messiah: Fragment of a Discourse', in *The Armed Hand: and other stories and pieces* by Fr. Rolfe, Baron Corvo: London, Cecil and Amelia Woolf, 1974.

9. The designation 'Baron Corvo' was used by Rolfe as a pseudonym, but he claimed to have acquired the title by gift from his friend the Countess Sforza-Caesarini, in whose power it would perhaps have been to bestow it.

Olive Custance
(1903)

OLIVE CUSTANCE

OLIVE CUSTANCE was one of a group of distinguished women writers who were associated during the Eighteen Nineties, and the early years of the present century, with The Bodley Head, the publishing house of John Lane, and were contributors to the *Yellow Book* and *Savoy* magazines, edited by Henry Harland and Arthur Symons respectively, with the collaboration of Aubrey Beardsley. Others in this group were Ella D'Arcy, Ada Leverson, George Egerton (Mary Chavelita Dunne), John Oliver Hobbes (Pearl Mary Teresa Craigie), and Katharine Harris Bradley and her niece Edith Emma Cooper, who collaborated to write the poetry of 'Michael Field'.

Oliver Eleanor Custance, who was born on 7th February, 1874, was the elder child and daughter of Colonel Frederic Hambledon Custance, of the Grenadier Guards and Weston Old Hall, Norfolk, and his wife Eleanor Constance Jolliffe. Mrs Custance's mother and father were both of distinguished descent. Her paternal grandfather was William George Hylton Jolliffe, secretary to the Treasury and privy councillor, who in 1866 was created the first Baron Hylton. On her mother's side she was descended from Francis Bacon, Baron Verulam and Viscount St Albans, philosopher and scientist.

Colonel Custance's father, Sir Hambledon Francis Custance, KCB, was High Sheriff of the County of Norfolk. In 1859 he had married Mrs Francis Nevill, the youngest daughter of Sir Edmund Bacon, and widow of the Reverend Henry Walpole Nevill. Colonel Custance was their only son, and in 1892 he inherited the family estate at Weston Longville, near Norwich. In 1776 the Reverend James Woodforde became rector of Weston Longville: various contemporary Custances and Bacons are mentioned in his diary.[1] A first cousin of Colonel F. H. Custance was Admiral Sir Reginald Custance, KCMG (1847-1935), who was retired from the Royal Navy in 1912 for outspoken criticism of Admiralty policy. The two cousins were close friends.

Colonel Custance was a Justice of the Peace, and chairman of the local bench of magistrates. He was a superbly skilful fisherman, and for over fifty years he was an expert breeder of trout, which he bred at his own trout farm. His one literary effort was the chapter on breeding in the 'Trout' volume in Longman's series of 'Fur, Feather, and Fin' books. He was a first-class shot, and often joined his friend and neighbour King Edward VII with the guns at Sandringham, Weston, or other Norfolk coverts.

Colonel Custance was, in fact, a fine old English gentleman (a phrase sometimes synonymous with fine old English autocrat). Chronic deafness made life difficult for him, and did not make for evenness of temper on his part. Beyond his estate and his country pursuits his range of interests was narrow; he would not have agreed with Bacon's dictum that 'Reading maketh a full man.' The tenantry held 'The Old Man', as they called him, in considerable awe; indeed, he was a formidable personality. A writer in the Norfolk newspaper the *Eastern Daily Press*,[2] has drawn a vivid picture of the Colonel driving through the Norfolk lanes in winter in his high, ancient De Dion Bouton motor car, muffled to the nose in a thick woollen scarf, his hands encased in mittens, and with a large ear-trumpet protruding from his greatcoat pocket. Being a fast driver, and practically stone-deaf, he sounded his horn so loudly that it could be heard at a considerable distance; a warning of his approach that was much appreciated. He was a martinet, expecting to be obeyed immediately and without question; but he was capable of kindness, and could even, on occasion, show a sense of humour. A soldier and an aristocrat, he had little understanding of how the rest of the world lived. His daughter Olive once told Sir John Betjeman how, when she was young, she was walking one day with her father on the outskirts of Cromer, where some new bungalows had been built. Contemplating one of these, Colonel Custance said to her: 'Good Lord, do you mean to say that people *live* in these things?'

His religion was conventional; by which I do not mean insincere. Negatively, he harboured a deep distrust of the Church of Rome and 'those priests'. He perhaps cared more about the war memorial on the village green at Weston than he did about the church. He had superintended its design, and chosen its site, carefully. It was unveiled by his cousin the Admiral; one of his last orders, given shortly before his death in 1925, was for its care and protection. As he grew older he gave increasing attention to his garden, and to the cultivation of roses. As another writer in the *Eastern Daily Press* said: 'For all who could sympathise with him in his deafness and see beneath the surface of his strongly marked personality there remains the impression of a gentleman of the old school, straightforward, humorous, and kindly.'[3]

In 1890, when she was sixteen, his daughter Olive met the young poet and civil servant John Gray[4], then aged twenty-five, at a party in London. Gray, whose working class parents, and their younger children, lived in Bethnal Green, was employed as a librarian in the Foreign Office, and was beginning to be known as a man of letters and of fashion. He was soon to meet Oscar Wilde, who was to encourage him and help to launch him on his career as the 'typical' poet of the Eighteen Nineties. Miss Custance was captivated by Gray, who was certainly one of the most beautiful young men in London at the time, and fell in love with him on the spot. Olive herself was by all accounts an extremely pretty and attractive girl. Richard Le Gallienne, in his *The Romantic Nineties*, speaks of her 'flower-like loveliness'. A photograph of her taken in 1903 shows a finely-featured young woman, with a mass of modishly arranged dark hair and one of those slightly elfin faces that are so appealing, and which usually indicate wit, intelligence, and sensitivity.

John Gray paid no particular attention to the girl on whom he had made such an impression. They seem to have met only once more, in London, on an occasion recorded by Olive in her diary for 8th January, 1896.[5] She and her father were staying in London, in Curzon Street. In the afternoon, she says, she put on her new green silk shirt '(like a smock) with a black skirt. The bell rang and Tanie [her former governess] was shown up—what happiness and I told her I had asked John Gray to tea; and very soon he came and brought me "Silverpoints" and was so kind and talked so beautifully—and looked so nice. He *is* my ideal Poet. And tea came—and we were I think a happy little trio—and what a lot of interesting things John Gray told us. But at last we all had to say goodbye—and he went home and sent me at once a lovely book and a charming little note.'

For a time they kept up a correspondence. (Olive was a great writer of letters; Aubrey Beardsley, whom she knew, found her something of a nuisance in this respect.) She consulted Gray about her poems, and sent him her books on publication.

Some years ago an interesting letter of hers referring to John Gray was found inside the pages of a secondhand anthology of poetry on the shelves of a London bookshop. This letter is undated, but must have been written before her second meeting with Gray. I have not been able to identify the friend to whom it is addressed.

Lulu. I send you a book and a song. For Christmas . . . A Poet—whom I once met as a child (I was about sixteen, and he was twenty-five) wrote to me the other day and sent me his book—privately printed—of Carols on the life of the Christ Child.[6]
I think I may have spoken to you about him as he has been for a long while my Prince of Poets. There is no one who can sing like him—his poems are so precious and so pure. . . He has lived a strange full life and now he writes
'At a certain time one is apt to want to live for grace. Soon the better ideal comes to live well and chance the grace. And is it not so with poetry? Have you come to the determination to write *well* at every risk? to put more fire into your work than anyone else could ever find out.'
Curiously enough, just before he first wrote—I—thinking of him made a little poem—this, together with one of his, I send you. . .
Ever your loving
WILD OLIVE

On a separate sheet of foolscap paper enclosed with this letter she had copied out John Gray's carol 'The True Vine', and the poem 'Sensation' from Gray's *Silverpoints*, published by John Lane in 1893. Below these she has added her own poem 'To John Gray', which was printed, under a new title, 'Reminiscences', in her second volume of poems, *Rainbows*, published in 1902.

TO JOHN GRAY

Just once we met,
It seems so long ago.
So long . . . and yet
Men would not think it so
Who count their time by years.
Just once we met . . .
And now we never meet . . .

Is it regret
(I lost a friend so sweet)
That stings my heart to tears?

I clasped your hand,
But scarcely said a word!
We stood as children stand—Whose souls are stirred
To great shy love they cannot comprehend.
I clasped your hand
And looked into your eyes.
My spirit spanned—Your spirit's mysteries,
But *feared* to call you 'Friend'!

In 1897, when she was twenty-three, John Lane published, at The Sign of The Bodley Head, Olive's first collection of poems: *Opals.* She had a strange passion for these stones, which are said to bring their owner or wearer ill fortune; and she liked to be called, and to call herself, Opal. In *Opals* there is a poem with the title 'Ideal'; but in the original manuscript it is headed

TO JOHN GRAY

We are not sundered for we never met.
We only passed each other in the throng,
We moved together, but not long . . . not long . . .
You were indifferent . . . and I may forget
Your profound eyes, your heavy hair, your voice
So clear, yet deep and low with tenderness,
That lingered on my ears like a caress
And roused my heart to make a futile choice.

O! Poet that passed me carelessly in the throng—
O! Soul that clamoured unto God in song!
How should I lose you thus and lack regret?

In this same year, 1897, Aubrey Beardsley designed a book-plate for Miss Custance, and in connexion with this he received several letters from her. In a letter of 7th January to his publisher, Leonard Smithers, Beardsley refers to 'Silly little O.'; and in a letter to Smithers written a month later he says: 'Eleven pages from Olive this morning plus two pages of verse.' His irritation is understandable; but he designed her a fine bookplate all the same. There was a certain kittenish quality about Miss Custance at this time, which showed itself in lengthy letters to her friends, written somewhat breathlessly, with erratic and idiosyncratic punctuation, and with a plethora of dashes and dots. Here are two more poems from *Opals*, inspired by her familiar Norfolk scene. These are simple, evocative verses; but the second poem reveals a skilful use of technique.

AN IMPRESSION

Sky like smoked mother-o'-pearl,
Dim background for bare trees
That lift against it stained twig traceries:
Smoke wreaths that curl
Upward from carved stone chimneys silently—
Twilight time . . . nigh!

Westward, wide scarlet bars
Belting day's silvery waist—
And Eastward sable clouds interlaced . . .
So—night lifts nearer, luminous with stars . . .

A LAMENT FOR THE LEAVES

The trees look sad—sad—I long for the leaves,
Green leaves that shimmer—and shelter the nests that
    the song-birds make.
The earth is glad—glad—but my spirit grieves.
Break forth from your buds and awake
        O! leaves!

I remember the woods last year and the thick fresh leaves
How they fluttered and flickered and sighed, rustled and
    quivered all day . . .
I almost fancy I hear their song to the breeze,

The fickle breeze that faltered and wavered, but would not
    stay.
        I long for the leaves!

I remember the sun-laced grass, where their shadows were
    flung
In a tangled web as they trembled—trembled a-tilt on the
    bough.
Now! they are fallen, alas! from the trees where they hung,
Withered, wind-wafted away . . . O! where are they now,
        The leaves?

Early in 1901, or possibly some time in late 1900,[7] the young
American – Parisian poet, novelist, and heiress Natalie Clifford
Barney was in London. Looking in at the Bodley Head offices in
Vigo Street, in search of a new translation of Sappho that Lane
had just published, she was persuaded by him to buy a copy of
Opals, the first book of a young poet from Norfolk, whose second
book he was hoping to issue very shortly. Miss Barney was much
pleased with these poems, and wrote to their author to express
her admiration, enclosing with her letter copies of her own two
books of verse, *Etudes et Préludes* and *Quelques Portraits-
Sonnets de Femmes*. Opal replied with a poem, which remains
unpublished except for these four lines:

    . . . For I would dance to make you smile and sing
    Of those who with some sweet mad sin have played,
    And how Love walks with delicate feet afraid
    'Twixt maid and maid.

This sounds a note nowhere to be found in Olive Custance's
published work. John Lane, cultivating safety and respectability
after William Watson's damaging attack on the morals of *The
Yellow Book*, published by Lane, would not have been prepared
to publish anything so frank; nor could it safely have been laid on
the occasional tables in the drawing room at Weston Manor.
    Natalie Barney was a close friend of the tragic French Sapphic
poet Renée Vivien—the assumed name of a francophile English
girl, Pauline Tarn. About this time Natalie suggested to Renée
that they should form around themselves, for purposes of mutual

inspiration, a group of poets such as had surrounded Sappho at Mytilene. Their first step was to invite Opal to visit them. She replied that she hoped to come with her mother to Paris in the spring. Again she enclosed for Natalie a poem, which began:

Her face is like the face the Dreamer sometimes meets,
A face that Leonardo would have followed through the
    streets . . .

The following spring Opal arrived with her mother for a month's stay. Accompanying them was a young man whom Natalie Barney describes in her *Souvenirs Indiscrets* as the 'vicomte de Canterbury'. In reality he was the Hon. George Montagu, later to become the ninth Earl of Sandwich.

After Mrs Custance and George Montagu had returned to England, Natalie and Opal, attended by a chaperone approved by Mrs Custance, left Paris for a holiday in Venice. Miss Barney records that Opal had with her in Venice a picture of Antinous, which she said reminded her of Lord Alfred Bruce Douglas, the third son of the Marquess of Queensberry, with whom she was, unknown to her parents, in love. Alfred Douglas ('Bosie', as he was known to his family and friends) was four years older than Opal, and was still under a cloud as a result of his disastrous friendship with Oscar Wilde, and the ensuing scandal. The statue of Antinous of which she had a photograph was probably the inspiration of her poem 'Antinous', which was printed in her second volume of poems, *Rainbows*, published by John Lane in 1902.

ANTINOUS

I spoke of you, Antinous, with her who is my heart's delight,
The while we watched the dawn of night through veils of dusk
    diaphanous.
I praised your gracious loveliness, as in cool marble it appears,
Your eyes that seem too sad for tears, your smile that is a
    sheathed caress.
And I, a freeborn singing child, in this dull sordid age of ours,
Cried to my friend, 'Oh flower of flowers, worship him with me!'

but she smiled.
She smiled, and said with soft disdain, 'His statue cannot see
   or hear:
If you should kneel forever, dear, he would not know; you kneel
   in vain.'
Yet all night long, oh, my Desire, I watched beside you, pale
   and dumb;
   And now the silver Dawn has come; the sky is stained with
     scarlet fire.
The faint light widens to fair day round a white statue: the
   birds sing,
But you will never wake, my King, though love should kiss your
   lips away.

This poem is one of three that she wrote on similar
themes. They are among her best, full of a perversity that makes
her a true poet of the *fin-de-siècle*. In *The Romantic Agony*
Professor Mario Praz places her with those other poets of the
Nineties who actually or supposedly cultivated themes of a
decadent and perverse nature: Arthur Symons, Richard Le
Gallienne, John Gray, Theodore Wratislaw, Lionel Johnson, and
Ernest Dowson. Her other poems of this kind are 'Statues' and
'The White Statue'.

STATUES

   I have loved statues . . . spangled dawns have seen
   Me bowed before their beauty . . . when the green
   And silver world of Spring wears radiantly
   The morning rainbows of an opal sky . . .
   And I have chanted curious madrigals
   To charm their coldness, twined for coronals
   Blossoming branches, thinking thus to change
   Their still contempt for mortal love, their bright
   Proud scorn to something delicate and strange,
   More sweet, more marvellous, than mere delight!

   I have loved statues—passionately prone
   My body worshipped the white form of stone!

And like a flower that lifts its chalice up
Towards the light—my soul became a cup
That over-brimming with enchanted wine
Of ecstasy—was raised to the divine
Indifferent lips of some young silent God
Standing aloof from all our tears and strife,
Tranced in the paradise of dreams, he trod
In the untroubled summer of his life!

I have loved statues . . . and at night the cold
Mysterious moon behind a mask of gold—
Or veiled in silver veils—has seen my pride
Utterly broken—seen the dream denied
For which I pleaded—heedless that for me
The miracle of joy could never be . . .
As in old legends beautiful and strange,
When bright gods loved fair mortals born to die,
And the frail daughters of despair and change
Become the brides of immortality.

THE WHITE STATUE

I love you, silent statue! for your sake
My songs in prayer upreach
Frail hands of flame-like speech,
That some mauve-silver twilight you may wake!

I love you more than swallows love the South.
As sunflowers turn and turn
Towards the sun, I yearn
To press warm lips against your cold white mouth!

I love you more than scarlet-skirted dawn,
At sight of whose spread wings
The great world wakes and sings;
Forgetful of the long, vague dark withdrawn.

I love you most at purple sunsetting:
When night with feverish eyes
Comes up the fading skies . . .
I love you with a passion past forgetting.

Perhaps most of us have, at least potentially, something of the 'Decadent' in us: taking Decadence to mean roughly what Arthur Symons meant by it in his famous essay 'The Decadent Movement in Literature'. Something in the atmosphere of the Eighteen Nineties, together with the influence and example of Poe, Baudelaire, and others, provoked an outburst of 'decadent' writing. Olive Custance made a small but highly individual contribution to it; she had caught the mood, and was affected by it. But it was a mood that she cultivated for a short time only.

Olive Custance and Alfred Douglas had first met, or at least had first seen each other, at the wedding of a cousin of Bosie's at Holy Trinity, Sloane Street. But when they next saw each other neither of them remembered the incident. Their second meeting was the result of a letter from Olive to Bosie, expressing her admiration for his poetry. Attended by her maid, Olive met Lord Alfred at his rooms in Duke Street—after they had somehow missed each other at an assignation in the South Kensington Museum.[8] They continued to meet, at a picture-gallery in Ryder Street owned by Robert Ross. (At that time Ross and Douglas were still friends.) A little later Olive was staying at Dinard with her cousin Lady Anglesey, who took her to Paris, where she met Bosie every day. In an undated letter to him written a little later she says:

My own Prince,—
. . . I miss you more than I can say . . . for I love you beyond everything in the world . . . and I think we shall never be happy together again . . . Write to me . . . soon and tell me you love your little Page and that one day you will come back to 'him' . . . my Prince, my Prince.
I found Mummy rather unhappy as 'Tannie' had told her that we met that time in London! however, Mummy has forgiven us and all will be well if she doesn't find out about Paris. . .
She would never forgive us *then,* I am afraid!
Goodbye my Darling . . . may all your dreams come true.
I cannot write more . . . Goodbye . . .

OLIVE

Bosie's affairs had now reached rock bottom, and he was being urged by his family to go to the United States in search of an heiress who might be willing to marry him. Desperation drove him to take this step, and he sailed for New York in the autumn of 1901. Natalie Barney says that Opal had tried to persuade her to enter into a *mariage blanc* with Lord Alfred, which would have left the way clear for a lasting liaison between him and Olive. But nothing came of this. When Bosie got to America he found that there would be no difficulty in finding a suitable and willing heiress; but his heart was not in the quest. Opal's love-letters were following him; and he did not feel at home in America. He encountered a certain amount of social antagonism there; and there was an unpleasant incident in Washington's most exclusive club, The Metropolitan.

In January 1902 he returned to England, and was thunder-struck to learn that Olive had become engaged to George Montagu. The match was enthusiastically approved by the Custance and Montagu families. It was, in fact, exactly the kind of marriage that a girl of her social position was then expected to make. A congratulatory telegram had been received from the King. There was only one drawback: Olive was not in love with her betrothed. She had accepted his proposal believing that Bosie either did not want to marry her, or could not.

Lord Alfred acted immediately. In his own words, 'The blood of a hundred Douglas ancestors surged up', and he said in his heart, 'No, you don't.' He arranged a meeting with Olive, pleaded his cause, and without difficulty persuaded her to elope with him and share a life of romantic poverty.

There was a short delay before the marriage could take place, and this letter of Olive's, undated as usual, reveals some of the stratagems they were forced to use.

My own boy prince—
. . . Don't stay away too long from London as I shall certainly be up on the 30th . . . and write to me to 19 Dover Street Piccadilly W . . . As your friend's writing is so utterly unlike yours they would never guess anything . . . tell him not to forget to put Miss *Olive* Custance . . . as then they cannot give them to Mummy by mistake.
A dreadful thing happened to your last wire! It was opened by Daddy! However, 'Bosie' conveyed nothing to him . . . so I said it was from Nathalie . . . and soon after sent myself a wire from her to say she was going to Italy as Mummy doesn't like her! I think you will laugh at all this . . . But oh why, why does fate make it so difficult for us to meet. . .

They were married by special licence at St George's, Hanover Square, at nine in the morning on Tuesday 4th March, 1902, and left immediately for Paris.

When the news was received at Weston, Colonel Custance was furious. That Lord Alfred Douglas should have acquired Colonel Custance as his father-in-law was a misfortune for both of them; and for Olive too. Apart from aristocratic birth Bosie and the Colonel had nothing in common except a strong mutual distrust. It was Olive who suffered the most from the feud that broke out between them, which virtually destroyed her marriage. At the time, after his first reaction, the Colonel behaved rather well. He had every right to be upset at his daughter's elopement and clandestine marriage to the disreputable and penniless Lord Alfred Douglas, still tainted with the Oscar Wilde scandal, after she had jilted a future earl with a prospective income of £30,000 a year. But he quickly reconciled himself to the *fait accompli*, and showed himself, for the time being, well disposed towards the young couple.

All things considered, the marriage began quite auspiciously; a son was born before the end of the year. But this child, Raymond, from an early age gave signs of instability. As a young man he was in the Guards for a time; but he became increasingly subject to severe brainstorms, and for long periods was confined in mental hospitals.

If the marriage began bravely, after the initial troubles, it was not long before tensions developed. In a letter written years later Olive said: 'Alas, our marriage ended in misery for both of us, whatever Bosie may say. But, at least, it did have a radiant beginning.' In his autobiography, which was published during his wife's lifetime, Bosie analysed the matter with some acuteness. He says that after their marriage he was more in love with her than she was with him, so that he lost his supreme position in her eyes. He attributes this to the fact that he was always trying to suppress and keep under the 'feminine' in him, and to become more manly. This was disastrous, for it was the feminine part of him that she especially loved. 'My only consolation, now that I at last understand,' he says, 'is that if she had married anyone else her disillusion would have been ten times more rapid, and quite as complete.'

However, at first things went smoothly. The Douglases were received at Weston, where Colonel Custance taught Bosie the art of fishing. He was an apt pupil, and could have had no better instructor.

In the year of her marriage Olive's second collection of poems, *Rainbows,* was published. One of these poems, 'The Girl in the Glass', could almost be a prophetic self-portrait.

THE GIRL IN THE GLASS

Girl in the glass! you smile, and yet
Your eyes are full of a vague regret;
For dreams are lovely, and life is sad,
And when you were a child what dreams you had!
Now, over your soul life's shadows pass,
    Girl in the glass.

Girl in the glass, an April day
Looks not more tearful, looks not more gay
Than your rose-flushed face with the wistful mouth.
For your soul seeks Love as a swallow flies south,
So, into your eyes Love's sorrows pass,
    Girl in the glass.

Another poem from *Rainbows*, 'The Masquerade', catches an authentic *fin-de-siècle* note, as in certain poems by Wilde, Symons, and Wratislaw.

THE MASQUERADE

Masked dancers in the Dance of Life,
We move sedately . . . wearily together,
Afraid to show a sign of inward strife,
We hold our souls in tether.

We dance with proud and smiling lips,
With frank appealing eyes, with shy hands clinging.
We sing, and few will question if there slips
A sob into our singing.

Each has a certain step to learn;
Our prisoned feet move staidly in set paces,
And to and fro we pass, since life is stern,
Patiently, with masked faces.

Yet some there are who will not dance,
They sit apart most sorrowful and splendid;
But all the rest trip on as in a trance,
Until the dance is ended.

In 1905 Lady Alfred Douglas issued a third volume of poems: *The Blue Bird* by Olive Custance. This was published by The Marlborough Press, which was the imprint of a mushroom firm run by Thomas William Henry Crosland, a tough Fleet Street journalist who had come to London from Yorkshire. Crosland was a poet of some merit himself, and his book *The English Sonnet*, published by Martin Secker in 1917, should be studied by all who aspire to attempt this most difficult of verse-forms. A wheezing, asthmatic, alcoholic wreck, of indomitable courage and persistent energy, hobbling around on two sticks, Crosland was the author of a series of highly popular, rather crude satirical works with titles such as *The Unspeakable Scot* (the first in the series), *The Egregious English*, and—it would hardly be publishable today, though really there was no harm in it, *The Fine Old Hebrew Gentleman*. From 1907 to 1910 he was to be the assistant editor of Lord Alfred Douglas's magazine *The Academy*. In 1905 he was editing *The English Review*, which ran only from October of that year to February, 1906. Crosland was an extraordinary character, a kind of 'Ancient Pistol', as Alfred Douglas described him. Like Lord Alfred, he was an incurable litigant, and was much feared by eminent King's Counsel such as Ernest Wild and F. E. Smith, who found cross-examining him no easy or agreeable task. A good example of Crosland's manner in the witness box occurred at the Old Bailey in June, 1914, when Crosland and Douglas were charged with conspiring to libel Robert Ross. When Crosland said that he did not want the jury confused on a certain point, F. E. Smith told him: 'The jury can probably take care of themselves.' Crosland riposted: 'I dare say they can, but I want them to take care of *me*—.' He won his case.

Why Olive should have entrusted her poems to Crosland for publication, rather than to John Lane once more, is hard to understand; but in 1905 her poems were appearing in the *English Review*, so she may have been motivated by friendship for the

Review's editor. The arrangement was not a good one. She received no royalties—even though the unusually generous figure of 20% had been offered and agreed on—and after a few months Crosland offered to sell her all the unsold copies of *The Blue Bird* for £15. Olive demurred, and offered him £5: which was accepted. She forbearingly wrote to him: 'A thousand thanks for the charming little birds . . . Do come and dine tonight—no dressing! I hope you are better. Yours very sincerely, Olive Douglas.'

So things went on. Bosie and Olive were often abroad, in the south of France and in Corsica; sometimes at Ostend. Their happiest times seem to have been spent, between 1904 and 1907, at Lake Farm, near Amesbury, in Wiltshire. Then in 1907 Edward Tennant, a brother-in-law of Margot Asquith, who was married to Bosie's cousin Pamela Wyndham, bought the *Academy* magazine, and appointed Bosie editor at a salary of £300 a year. Olive's poems then began to appear in this brilliant and polemical periodical.

In 1911 Olive's fourth and last book of poems, *The Inn of Dreams*, appeared, published by John Lane. She seems to have sensed impending disaster. Her poem 'The Prisoner of God' reflects her mood at this time.

THE PRISONER OF GOD

Once long and long ago I knew delight.
God gave my spirit wings and a glad voice.
I was a bird that sang at dawn and noon,
That sang at starry evening time and night;
Sang at the sun's great golden doors, and furled
Brave wings in the white gardens of the moon;
That sang and soared beyond the dusty world.

Once long and long ago I did rejoice,
But now I am a stone that falls and falls.
A prisoner, cursing the blank prison walls,
Helpless and dumb, with desperate eyes, that see
The terrible beauty of those simple things
My soul disdained when she was proud and free.

And I can only pray: God pity me,
God pity me and give me back my voice!
God pity me and give me back my wings!

In 1911 Alfred Douglas was received into the Roman Catholic church. His conversion, and repentance of former errors, were most sincere. In taking this step he was following many of the aesthetes and decadents of the Eighteen Nineties; among them Aubrey Beardsley, John Gray, André Raffalovich, Ernest Dowson, Lionel Johnson, Frederick William Rolfe, Henry Harland, Mrs Craigie, and Oscar Wilde. Most of these converts, and Bosie was no exception, seem to have been drawn by the firm moral and penitential discipline of the church.

Olive Custance eventually took the same step; but not until 1924. After three years she lapsed, and ceased to practise her religion. In February 1944, just five weeks before her death, she expressed deep regret for this.

Colonel Custance shared the general mistrust of Catholicism and of Catholics that was then common. He bitterly resented the idea of his grandson being brought up in this alien religion, as he thought it, and his hostility to his son-in-law broke out again with added bitterness. For him this change of faith was just another example of Bosie's instability and untrustworthiness. The boy Raymond had become the centre of Colonel Custance's affections. Always regretful of his own lack of a son, his hopes were now fixed on his grandson as the eventual heir to the family estates and inheritance. He immediately set about persuading Olive to agree to a resettlement of the estates, which were entailed on her, in favour of Raymond. By doing this he hoped to ensure that Alfred Douglas should never derive any benefit from them. Next, he exerted strong financial pressure on Olive to make her put the boy under his guardianship. Such tactics were common enough with outraged upper-class parents in those days; in fact, the Marquess of Queensberry had behaved in very much the same way towards Bosie. The Colonel saw Bosie as a bad and fanatical man, of dubious morals; Bosie saw the Colonel's conduct as base and dishonourable. The breach between the two men was to prove irreparable; Olive was torn between them. Early in 1913 she left her husband and returned to her parents at Weston. On

14th January Bosie was declared bankrupt.

Writing to her mother-in-law, Lady Queensberry, on 14th January Olive said:

Bosie was cruel to me before I went to Weston, and I have often been very unhappy with him, but I love him above everything, and would never have left him if he had not taken away Raymond. Everybody knows I take my father's part, and, God help me, I don't know where to turn for advice and comfort. My father is angry all the time because I love Bosie still—and I am utterly miserable. But would it do Bosie any good if I am turned out to starve? I am utterly helpless since I made those settlements. Perhaps it would be better for Bosie to divorce me for desertion? I only wish I had courage enough to kill myself.

On 26th February, 1913, Lord Alfred Douglas was committed for trial on a charge of criminally libelling Colonel Custance. On 29th April he surrendered, pleading in mitigation of his libels that he had been under great stress; and he tendered an apology. This was not in accord with the Queensberry fighting spirit that he normally showed when under attack; but he had been deeply depressed by Olive's leaving him, and by the loss of the Arthur Ransome libel case, a case that he should have won. His defeat was due to the machinations of Robert Ross, his enemy since he had discovered that Ross had not delivered to him, as he had been instructed to, the copy of Oscar Wilde's long letter to Alfred Douglas written in prison, and known to us under the title *De Profundis*. Instead, Ross had consigned it to the British Museum, with an embargo on its being made available to the public for a long period of time. (Ross's admirers deny this; but they cannot prove their case, and to my mind the weight of evidence lies the other way.) In the Custance case Lord Alfred was bound over in the sum of £500. If he had pleaded justification he would probably have secured a verdict in his favour.

For the rest of his life Bosie regarded Colonel Custance and Robert Ross, together with the lawyer Sir George Lewis, as his principal enemies. He says in *The Autobiography of Lord Alfred Douglas*: 'I also wish to place it on record that I forgive George Lewis, and it is a fact that for at least twelve years I have prayed for him and Colonel Custance by name as my greatest enemies every day of my life.' In the same chapter of his autobiography, published in 1926, Douglas says that he has long ceased to feel any resentment towards Colonel Custance, and that when the Colonel was dying, in 1924, he had hoped to be reconciled with him. 'However, he remained implacable, though from what he said just before he died I believe that he recognized that he had done wrong in the line of conduct he had followed in regard to my son.'

After 1911 Olive Custance published no more poetry. No manuscripts of hers written after that year are known to exist.

The struggle for Raymond was still raging in 1915, when Olive and Bosie applied for sole custody of the boy in the court of Chancery. The petition was dismissed by Mr Justice Eve, whose decision prompted the writing of Lord Alfred's scathing poem 'Eve and the Serpent'. Had the petition been granted, their marriage might have been saved. By then Olive had left her father's house; in 1920 she settled at Bembridge, in the Isle of Wight. Sir Osbert Lancaster recalls that on the gate of her cottage were inscribed the words 'Safe haven, after a stormy passage'.[9] Let us hope that it was so. Here each summer she had her husband— described by Sir Osbert as 'a deplorable old wreck who had treated her abominably'[10]—to stay for a fortnight. In 1930 or thereabouts she moved to London, where she settled in Westbourne Terrace W11; in 1932 she moved to Hove, where Lord Alfred had been living since 1927. They continued to live apart, but they met almost every day. She died on 12th February, 1944, at Viceroy Lodge, Hove. Her husband survived her by one year.

Sir John Betjeman remembers Olive Custance as extremely entertaining and animated in conversation. 'Bosie', he says, 'grew quiet in her company. The last time I saw them together was when she had a flat in Westbourne Terrace and we had a Christmas luncheon party of the three of us. Her hero was Byron. She was large, curved and jovial, and not at all the wispy, sad, inward-looking person her excellent poetry might lead you to believe. She thought very highly of Bosie's own poetry and did not speak of her own.'

Lord Alfred Douglas used to speak of his wife as 'a distinguished poet'. He could speak with authority, and his judgement in this matter was not a partial one. It is a great pity that her collected poems have never been edited and published; her work is not known as it deserves to be, although some of her poems continue to be reprinted in anthologies.

Mr John Dixon Hunt has cited one of her poems from the *Yellow Book*, in his valuable work *The Pre-Raphaelite Imagination*, as an example of the kind of feebleness shown by many poets who have been influenced, but not for good, by Dante Gabriel Rossetti. In this particular instance the criticism is valid; but the poem is not typical of her work. Mr Hunt cites two lines from another of her *Yellow Book* poems, 'A Mood', as an example of the popular use by poets of the Nineties of twilight as the appropriate landscape for an uneasy soul; another post-Rossettian trend. These poems that voice the poet's reactions to the weather or the time of day may not be among her best; but they do, as a rule, contain good lines that one tends to remember. And even those of her verses that at first sight seem to be no more than a late Victorian young lady's conventional poetic exercises are often surprisingly effective when read aloud.

I hope that the poetry of Olive Custance will be rediscovered, and that she will come to be recognised as one of the most distinctive and attractive, and by no means the least powerful, of the poets of the *fin-de-siècle*.

NOTES

1. Cf. *The Diary of a Country Parson: The Reverend James Woodforde 1758-1781*, edited by J. Beresford: Oxford, 1924-31, and 1968. Ronald Fletcher's *In a Country Churchyard* (London, 1978) quotes some Custance passages from the *Diary*, and prints a drawing of Weston Longville church by Woodforde's nephew William.

2. Ida Fen, 'The Old Man: Encounters with Squire Custance', *Eastern Daily Press,* 6.3.1964.

3. John Cromer, 'The Weston Estate: More goings-on in the Woodforde Country', *Eastern Daily Press*, 22.5.1964.

4. For John Gray see *Two Friends: John Gray and André Raffalovich,* a symposium edited by Brocard Sewell: Aylesford, St Albert's Press, 1963. Also, by the same, *Footnote to the Nineties: a Memoir of John Gray and André Raffalovich:* London, Cecil Woolf, 1968.

5. The diaries of Olive Custance are now in The Berg Collection of the New York Public Library. I am indebted to Miss Mary Ellen Evans for examining them on my behalf, and for supplying me with this extract, which is cited by kind permission of the Curator, Dr Lola Szladits.

6. *A Book of Carols invented and writ by John Gray Forty-three Park Lane London Privately Printed and Not for General Distribution The Twenty-fourth of December 1894.* This tiny booklet, in light blue paper covers, is the first of the 'Blue Calendars' issued by John Gray to his friends at Christmas from 1894 to 1898.

7. In his autobiography Lord Alfred Douglas gives the year as 1901, but his chronology seems to be uncertain.

8. Now known as the Victoria and Albert Museum.

9. Private letter.

10. Private letter.

THOMAS HARDY AND G. K.
CHESTERTON: A CONTRAST

THE ONE THING that most admirers of Thomas Hardy seem
to know or to remember about Gilbert Chesterton is his 'clever
and facile jibe' at Hardy as the 'village atheist brooding and
blaspheming over the village idiot'.[1] One sees what Chesterton
meant; but it was not a tactful way of putting it. It looks as if he
came to regret the remark. In his *Autobiography,* published after
his death in 1936, but most of it written several years before, he
says that this supposed attack on Hardy is not really an attack, but
a defence. The whole case for Hardy 'is that he had the sincerity
and simplicity of the village atheist; that is, he valued atheism as a
truth and not a triumph.' Taken by itself, this may not seem very
convincing; but it should be read in its context, two whole pages
about Hardy, markedly sympathetic and generous in tone.

Chesterton knew Hardy, but only slightly. Hardy was his
senior by thirty-four years; in the *Autobiography* he says that
Hardy was the first great Victorian he ever met. He does not tell
us the year of their meeting, but says that Hardy had already
written *Tess of the Durbervilles*, and was famous everywhere.
Tess was published in 1891; so probably Chesterton was about
twenty when he met Hardy, in a London publisher's office. For
about five minutes he engaged Hardy in argument about his
alleged pessimism, which Hardy defended, 'but somehow with
the innocence of a boys' debating club'. He impressed Chesterton
as being a humble man.

After the outbreak of war in 1914 Hardy and Chesterton were
among the writers who agreed to serve on the committee set up to
advise the Government on propaganda, especially to neutral
countries. A meeting of the committee was held in London, at
Wellington House, on 3rd September. Arnold Bennett was
present, and afterwards noted in his diary: 'Zangwill[2] talked a
great deal too much. The sense was talked by Wells and Chester-

ton . . . Thomas Hardy was all right.'

In the previous year there had been an occasion when Hardy and Chesterton might well have met, but there is no evidence that they did. In 1893 J. M. Barrie had written to Hardy to ask him to write a companion piece to accompany two one-act plays, by Barrie and Conan Doyle respectively, that were to be produced in London in June. Hardy sent Barrie *The Three Wayfarers*,[3] 'a pastoral play' adapted from his story 'The Three Strangers' (in *Wessex Tales*). In 1913 *The Three Wayfarers* was produced again in London, at The Little Theatre, on 21st November. Accompanying it was Chesterton's play *Magic,* which was much enjoyed by George Moore, who was to become one of Hardy's severest critics. What Moore thought of *The Three Wayfarers* is not known.

Chesterton never visited Max Gate, Hardy's home outside Dorchester; but Sir John Squire once took Hilaire Belloc to Max Gate, it would seem in 1922. When the visit was suggested to him by Squire, Hardy said: 'What, do you mean that Catholic journalist?', and when Squire proposed it to Belloc, Belloc said: 'What, do you mean that atheist novelist?'[4] The visit appears to have been a great success. The principal topic of conversation between Hardy and Belloc was the great storm, early in the nineteenth century, which had blown ships right across the Chesil Bank, the narrow strip of shingle that joins the Isle of Portland to the mainland.

This charge of pessimism was constantly levelled at Hardy, and it irked him. In his conversation with the young Chesterton in the publisher's office Hardy had gently said that he did not think he was wholly a pessimist; but usually he denied it more strongly. In the Preface to *Late Lyrics and Earlier* (1922) he says:

If I may be forgiven for quoting my own old words, let me repeat what I printed in this relation more than twenty years ago, and wrote much earlier, in a poem entitled 'In Tenebris':
 If way to the Better there be, it exacts a full look at the Worst: that is to say, by the exploration of reality, and its frank recognition stage by stage along the survey, with an eye to the best consummation possible: briefly, evolutionary meliorism. But it is called pessimism nevertheless; under which word, expressed with condemnatory emphasis, it is regarded by many as some pernicious new thing (though so old as to underline the Gospel scheme, and even to permeate the Greek drama); and the subject

is charitably left to decent silence, as if further comment were needless.

Hardy ended the introductory note to his posthumously published *Winter Words in Various Moods and Metres* by saying: 'I repeat what I have often stated on such occasions, that no harmonious philosophy is attempted in these pages—or in any bygone pages of mine, for that matter.'

A reflective comment on Thomas Hardy's 'pessimism' occurs in *The Art of Thomas Hardy*, by the poet Lionel Johnson, which was published in 1894. Johnson says:

Much of Mr Hardy's work is an austere descant upon 'the dust and ashes of things, the cruelty of lust, and the fragility of love': very unwelcome truths; and not all the truths there are. But they are very old and very grave truths: and Mr Hardy presents them with a consciousness of their greatness. By the severity of thought and style . . . he takes his place among those writers who, from the early ages of literature, have expressed in art a reasonable sadness. That deep solemnity of the earth in its woods and fields, and lonely places, has passed into his work: and when he takes it in hand to deal with the passions of men that spirit directs and guides him. I do not find his books quite free of offence, of anything that can hurt and distress; but I never find them merely painful: their occasional offences are light enough, and unessential; the pain they sometimes give is often salutary.[5]

Hardy was not, and did not profess to be, a philosopher. 'When we speak of philosophy in Hardy,' says A. O. J. Cockshutt, 'we mean his general temperamental approach to the universe.'[6] By temperament Hardy was religious; as a young man he had contemplated taking Orders, but the Darwinian theory and the new discoveries concerning the origin of man and the age of the earth, with their devastating effect on the literal interpretation of the Book of Genesis, combined with his readings in Nietzsche and Schopenhauer, undermined his religious faith. As a result, he wisely chose architecture instead of the Church as his profession.

A more recent poet than Lionel Johnson, John Heath-Stubbs, has this to say about Hardy's 'philosophy':

Hardy's ironic pessimism is personal, but it can also be traced to his intuitive perception of the social decay of the countryside in which he grew up. From the philosophical point of view it has its roots in that combination of a narrow scientific materialism with an impoverished Puritanism which, for want of a better faith, the late nineteenth century forced upon him. The ruler of Hardy's universe is the cruel

predestinating deity of Calvinism, stripped of his anthropomorphic
qualities and theological trappings. He is also the amoral evolutionary
law of Huxley and Darwin . . . Yet spiritually impoverished as Hardy's
world is, his verse lives by its obvious sincerity. Hardy's world . . . is a
legendary one, in which traditions of a past generation are a thing more
living than the actuality of the writer's day.[7]

Chesterton's celebrated quip on Hardy has often been blamed
on his Catholicism;[8] but when *The Victorian Age in Literature*
was published he was still an Anglican, and would so remain for
another ten years.

If, then, the view of Hardy as a pessimist may not be entirely
accurate, the widely diffused image of Chesterton as a noisy
optimist also requires revision. For one thing, as an orthodox
Christian he believed in the doctrine of Original Sin, a doctrine
which excludes any idea of the natural perfectibility of the human
race. In orthodox Christian belief human nature, though
fundamentally good, is radically flawed. It is quite true that
Chesterton possessed the quality of innocence in a remarkable
degree; but those who think that his innocence meant that he was
ignorant of the darker shades of human nature and human life are
wrong. Garry Wills, in his book *G. K. Chesterton: Man and
Mask*, was the first to stress the spiritual and psychological night
of the soul that plagued Chesterton when he was a young student
at the Slade School of Art. He went to art school in 1892, and
found it filled with *fin-de-siècle* gloom and decadence, and even
diabolism. He found himself going through what today we would
call a crisis of identity; disturbed by solipsist fancies, he began
almost to doubt his own sanity.

Chesterton seems always to have had, except for a brief time
when he lost it, a profound intuition of what he calls 'the blaze of
Being'; it was probably the recovery of this perception that
rescued him from the solipsist miasma. Although untrained in
philosophy, he was a natural Thomist; the 'amateur' study of St
Thomas Aquinas that he published in the nineteen thirties was at
once acclaimed as a masterpiece of exposition and interpretation
by such leading Neo-Scholastic philosophers as Etienne Gilson
and Jacques Maritain. Hardy had never studied, even cursorily,
the thought of Aquinas. Chesterton, on the other hand, was
acquainted with the writings of Nietzsche and Schopenhauer,

which had had such a powerful influence on Hardy.

Chesterton says that the whole system of Aquinas 'hangs on one huge and yet simple idea; which does actually cover everything there is, and even everything that could possibly be. He [St. Thomas] represented this cosmic conception by the word *Ens*; and anybody who can read any Latin at all, however rudely, feels it to be the apt and fitting word.' *Ens*, means Being; absolute, unconditioned, eternal, self-sustaining Being (or Existence). And, as St Thomas says, 'This is what we mean by God.' Being *(Ens)* is by definition good; or rather, is absolute Goodness. Once this notion of Being has been intuited, it is impossible for the mind to think otherwise. Chesterton affirms that the primary and fundamental part of this *philosophia perennis* is 'entirely the praise of Life, the praise of Being, the praise of God as the Creator of the world. Everything else follows a long way after that, being conditioned by various complications like the Fall.'⁹ Thomas Hardy's mind seemed able to dwell on man's fallen state only.

In his earlier book *Orthodoxy* (1908) Chesterton had said that as a boy the words *optimist* and *pessimist* puzzled him, for the ordinary explanation seemed to be that the optimist thought his world as good as it could be, while the pessimist thought it as bad as it could be. Neither statement made sense to him.

My acceptance of the universe is not optimism, it is more like patriotism. It is a matter of primary loyalty. The world is not a lodging-house at Brighton, which we are to leave because it is miserable. It is the fortress of our family, with the flag flying on the turret, and the more miserable it is the less we should leave it. The point is not that this world is too sad to love or too glad not to love; the point is that when you do love a thing, its gladness is a reason for loving it, and its sadness a reason for loving it more. All optimistic thoughts about England and all pessimistic thoughts about her are alike reasons for the English patriot. Similarly, optimism and pessimism are alike arguments for the cosmic patriot.¹⁰

This was not at all how Thomas Hardy saw things. In 1920 a report in the *Morning Post* of a lecture of Alfred Noyes on 'Poetry and Religion' attributed to Noyes a statement to the effect that according to Thomas Hardy's philosophy 'the Power behind the Universe was an imbecile Jester'. Hardy sent Noyes a letter of protest, saying that he held no such 'philosophy', and asking Noyes where he had got this idea from. In a courteous reply Noyes cited various passages from Hardy's writings that seemed to him to tell in that direction; to which Hardy responded that in his opinion a writer's works should be judged as a whole, 'and not from picked passages that contradict them as a whole—and this especially when they are scattered over a period of fifty years'. He also stressed the vast difference between fancy and belief, and summed up his state of mind as follows:

My imagination may often have run away with me; but all the same, my sober opinion—so far as I have any definite one—of the Cause of Things, has been defined in scores of places, and is that of a great many ordinary thinkers: that the said Cause is neither moral nor immoral, but *un*moral: 'loveless and hateless' I have called it, 'which neither good nor evil knows'—etc., etc.—(you will find plenty of these definitions in *The Dynasts* as well as in short poems, and I am surprised that you have not taken them in). This is quite in keeping with what you call a Pessimistic philosophy (a mere nickname with no sense in it), which I am quite unable to see as 'leading logically, to the conclusion that the Power behind the universe is malign'.[11]

Since Hardy's and Chesterton's philosophies, and first principles, were so totally opposite, Chesterton's dictum about the village atheist brooding over the village idiot is entirely comprehensible, even if, as a summary of Hardy's outlook, it is inadequate or unjust. But in the course of his life Chesterton said a number of other things about Hardy, and one never sees them mentioned.

Hardy's first novel, *The Poor Man and the Lady*, was withdrawn before publication on the advice of George Meredith, who was at that time a reader with the firm of Chapman and Hall. Meredith was born in 1828, and so was Hardy's senior by twelve years; but as novelists they were to some extent contemporaries. Hardy's novels seem to have achieved a lasting popularity, while most of Meredith's are no longer much read. Chesterton preferred Meredith to Hardy; he explains why in an essay 'On George Meredith' in his book *The Uses of Diversity* (1920).

The name of that powerful writer Mr Thomas Hardy was often mentioned in company with that of Meredith; but the coupling of the two names is a philosophical and chronological mistake. Mr Hardy is wholly of our own generation, which is a very unpleasant thing to be. He is shrill and not mellow. He does not worship the unknown God: he knows the God (or thinks he knows the God), and dislikes him. He is not a pantheist; he is a pandiabolist. The great agnostics of the Victorian age said there was no purpose in nature. Mr Hardy is a mystic; he says there is an evil purpose. All this is as far as possible from the plenitude and rational optimism of Meredith.

This is surely much more severe, and perhaps unfair, than the remarks about the village atheist and the village idiot; but it seems to have drawn no protests from either Thomas Hardy or his admirers.

Occasionally, Hardy called himself a pagan. In October 1893 he was passing the weekend at some fashionable country house. Among his fellow guests was his friend Mrs Craigie (the novelist John Oliver Hobbes). Writing to a much closer friend, Mrs Florence Henniker, from Max Gate on 6th October, Hardy says: 'Mrs C. being a R.C., and I being a Pagan, we were obliged to go for a walk in the woods on Sunday when the others went to church.'[12] But in an essay on 'The Moral Philosophy of Meredith' Chesterton says: 'Thomas Hardy is not a Pagan; he is a Nonconformist gone sour. It is not pagan to revile the gods.'[13]

In an essay on 'Books for Pessimists', written in 1934, Chesterton contrasts Hardy with Walt Whitman. Hardy and Whitman, he says, were both Freethinkers; both had the same facts of the material world before them; but each gave a different answer to the question, 'Is life worth living?' He continues:

It looks to me as if the old inquirers, from Job to John Galsworthy, wanted to be convinced that it was all right. It looks to me as if many modern inquirers wanted only to be convinced that it was all wrong. To bring them news is to bring them bad news . . . Now I do not believe that Thomas Hardy really wanted to be a pessimist. On the contrary, it seems to me that he took every incidental opportunity to avoid being a pessimist. Whenever he could describe the glories of the glowing southern landscape of England, he described it for the sake of its own beauty; he made his hills and valleys even more vivid than his own men and women. There are passages in his novels which I still remember, alas! long after I have forgotten the novels. I can remember an impression of sweeping and splendid pasturage, ending with a line of noble and uplifted trees. But to the new pessimists it would seem a stretch of flat vegetation ending in some unusually large vegetables . . . To put the matter very crudely: in Victorian times even the atheists could be optimists.[14]

Hardy was not a controversialist; he did not share Chesterton's delight in discussion and argument. He was much less involved in current affairs than was Chesterton; in this sense he was much less of a public figure. When Hardy was about six or seven he had, one summer's day, a curious experience, which is described in his 'secret' autobiography, *The Life of Thomas Hardy*,

attributed to his second wife, Florence Emily Hardy. (It may seem
unfair of Hardy to have made her his 'ghost' in reverse, as it were;
but if she had not consented to the stratagem, Hardy would very
likely not have had the energy to get the book done. She deserves
a certain amount of credit, I would think, for her part in this
operation. Hardy might perhaps have done better to let her write
the book herself, in her own way. Her modest published works
evince no great literary talent, but she could hardly have written a
duller biography of Hardy than he did himself. But still, it might
not have been a success since there were episodes that she was as
anxious to conceal as he was.) Of this childhood experience the
Life of Thomas Hardy tells us that 'He was lying on his back in
the sun, thinking how useless he was, and covered his face with
his straw hat. The sun's rays streamed through the interstices of
the straw . . . Reflecting on his experiences of the world so far as
he had got, he came to the conclusion that he did not wish to
grow up . . . but he did not want at all to be a man, or to possess
things, but to remain as he was, in the same spot, and to know no
more people than he knew already (about half a dozen).' This
attitude of detachment and uninvolvement recurs in some of
Hardy's poems; for instance, 'Wessex Heights' and 'I Travel as a
Phantom Now'. Commenting on this incident the critic Hillis
Miller says:

Though Hardy finds that his consciousness separates him from the
world, he does not turn away from what he sees, to investigate the realm
of interior space. He and his characters are distinguished by the
shallowness of their minds. They have no profound inner depths leading
them down to the 'buried self' or to God. They remain even in
detachment oriented towards the outside world, reflecting it, mirror-like.
Though Hardy remains turned towards the exterior, looking at it or
thinking about it, his movement of retraction separates him from blind
engagement and turns everything he sees into a spectacle viewed from
the outside.[15]

Chesterton was much more publicly involved and committed
than Hardy, and was a lifelong publicist. His chosen profession
was the gregarious one of journalism; he was at home in Fleet
Street in a much more definite way than Hardy had been in the
world of architects and architecture. Chesterton thought that
Battersea was a lively and exciting place to live in; Hardy did not
view Westbourne Grove in any such light. When Chesterton was

removed by his wife, anxious for his health, from London to Beaconsfield, Top Meadow, a house built very much to G. K. C.'s own specifications, was a very much pleasanter residence than Hardy's self-designed Max Gate, and a far more friendly and sociable *foyer*.

Chesterton remained always very much the Londoner that he had been born, and many causes centred on London engaged his interest. As a young man he was solidly behind his brother, Cecil, and Hilaire Belloc, in their campaigns against political and financial corruption; after Cecil's death, in 1918, Gilbert carried on his paper, *The New Witness*, which supported the same causes. The policies of the *New Witness* were continued after 1925 in *G. K.'s Weekly*, and by the Distributist League, of which Gilbert was the President. High among Distributist aims was the restoration of British agriculture, to be based on widespread small ownership of farms and holdings.

Hardy was fully aware of the plight of the English labourer, and more especially the agricultural labourer. In 1883 he had contributed to *Longman's Magazine* an article on 'The Dorsetshire Labourer', a long essay on the economic condition of the agricultural worker. It has been said that in this essay Hardy 'displays curiously little sense of the real position, and can have fired little indignation in those accustomed to regard him as the man who put the Dorset "peasant" on the public map'.[16] Michael Millgate comments that Hardy's 'concern with the fate of the agricultural community . . . had relatively little significance in socio-political terms', and that he was 'reluctant to venture into the areas of politics and social philosophy'.[17]

It is not really possible to compare Hardy and Chesterton as writers, since for the most part they were attempting quite different things. Chesterton was not a great novelist; Hardy was. Hardy was a great poet also; Chesterton was scarcely that, though he wrote some fine poems. But it might seriously be argued that Chesterton was a better *writer* than Hardy, in the sense that he had a much greater gift for writing a clear expository prose with a strong individual note. Marshall McLuhan described Chesterton as 'a master of analogical perception and argument, whose real strength as a prose writer lies in his power of rhetorical paradox and epigram'.[18] Hilaire Belloc believed that Chesterton's writing derived its power largely from 'a unique capacity for parallelism', by means of which he 'continually illumined and explained realities by comparisons.'[19] Hardy at his worst is a worse writer than Chesterton ever was, even at his most careless. George Moore was not far wrong when he said: 'The best prose is usually written by poets . . . and I do not think I am going too far when I say that Mr Hardy has written the worst.'[20]

The examples which he gives amply justify the charge. The fact remains, however, that fifty years after Hardy's death his novels are as popular as ever, while George Moore's perfect prose, of which he was so proud, seems as dead as Walter Pater's. Hardy and Chesterton both had a great gift for story-telling; but Chesterton could not create character as Hardy could. His heroes tend to be personifications of ideas rather than real human beings. Certainly in Father Brown he succeeded in creating a character who is as familiar to us as Sherlock Holmes; but it is with difficulty that one recalls even the names of the heroes of some of his novels. His heroines are mostly of a red-headed Pre-Raphaelite type, with little to distinguish one from another. Hardy's novels are immeasurably more powerful than Chesterton's, partly because so much of their action is 'derived from the pull of sexual attraction across social barriers'.[21] But outside his Wessex themes and scenes Hardy could be a very dull writer, in a way that Chesterton never was. *The Life of Thomas Hardy*, largely dictated by him, and eked out with extracts from his diaries, is on the whole about as flat-footed a piece of biographical writing as can ever have been composed. Throughout the book Hardy remains a curiously withdrawn, colourless figure, with little that is of interest to say about himself or anyone else. By contrast, Chesterton's *Autobiography*, reticent though it is on a number of matters of which we should like to know more, crackles with life from beginning to end, and is a storehouse of lively anecdote about a great number of people, many of them famous, others quite obscure persons, who would have remained obscure if Chesterton had not found in them something that interested or amused him. For instance, in just a few sentences he gives us a most lively picture of that eminent man of letters Sir Edmund Gosse, of whom he says he was very fond. Gosse was one of Hardy's closest friends, yet in *The Life of Thomas Hardy* he is a mere stick, little more than a name.

Thomas Hardy died on 11th January, 1928. In the next issue of the *Illustrated London News* Chesterton devoted the whole of his weekly article, 'Our Notebook', to a long essay on him. In this article he said that:

Thomas Hardy, the maker of great tragedies, had through all his life learned the noble lesson of the grand Greek tragedies of whose high thunders his voice was perhaps the last reverberation. He may be called a heathen rather than a heretic; for he was never near enough to Christianity to contradict it. But in none of his contradictions, such as they were, was there anything of that special sort of insolence against which the Greek tragedy warned heroes and kings. He was often provocative; but he was never proud. Down to the last days when he received a universal veneration as the greatest of living Englishmen, he retained a splendidly unconscious simplicity.

Hardy, he says, was not a neutral or a non-combatant; and would not have wished to be treated as one. 'I will not pretend to sympathise with his philosophy as a truth; but I think it quite possible to sympathise with it as an error; or, in other words, to understand how the error arose.' He thought that Hardy had mellowed with age:

His own personality was always in the best sense gracious, being full not only of humanity but humility. Bitterly as he had quarrelled with a demon who did not exist, he never quarrelled with the human beings who do exist, and are therefore so much more aggravating. And he seems himself to have come to doubt whether he had not wasted on the former quarrel a fire that should have been given entirely to the latter sympathy:

> 'You have not said what you meant to say',
>   Said my own voice speaking to me:
> 'That the greatest of things is charity.'

Certainly there is no greater thing to say, and he often said it greatly.

When Hardy died Chesterton published a short unsigned article on him in his own paper, *G. K.'s Weekly*. In it he expressed his regret that Hardy's last wish—to be buried in the place where he was born—should have been denied him,

out of respect for a sort of newspaper noise which it was certainly his noblest quality to despise. If ever a man showed, in his testamentary directions, a fine and fitting sense of what he was and where he ought to return to the dust, it was he . . . Whatever else, he was a local patriot; and he ought to have been buried like a patriot, within the frontiers of his small nationality. The heavens were not clean in his sight; but all the mud and mire of the Dorset lanes were clean. He ought to have been given back in death, as he desired, to the things that he really did understand; and which really did make him a great Englishman. He had slandered the Cosmos, but he had honoured the County . . . He is now being noisily and extravagantly praised for everything in which he was most wrong. But this was the only thing he ever stooped to ask his admirers. It has been refused.[22]

In the *Autobiography* Chesterton quotes a poem by an Irish lady, Molly O'Fogerty, which appeared in *G. K.'s Weekly* after Hardy's death.

THOMAS HARDY

Who can picture the scene at the starry portals?
—Truly, imagination fails—
When the pitiless 'President of the Immortals'
Showed unto Thomas
The print of the nails.

Here is Chesterton's comment on the poem. 'I hope', he says, 'it is not profane to say that this hits the right nail on the head. In such a case, the second Thomas would do exactly what Prometheus and Satan never thought of doing; he would pity God.'

NOTES

1. G. K. Chesterton, *The Victorian Age in Literature*: London, 1913.

2. Israel Zangwill: 1864-1926, novelist and Zionist: author of Jewish novels and plays, his best known novel being the partly autobiographical *Children of the Ghetto* (1892).

3. *The Three Wayfarers*: cf. Richard Little Purdy, *Thomas Hardy: A Bibliographical Study*: London, 1954.

4. Robert Speaight, *The Life of Hilaire Belloc*: New York, 1957.

5. Lionel Johnson, *The Art of Thomas Hardy*: London, 1894; new edition, 1923.

6. A. O. J. Cockshutt, 'Hardy's Philosophy', in *The Genius of Thomas Hardy*, edited by Margaret Drabble: London, 1976.

7. John Heath-Stubbs, *The Darkling Plain:* London, 1950.

8. A perceptive comment on Chesterton's quip about Hardy will be found in chapter 3 of Henry Williamson's novel *The Golden Virgin* (London, 1957).

9. G. K. Chesterton, *St Thomas Aquinas*: London. 1933.

10. G .K. Chesterton, *Orthodoxy*: London, 1908.

11. Quoted in Florence Emily Hardy, *The Life of Thomas Hardy 1840-1928*: London, 1962.

12. Cf. *One Rare Fair Woman: Thomas Hardy's Letters to Florence Henniker 1893-1922*, edited by Evelyn Hardy and F. B. Pinion: London, 1972. For Mrs Craigie, see Margaret Maison, *John Oliver Hobbes; Her Life and Work:* London, 1976.

13. G. K. Chesterton, 'The Moral Philosophy of Meredith', in *A Handful of Authors* by G. K. Chesterton: London, 1953.

14. 'Books for Pessimists', in G. K. Chesterton, *Avowals and Denials*: London, 1934.

15. J. Hillis Miller, *Thomas Hardy, Distance and Desire*: Cambridge, Mass., 1970.

16. Denys Kay-Robinson, 'Hardy's Wessex', in *The Genius of Thomas Hardy*, ed. Margaret Drabble: London, 1976.

17. Michael Millgate, *Thomas Hardy: His Career as a Novelist*: New York, 1971.

18. Marshall McLuhan, Introduction to Hugh Kenner, *Paradox in Chesterton*: New York, 1974.

19. H. Belloc, *On the Place of Gilbert Chesterton in English Letters*: New York, 1940.

20. George Moore, *Conversations in Ebury Street*: London, 1924.

21. Michael Millgate, *Thomas Hardy: His Career as a Novelist*.

22. *G. K.'s Weekly*, 21st January, 1928. In addition to his weekly full-page article, under the heading 'Straws in the Wind', Chesterton contributed to each issue of his own paper two short unsigned articles, which between them filled a page. The first was headed 'Top! . . .', the one below it 'And Tail.'

Father Vincent McNabb O. P.
(c. 1940)

FATHER VINCENT McNABB

THE 1920s and 1930s in Britain are a remarkable time to look back on. In literature it was a time of extraordinary brilliance. In 1927 Thomas Hardy was still alive. John Galsworthy, Arnold Bennett, H. G. Wells, Gilbert Chesterton, Hilaire Belloc, Bernard Shaw, Compton Mackenzie, Joseph Conrad, John Cowper Powys, Theodore and Llewelyn Powys, and Virginia Woolf and Dorothy Richardson were all flourishing. By 1930 T.S. Eliot, Henry Williamson, Evelyn Waugh, and Graham Greene were all established writers, or well on the way to becoming so. Socially the country was in a bad way; it had not recovered from the first world war, which was soon to be followed by the second. Things were going from bad to worse; unemployment was mounting. The political leaders of the three major parties had all failed to do anything about this. A number of other political movements were proposing remedies; some of these bodies attracted a very large following, but most of them never became more than 'fringe' movements. Among these groups were the Independent Labour Party, led by James Maxton, the Communist Party of Great Britain, led by Harry Pollit, the New Party, which was succeeded by Sir Oswald Mosley's British Union of Fascists, the Henry George 'Single-Tax' movement, and the Social Credit movement of Major Douglas and Professor Soddy, from which sprang the Duke of Bedford's British People's Party. The churches were still a power in the land. Archbishop William Temple, with his out-spoken attitude on social questions, was making people see, as someone put it, that the Church of England was not just the Tory Party at prayer. The Catholic and Roman church was distrusted by the mass of the nation; but in some respects its prestige stood high, as Cardinal Bourne presided with confident dignity over a docile and submissive flock. And in the '20s and '30s there was an extraordinary upsurge of intellectual Catholicism, with the brilliant apologetic of Belloc and Chesterton, the controversial wit of Ronald Knox, the Dominican revival (for which Father Bede

Jarrett was largely responsible), the foundation of the publishing firm of Sheed and Ward, which introduced the writings of Jacques Maritain to the British public, and Bernard Wall's review *Colosseum*.

Somewhere in the middle of all this was the Distributist movement: not actually a Catholic movement, but a movement in which Catholics were numerically preponderant. This was inevitable, as Belloc and Chesterton were the principal exponents of Distributism, a social and economic theory which aimed at securing a just, free, and happy human society by means of a system of widely distributed small ownership of private property, which would abolish the proletarianism common to both Capitalism and Communism. After Belloc and Chesterton the best known Distributists were Eric Gill and Father Vincent McNabb. In London Father McNabb had become a familiar and popular figure; he always wore the white habit and black *cappa* of the Order of Preachers, and walked everywhere, avoiding the use of public transport. This he found saved both time and money. Through his public wearing of the religious habit—a practice long abandoned by most monks and friars—he had become something of a public 'character' in the London streets (like Prince Monolulu, the racing tipster, and Count Potocki de Montalk, the *de jure* King of Poland, both of whom affected picturesque attire).

Vincent Joseph McNabb was born in Ulster, whose brogue he kept, in 1868. His father was a sea-captain in the merchant navy, and in due time the family settled in the port of Newcastle-on-Tyne, in the north of England. Their home was in the Dominican parish of St Dominic's, and that is how this very young Irishman came to enter the English Province of the Order of Preachers (Dominicans), at the age of sixteen, in 1885. He was found to be a brilliant student; after his ordination, in 1891, he was sent to the university of Louvain, for higher studies. On his return to England in 1894 he was assigned to a succession of teaching posts. What we may call his public career did not begin until 1908, when he was elected prior of Holy Cross Priory, Leicester. In Leicester he soon began to be known as a fine preacher, and as an able lecturer on English literature in the city's centres of adult education. In Leicester, too, he became aware of the wretched housing conditions of the working classes, and of their depressed conditions of labour. He learned a good deal about human nature from what he saw and heard as Catholic chaplain to Leicester Gaol. (An early volume of his essays, *The Wayside*, contains, under the title 'An Innocent', a vivid and sympathetic impression of a young Irishman, Patrick Glennon, who had been sentenced to death for murder.)

The writer of Father McNabb's obituary in *The Times*, in June 1943, noted his early interest in literature. On 10th December, 1925, years after he had left Leicester, he gave a lecture in the Free Library there on 'Poets I have Known'. These will have included Alice Meynell, Hilaire Belloc, Katharine Tynan, and G. K. Chesterton; and also the two ladies who wrote the poetry of 'Michael Field', who had been introduced to him by Father John Gray, who had himself, before taking orders, been considered the 'typical' poet of the 1890s. The Michael Fields—Katharine Harris Bradley and her niece Edith Cooper—had been captivated by the poetry of Father McNabb's sermons at Leicester, from which they compiled a selection of passages which they published under the title *The Orchard Floor*.

In 1907 Father McNabb gave a course of sermons, with a strong 'social' content, in Westminster Cathedral, and these at once placed him among the foremost preachers of the day. But there were complaints; he was accused of 'Socialism'. His later celebrity notwithstanding, he was not asked to occupy the cathedral pulpit again.

In 1898, before his appointment to Leicester, he had been for a time procurator at Hawkesyard Priory, a house of studies at that time deep in the Staffordshire countryside. Here he found himself responsible for the administration of a farm. He took no special interest in this part of his work; but when he returned to Hawkesyard as prior in 1914 he at once saw it as a patriotic duty that his community should, at least as a wartime measure, support itself from the produce of its own land, and he spent two to four hours every day working on the farm. This had the happy effect of easing the nervous tensions from which he then suffered, and which at times made him difficult to live with. At Hawkesyard, as he recorded in the little book, *Eleven, Thank God*— Mrs McNabb's response when asked how many children she had—that he wrote about his mother, he suddenly saw 'that the town as man made it was not only unproductive, but was essentially based on wasted material and wasted time. Then something began to say, and indeed sing, within me, "When we come back to the earth as God made it, and as God made it for us, we need never waste an ounce of material or a moment of time."' Father McNabb's biographer, Father Ferdinand Valentine, was right when he said that Hawkesyard always remained for Father Vincent 'a holy place, where, as in a vision, he had seen all things new.'

As early as 1911 Vincent McNabb was contributing articles to Hilaire Belloc's weekly *The Eye-Witness*, and was supporting the Distributist policies of that paper, which were to be continued in Cecil Chesterton's *The New Witness*, and finally in *G.K.'s Weekly*. Self-support from the land, both for the country and for family units, was the basic Distributist demand; also widespread small ownership by craftsmen of their own tools and workshops, and widespread small ownership of retail shops and businesses of every kind, backed up by anti-trust and anti-monopoly legislation, and penalisation and discouragement of 'big business', by taxation and other means. The aim of the movement was to be the Restoration of Liberty by the Distribution of Property. The whole idea may be studied in Belloc's books *The Servile State*, *Economics for Helen*, and *The Restoration of Property*. Clearly such a programme is hostile to mass production and factory industrialism, except where such may be unavoidably necessary. Distributists were, in fact, divided in the degree of their dislike for modern machinery; Belloc and Chesterton did not give this matter much of their attention, but for Vincent McNabb and Eric Gill it was important. For McNabb it became a major preoccupation; but even so, for him it was the Land, for which he developed a real mystique, that was at the basis of it all. In the creation by Eric Gill and Hilary Pepler of the Guild of Catholic craftsmen at Ditchling Father McNabb saw the practical fulfilment of the ideas adumbrated in the *Eye-Witness*, some of which he had attempted, in a small way, to put into practice at Hawkesyard. Ditchling too became for him a holy name and a holy place. Indeed his guidance was a decisive factor in the early days of the Guild. But in the end Ditchling became something of an occasion of sorrow to him, and he was seen there no more. In 1924 Eric Gill left Ditchling, largely because of disagreements between himself and Pepler. Financial matters were involved; Father McNabb was invited to arbitrate. Sensibly, he declined. But his relationship with Hilary was not affected; indeed, I think he admired him for holding on at a time when the ship seemed to be sinking. In a letter written to him in February 1931 he says: 'I hardly know where my resoluteness and definiteness of thought would be had you and your ideas not come into my life.' And in May of the same year he writes:

My dear Hilary,
    Your gift of Whitsun cream was more than welcome!
    How irresistably it brought back the Ditchling I first knew, and loved with the intensity of a first love. I can imagine that many a man marries the girl he loves not merely because he loves her, but because his love of her, or her love of him, has saved him from some fall. I sometimes wonder whether the vision of realities I was beginning to see and to speak would not have faded into a mist of despair. . . .

But soon after the events of 1924 Father McNabb's relationship with Eric Gill underwent a change; partly because of Gill's defection, as he viewed it, from the Ditchling community, and partly because of what he thought a dangerous element of eroticism that he had detected in some of Gill's writings and engravings. Gill was puzzled by this Irish puritanism, as he thought it; but to the end of his life, he revered Father McNabb as one of the holiest men of his time.

If Father Vincent's relationship with Hilary Pepler remained unchanged, it was not so with his relationship with the Ditchling guild. He seems never quite to have understood that the Guild of SS. Joseph and Dominic was an association of craftsmen, not of farmers. With his intense 'back-to-the-land' mystique, he was deeply pained when he saw the gardens or plots of ground outside the guildsmen's houses neglected or uncultivated, and felt that primary things were being neglected for secondary. The sight of this untilled land became more than he could bear, as he explained in a letter to Pepler written in 1930. It took a very urgent appeal from Hilary to bring him there, for what proved to be a final visit, of a few hours only, in 1934.

Whatever he was talking about, even when in the pulpit, the

land was never far from his thoughts, and he was constantly urging an exodus from the cities to the then untilled fields of England. Among his papers preserved in the Dominican provincial archives is this note: 'A man in the crowd at Regent's Park on hearing me speak of the evil of modern conditions especially in London said: "You seem to dislike London." I answered quickly: "Yes, I dislike London. Because—I love the people of London and London treats its people so shamefully. I know what it is to live otherwise than London lets its people live!"'

Father McNabb's anger at the conditions under which the urban poor were condemned to live did not affect his views on the birth control question. He followed unswervingly the then unanimous teaching of the moral theologians as to the immorality of artificial birth control, and some of his reasoning on this subject—as in the notes to his edition of Pope Pius XI's encyclical on Christian marriage—may now seem less than convincing; but where he differed from other theologians was in his insistence that for the poor in the slums of modern cities the observance of this teaching requires heroic virtue; and, he would stress, heroism is something that cannot be demanded. Therefore the living-conditions of the poor must be changed.

Father McNabb was an unashamed showman; he was not averse to making himself conspicuous, or even ridiculous, whether on the platform or in the pulpit. At times he would descend to vulgarities; as when, at a meeting held to raise funds for the Apostleship of the Sea, at which several bishops were present, he gave a noisy imitation of the master of a vessel speaking from the bridge through a megaphone. (The son of a sea-captain, he was fond of nautical allusions. In the course of a retreat he once said: 'When a seaman makes a contract with a ship-owner for an outward voyage and a homeward voyage, he is said to "sign on". Those who take religious vows may well be said to "sign on" to make the outward and homeward journey with Jesus.') 'McNabb's stunts', as some people called them, sometimes jarred on his hearers and embarrassed them; but by and large they were effective, especially when he was speaking in the open air, where audiences sometimes need to be shocked into attention. But over the years he gained in experience and wisdom, and came to rely less on such tactics.

Quintilian says that the orator must instruct, move, and delight his hearers. This Father McNabb did, whatever the subject of his discourse. He had a most effective gift of humorous repartee and comment. Many of his witticisms have been preserved, but often they tend to go flat in print. Some of them were similar to the kind of remarks that Chesterton attributes to Father Brown; thus, for example, Father Vincent's dictum that 'You don't need any intellect to be an intellectual.' These sallies were usually accompanied by something that was a cross between a grin and a smile—a sort of gratified smirk which seemed to say, Does that please you? Such mannerisms also he to a large extent grew out of, or outlived.

Perhaps he was not deliberately dramatic, but was a natural actor and was dramatic because he really felt like that. A French priest once called him 'Père Sed-contra': an allusion to the dialectical method of St Thomas Aquinas. He enjoyed that form of argument, conducted by socratic questioning, which leads one's opponent on to self-destruction. When Father McNabb had got his opponent in debate to utter the desired fatal admission, he would utter an incisive 'Thank you!', which would be accompanied by a seraphic smile.

Father McNabb was so public a figure that he could almost be said to have lived in the glare of the footlights. But no man was less self-centred, no one more unselfish. As a nun wrote in a letter: 'He was a very humble priest, who would go to the ends of the earth to help a soul.' A humble man may perhaps be vain, but he will not be proud. In Father McNabb's cell at St Dominic's Priory, NW5, there was no mirror. In fact, there was practically nothing in his room except his bed—which he never slept in, he used the floor—a hard straight-backed wooden chair, his Bible, the *Summa Theologica* of St Thomas Aquinas, and his notebooks and files of papers.

He enjoyed controversy; but it was never pursued for its own sake, or with violence. From the Catholic Evidence Guild platform in Hyde Park on Sunday afternoons he used to give lucid explanations of Catholic doctrine which were often a kind of commentary on some passage from the Gospels, or other scriptural texts, which he would read out at the beginning of his talk. Controversy began only at question time, or in response of the interjections of hecklers. Sometimes his outdoor addresses were more like short sermons, or the kind of 'meditations' that retreat conductors give.

He did not approve of the idea that it is not what we preach or do, but what we are, that saves souls. This he described as 'a superstition of humility', and said that 'The truth is that we save souls neither by what we do nor by what we are, but by what God does and by what God enables us to do.'

An assistant priest at the old church of Our Lady of Victories in Kensington High Street—it was bombed out during the last war—once described to the late Father Bernard Delany, O.P., a sermon that Father Vincent had preached there one Good Friday evening. He had timed his arrival to a nicety. The thronged congregation was waiting expectantly for the well known figure. Father Vincent entered by the main door, having walked from Hyde Park where he had been preaching the Stations of the Cross. With his battered old hat in his hand and his knapsack—or 'McNabb-sack', as he called it—on his back, he walked rather wearily up the aisle. The pulpit was a very lofty one, entered by a regular staircase. He went slowly up the stairs, took out his Bible from his knapsack, placed knapsack and hat on the pulpit floor, and surveyed the hushed congregation. Then he made the sign of the cross and said, rather stridently and defiantly:

I've got a headache; and I hope you've all got headaches too. If you haven't got headaches, it's your own fault. If you have fasted, as you should on this most holy day; if you have been to the Good Friday Mass, read the Passion of our dear Lord, and made the Stations of the Cross, then you've got headaches. It's the proper thing to have on Good Friday evening. It means you've tried to do your duty. You're meant to have a headache today. I can't bear hearing people say: 'Oh, I do enjoy Holy Week.' [Here there was almost a snarl in his voice.] How dare you enjoy Holy Week? Would you enjoy being crucified? Because that's what Good Friday means!

So he went on for about twenty minutes, jerking out staccato sentences, every one of them a stab.

But it must not be thought that he was always scolding. To pierce the tough skin of conscience with sharp stinging words—that Ronald Knox thought to be the true work of the preacher. But it is far from being the whole of preaching. Those who attended his retreats experienced quite another side of this priest.

Under his ascetic appearance, and under his austerity, there was a most tender heart. At the end of his sermon at the funeral of Father Bede Jarrett, at Blackfriars, Oxford, in 1934, he broke into sobs, and almost ran back into the sacristy. Father Bede he held in highest veneration. Bede Jarrett had served three consecutive terms of office as Prior Provincial, he had brought the Dominicans back to Oxford, and had been thought likely to have been a future archbishop of Westminster, unless he were made Master-General of his Order first. Father Bernard Delany, who succeeded Father Bede as Provincial, once said to Father Vincent: 'Father Bede is amazing. He trusts everybody—even the untrustworthy.' Father Vincent replied: 'Yes, I know. God forgive me—he even trusts me.'

As a debater he was in the first class. He was one of the few men in England who could debate with Bernard Shaw on equal terms. Among his manuscript notes occurs the following:

I have now argued several times with members of the Metropolitan Secular Society on their thesis 'Atheism is more rational than Theism.' Last night, 12th October 1924, I again discussed the question before a large audience in Woolworth Buildings, Edgware Road. I summed up the positive side by saying: The doctrine of a personal God is more rational because it more thoroughly (consistently) accepts the ideas of Causality, Purpose, Evil.

His notes contain this on the problem of evil: the basic question in the theist-atheist debate:

Evil: is it merely a problem?
A problem is an intellectual difficulty. Now, just as ethics (moral science) is not so much a moral science as a moral life, so is Evil not so much an intellectual difficulty as a moral difficulty.
If there is no God, evil still is; and is supreme.
To admit the existence of God is not to deny the existence of evil, but to deny the supremacy of evil.
To deny the existence of God is not to deny the existence of evil, but to deny the existence of a final remedy for evil.
To admit the existence of evil is not to deny the existence of God.

This is typical of his method of disputation.
Men accustomed to less closely reasoned and less vigorous

kinds of discussion sometimes thought, wrongly, that he was proud and opinionated. The proof of his humility was to be seen in his obedience. One of his former superiors said that being Father Vincent's prior was like leading a lion on a string. 'But the string never broke.'

He used to say that it was a great mistake to identify authority with autocracy, as if every superior was inevitably an autocrat. For authority itself he had the greatest reverence, irrespective of the qualities of the man in whom it was vested. He had ways of showing respect to his superiors which were infinitely courteous; he was careful to keep to the path of obedience even in small matters. At St Dominic's Priory, although his work obliged him to spend almost as much time away from the house as in it, and although he held the office of subprior, he never left the monastery without seeking the Prior's blessing. Always he asked permission for anything unusual or uncustomary that he wished to do. His brethren knew that he was not cast in the same mould as they were, and that the standards of religious observance that he set himself often went beyond their own standards: at least in the sense that what one religious may find useful or necessary as aids to perfection may not be so to others. They knew that he was some kind of genius, perhaps some kind of saint; and that they, for the most part, were men of average ability. A few, however, thought otherwise, and were inclined to consider him a crank or poseur. Those who were unable to appreciate his qualities, and to make allowance for characteristics that struck them as tiresome, sometimes found his behaviour maddening; as did a certain Father who was once driven to exclaim, in a fit of exasperation, 'I'll get even with McNabb before I die!'

Father Vincent, intensely individual though he was, did his best to live as a 'good community man', and was unshakably loyal to his brethren. In those days, and here and there even now, a monastic common-room often had a tobacco-laden atmosphere like that of a second-class railway compartment with the windows shut—a considerable mortification for a non-smoker to put up with. He never complained. Nor did he ever go on holiday cruises (priests can sometimes get free passages as chaplains), or stay in good-class hotels when he was travelling. He knew, of course, the traditional teaching on the dangers attaching to 'singularity' in community life, which was one reason why he was always so careful about asking permissions. Certainly he had a technique of 'trying it on' and seeing how far he could go; but he always took no for an answer, without any demur. In the matter of wearing the habit in public—a practice not viewed with favour by most of the brethren—he got away with it. Father Bede Jarrett once decided that it had gone on long enough and that he had better stop it. He arranged for Father Vincent to accompany him to a tailor's to be measured for a black suit; but he looked so ludicrous when he tried on one or two of his confrères' suits which they had offered to lend him for the occasion that Father Bede thought better of it. No one can be measured for a suit while wearing the costume of the thirteenth century; so the project was dropped.

In 1935, the year of his golden jubilee as a Dominican, Father Vincent wanted to walk to Rome to see the Pope—a pilgrimage to be made somewhat in the spirit of Belloc's *The Path to Rome*. His idea was to do thirty miles a day, sleep where he could, and end up by renewing his vows in the hands of the Pope, receiving the pontiff's blessing, and then returning home by train. The Provincial vetoed the idea, fearing that it would be too much for the health of a man of seventy. In any case, for a Dominican to visit Rome the permission of the Master-General of the Order is necessary. When the General heard about it later he said that if he had been asked he would not have given permission.

After Father Vincent's death the special arrangements that he wanted for his funeral, which he had planned as a kind of acted parable, or sermon in action, were for the most part vetoed. This was a pity, for it would have been the best sermon he had ever preached.

His motto, which he commended to others, was 'Do all you can. Do without all you can.' (A simple summary of Christ's teaching in the Gospels.) So he did without radio and television, and never went to the cinema. These things, in his view, wasted time. Labour-saving devices,' he used to say, 'cause more labour than they save.' A prolific author and contributor to magazines, he never used a typewriter, because he wished to preserve the dignity of handwriting and the noble art of making letters. He had a big post every day, and every letter was answered, in his fine square script, by return. How he did it is a mystery, in view of all his commitments. For this purpose he used one of those brick-red outsize Parker fountain-pens that were common before the second war, but are now no longer made. He did not, as Dudley Barker says in his biography of Father McNabb's friend G. K. Chesterton, make his own monastic habit. It was made for him from the hand-woven cloth of Valentine KilBride, the Ditchling weaver. Obviously it was more expensive than the machine-made material used for his brethren's habits, but since it lasted twice as long there was no infringement of holy poverty. In London he walked everywhere, using heavy Army-surplus boots, and left the traffic-jams standing as he knew all the short cuts and byways.

During his twenty-three years' residence in London he held the posts of subprior and librarian in his convent; this left him free to accept engagements to preach sermons and conduct retreats up and down the country; tasks at which he excelled, and for which he was in great demand. Many of his confrères regarded his preoccupation with social questions as just some kind of private fad. Quite a number of Catholics disapproved of him, and thought he was a crank and a fanatic in his attitude to industrialism and in his back-to-the-land propaganda. Canon John Gray, the most distinguished priest in Scotland, and himself a Dominican tertiary, once said: 'What a pity it is that Father Vincent doesn't stick to his philosophy and theology, where he is a great success, instead of insisting on being such a failure at the other thing.' He must at times have thought himself a failure. If he were alive today he would be surprised and pleased at how much better some of his ideas are understood; his denunciations of industrialism now claim wide agreement. He was a forerunner of our present-day ecologists, and his denunciations of the evils of modern urban life are now amply vindicated. How he would have rejoiced to see the spread of the 'Small is Beautiful' idea. The pith and essence of his thought on these matters will be found in his two books *The Church and the Land* and *Nazareth or Social Chaos.*

We still have no adequate biography of this extraordinary man. That by his confrère Father Ferdinand Valentine is a valuable testimony, a piece of essential witness; but it is more of a memoir than a real biography; and as a psychological study its success is doubtful. Of the biography begun by the late Father Bernard Delany, whose notes I have been generously allowed to consult, very little was achieved. Very soon Father McNabb will have been dead forty years. It is surely time that a 'definitive' biography—in so far as there can be such a thing—is written before it is too late.

H. D. C. Pepler
(c. 1950)

H.D.C. PEPLER

I FIRST HEARD of Hilary Pepler when I was fifteen, and still at school. The school was Weymouth College, an Anglican 'low church' foundation, one of three minor Public Schools maintained by a charitable trust, Evangelical Church Schools Ltd. It was a good school, and produced many distinguished alumni. In 1927 the Senior English Master was Lionel Gough, a Master of Arts of London University, and an exceptionally gifted teacher. Gough was an ardent Anglo-Catholic, and the very plain liturgy in use in Weymouth College Chapel tried him a good deal. He could joke about it with the Chaplain, Victor Tanner, one of the great schoolmasters of the century as he has been called, who was not lacking in a sense of humour. Gough could tease him about his 'north end' stance when celebrating the Holy Communion, and playfully urge him to be bold and introduce coloured stoles, to replace his sombre black tippet; but he could not have advocated such things seriously and openly without risk of losing his job. In his English classes his Catholic sympathies would sometimes emerge when we discussed such writers as Dryden and Newman, or Chesterton and Belloc. Gough subscribed to Chesterton's paper, *G. K.'s Weekly*. This was not a Catholic periodical, but it had many Catholic contributors. Occasionally he would read us a poem, or part of an article, from *G. K.'s*, and he would sometimes lend me a number to take away and read by myself.

The magazine carried every week a collective advertisement for a group of craftsmen on Ditchling Common, in Sussex. These were a weaver, a carpenter, a stone-mason, and, last on the list, 'H. D. C. Pepler, printer, St Dominic's Press'. A footnote said that there were vacancies for apprentices in these workshops. Just at this time my father had warned me that I would soon have to leave school as he would not much longer be able to afford the fees. What to do? A total incapacity for Mathematics ruled out the possibility of being admitted to a university. Or so it seemed at the time. Careers masters had hardly been thought of in those days, and there was no one to tell me that Logic—a more amenable subject—could be substituted for Mathematics in the London University matriculation examination. The Church was out of the question, as I was not at all sure that the Church of England, in which I had been brought up, was all that her credentials claimed her to be. The Bar was no alternative because of the high cost of qualifying. The notion of a career in the Armed Forces did not appeal. Studying the advertisement in *G. K.'s Weekly*, I wondered if printing might not be a possible occupation. A letter of inquiry was sent to Mr Pepler, who invited me to visit him during the summer holidays.

So one day in August 1928 I took a train from London, Victoria Station, to Burgess Hill, only a mile and a half distant from Ditchling Common, which is reached by way of Folders Lane, a thoroughfare just beyond the town. At the end of the lane, just before it joined the crossroads in the middle of Ditchling Common, a sign on the right indicated a path leading to 'The Guild of SS. Joseph and Dominic'. Here, around a small grass plot, were the workshops of the craftsmen who made up the Guild. Most of these workshops were simple wooden structures, some of them former Army huts; but on the further side of the quadrangle which they formed was a solid two-storey brick building which a small painted name-board identified as 'Saint Dominic's Press'. Knocking on the door and being told to come in, I was greeted by Mr Pepler himself, a tall, handsome man, of rather grave appearance, but with a twinkle in his eye indicative of good humour. He was then fifty years old, but hardly looked it. His speech seemed measured and thoughtful, hinting perhaps at his upbringing among the Society of Friends. Of that, of course, I knew nothing; but I did know that he was a Roman Catholic. He was, I think, the first Catholic layman I had ever met, or at least knew to be such.

In entering the premises that housed St Dominic's Press I was entering a new world. I had some vague idea of what an ordinary small-town commercial printer's premises looked like, but this was something quite different. When you entered St Dominic's Press you stepped straight into the composing room. (There was no vestibule or waiting room for the reception of customers or other visitors.) Apart from a 'tortoise'-type stove for winter heating, the composing room was filled with the frames containing cases of type, with large wood-letter type for printing posters arranged in racks on the wall. On the west wall, to the right of the door, hung a large chart or diagram of the layout of the type-cases, with the 'boxes', or compartments, for the individual letters arranged somewhat after the fashion of a typewriter keyboard; the biggest box, for the letter most commonly used, 'e', being within immediate reach of the compositor's right hand; the less frequently used signs and symbols being distributed round the edge of the case. (Actually there are *two* cases, both placed at a convenient angle above the frame, at a convenient height. The upper case contains the capital letters, small capitals, etc., the lower case the small letters. The trained compositor, of course, knows their positions by heart.)

From the composing room an open arch led straight into the long press room. Here, for the first time, I saw iron hand-presses, the immediate successors to Gutenberg's and Caxton's wooden presses: a Stanhope press—the first iron press ever made—dating from 1790, and said to have belonged to William Morris; a folio Albion press; and that most decorative of all presses, a Columbian. On the walls of the press room were posters that had been printed on these presses: posters of a bold originality of design that set them quite apart from the usual run of such things.

Within a few minutes of my arrival Mr Pepler handed me a setting-stick (also known as a composing-stick), and began to teach me how to set up type by hand. He was a good instructor, and he seemed to perceive in me some aptitude. At any rate, at the end of my stay, a day or two later, he said that he was satisfied with my progress, and that he would take me on later as an apprentice if I applied. However, nothing further came of this for some time, since shortly afterwards I was offered a job on *G. K.'s Weekly*, and succumbed to the attractions of journalism. But in 1932 I did go to work at the St Dominic's Press, and I remained there for five years.

HARRY[1] (HILARY) DOUGLAS CLARKE PEPLER was born at Eastbourne on 14th February, 1878, the elder son of George

Henry (Harry) Pepler and his wife Florence Mills. The Peplers are an old Wiltshire family from the village of Headington. By the end of the nineteenth century some of them had left Wiltshire for London, where, like Galsworthy's Forsytes, they had 'done well for themselves and were what is called "of a certain position". They had shares in all sorts of things, and had inherited a talent for bricks and mortar.'

Hilary's father, George Henry Pepler, had been a partner in the firm of Diplock, brewers, of Eastbourne, from which he retired as soon as he could because he disliked making his living from something that made the poor poorer. He then moved to Croydon, but died soon afterwards. His widow married again, and her second husband was a Quaker. That is how Hilary and his younger brother George, later to be knighted for his services to town-planning, came to be entered at Bootham School, York, the well known foundation of the Society of Friends.

At Bootham the two boys made a lasting friendship with the Yorkshire family of Mennell, which is closely related to the better known Meynells. His school-fellow Harry Mennell became a close friend of Hilary's, and another was T. Edmund Harvey, later M.P. for the United Universities, and a lifelong worker in the cause of peace. When Hilary left Bootham in 1894, Harvey, his senior, had already graduated at Oxford. A few years later they were working together in London, at Toynbee Hall, in the East End, where Harvey had been appointed Deputy Warden. On leaving Bootham, however, Hilary first spent a year in Switzerland, learning to speak French, and enjoying himself. Returning to England, he was apprenticed to Sir Reginald Hanson, a Merchant Taylor in the City; but soon afterwards he transferred to the tea trade, probably under the influence of Harry Mennell, who was now in London, and in that line of business. At first Hilary was with the firm of Travers, wholesale grocers in Cannon Street, where he was put in charge of the cigar department. Seeking greater independence, he then bought for £250 a pewterer-engineer's business employing seven or eight men in casting pewter moulds for making candles and ice-cream. He enjoyed running this enterprise, but his machines were out of date, and after two years he sold out to a competitor from the United States.

In 1901 he was elected a Liveryman of the Merchant Taylors Company, and was granted the Freedom of the City of London, probably under the sponsorship of Sir Reginald Hanson. He now seemed all set for a successful commercial career, destined to become an Alderman, and very possibly Lord Mayor. He was living in Great Albany Street, sharing rooms with Harry Mennell, whose parents' former housekeeper looked after them. Through Harry, Hilary became a regular visitor to the home of Wilfrid and Alice Meynell, in Palace Court, off the Bayswater Road. He became very friendly with the Meynell children, and for a short time was 'almost' engaged to one of the daughters. He developed an enthusiasm for amateur theatricals, and joined the O.P. Club, which was chiefly made up of first-nighters, and also a Shakespeare Society. He took part in the productions put on by these societies, but was not allowed to appear in romantic rôles, as was his ambition, but had to content himself with parts such as Sir Toby Belch in *Twelfth Night* and Don Amado in *Love's Labour's Lost*. Evidently he had a talent for comedy. One of the Meynell girls who knew him at that time remembered him, in 1965, as 'a very amusing and attractive young man: I always remember him as a good skater, and a very good manager of a boat on wonderful days on the river, and an actor always in demand for amateur Shakespeare productions'. He remained close to the Meynell family for the rest of his life.

In 1903 Hilary met his future wife, Clare Whiteman, who was studying painting, with Herkomer, and was, like Hilary, a Quaker. A year later they married, and spent their honeymoon visiting Paris, Florence, and Rome. After the honeymoon he decided that his real vocation was land surveying; so a year was spent at Tunbridge Wells while he learned the business. In the same year, 1905, his and Clare's first child was born, a boy, who was given the names of David Whiteman Pepler. His own comment on this period is: 'Good heavens. I *was* a rolling stone. I remember Queen Victoria's funeral (seen from the Green Park), and first reading G. K. C.—*Daily News*, 1903-4; but I did not meet him until 1909.'

His land surveying aspirations do not seem to have lasted very long, and his next step was to accept an invitation from Edmund Harvey to work with him, as his personal assistant, at Toynbee

Hall, the East End 'settlement', founded by Canon Barnett, whose purpose was to provide the amenities of adult education and healthful recreation for the poverty-stricken inhabitants of the slums. In 1907, as a result of his Toynbee Hall experience, he was engaged by the London County Council as a professional social worker, with special responsibilities in the field of child welfare. An LCC General Purposes Committee Report of 1950 recorded that 'The establishment of a staff of two organisers of care work began in 1907 when the Council appointed two temporary organisers, Mr H. D. C. Pepler and the late Miss T.M. Morton, who reported on the method of selection of necessitous children; and officially recognised care committees were then set up.' Pepler, who was joined by Miss Morton a little after his own appointment, was the first organiser of meals for children in the London County Council schools. As the report says: 'These pioneers did much that is now forgotten.'

In 1907, or early 1908, Pepler acquired a house, Number 14 in Hammersmith Terrace, West London. By now, he had a second son, Stephen, and himself and Clare were hoping for more children. Hammersmith, on the upper reaches of the Thames, was still something of a village, and was about as good a place as could be found in London for the bringing up of a family. The Terrace had among its residents some interesting personalities, Frederic Stevens, the Pre-Raphaelite painter, May Morris, daughter of William Morris, and Morris's friend and associate, Emery Walker. Among younger neighbours in the Terrace were the calligrapher Edward Johnston, who was teaching at the Central School of Arts and Crafts in Holborn, and his family, at Number 8; a Quaker friend of Hilary's, Fred Rowntree, architect, was at Number 11; and Warwick Draper, barrister-at-law and historian of Hammersmith at Number 13, later to be occupied by Edmund Harvey and his family. Round the corner, a cottage in Black Lion Lane was occupied by Eric Gill, then a more or less unknown sculptor and stone-carver, and his wife Mary. The Peplers and the Johnstons quickly became friends; but as yet there was no special entente between the Pepler and the Gill families, although Eric did give Hilary some lessons in stone-carving.

In some reminiscences entitled 'Forty Years Back,'[2] Pepler recalls that Edward Johnston 'was averse from all forms of publicity, and was physically incapable of exploiting his own talents; he was repelled by any kind of organisation, even of his own time . . . There was an atmosphere in the Terrace which was thoroughly in keeping with the sheltered life for which Johnston was clearly cast. The ageing forms of the last Pre-Raphaelite (Frederic Stevens) and his wife and Miss May Morris belonged to the past; they were visible just often enough to suggest a refuge from the shattering trams of the Broadway . . . The Black Lion guarded the Terrace . . .; but strangely enough "The Lion" was not part of our lives—a fact which illustrates the Victorian atmosphere we still preserved. . . Facing our backs was an old and small stable then being used as a workshop by Eric Gill (later to be taken over by Romney Green[3]).'

Also living in Hammersmith just then were T. J. Cobden-Sanderson, of Doves Press fame, and the artists Roger Fry and Frank Brangwyn. Pepler was introduced to Brangwyn by the painter Sir William Richmond, RA.

His work at Toynbee Hall and for the LCC had brought Pepler into very close touch with the London poor, who were poor beyond anything that can be experienced in this country today. He was keenly aware of the gospel of 'Social Service' preached by John Ruskin and William Morris, and his conscience, nourished on the charitable traditions of the Society of Friends, had been stirred. This stirring of conscience now led him to join with his neighbours Fred Rowntree (of the York Quaker family) and Warwick Draper (Anglican) to found a non-denominational club for working men which would do for Hammersmith, though on a smaller scale, what Toynbee Hall was doing in the East End. For this purpose they acquired Hampshire House, a pleasant, panelled manor house, close to William Morris's Kelmscott House in Upper Mall. The Hampshire House Club, as it was called, proved a great success. Among its many activities was a mock Parliament, in which Cecil Chesterton, GKC's brilliant younger brother, served as a Socialist member; the Club's panel of lecturers included Gilbert Chesterton, Hilaire Belloc, William Rothenstein, Edward Carpenter, and G. P. Gooch. There was a dramatic society, in one of whose productions Ellen Terry appeared as Portia in *The Merchant of Venice*; and there was an annual exhibition of paintings by local artists, to which Brangwyn, Richmond, and Muirhead Bone contributed. In one year the content of the show was widened to include examples of printing and bookbinding from the Doves Press, embroidery by May Morris, lettering by Edward Johnston, sculpture by Eric Gill, and wood-carving and furniture by Romney Green. A stalwart helper was the Club's secretary, E. H. Haywood, a resourceful Cockney from Whitechapel, who had begun life, after leaving school, as a postman. Pepler had spotted his potentialities, and helped him to enter Ruskin College, Oxford, in pursuit of knowledge and education. Haywood, who remained a Freethinker all his life, was devoted to the memory of Cardinal Manning, not as priest, but as a power on the side of Labour and the poor, especially during the great London Dock Strike. Later he was a devoted admirer of Father Vincent McNabb, another champion of the poor. He rose to become a high official of the Workers' Travel Association, and was an habitué of the upper and inner circles of the Labour Party, with all whose leading figures in the 1920s and '30s he was on familiar terms. Haywood could have entered Parliament himself at any time, but he chose not to. He was a very popular figure at meetings of the Distributist League.

During this Hammersmith period Pepler was attending regularly at meetings of the Fabian Society, of which he was a member, as was Eric Gill. At these meetings he often met Hilaire Belloc and Cecil and Gilbert Chesterton, whom he was to follow in rejecting the Socialist creed in favour of Distributism, the doctrine of widespread small ownership as the basis of freedom, and the only viable alternative to the twin evils of Capitalism and Collectivism.

For Pepler this distributist line of thought sharpened his already growing distaste for the bureaucratic aspects of the LCC's policies for dealing with the poor, and especially with the children of the poor. In 1912 he published a book, *The Care Committee, the Child, and the Parent*, which upset some of his employers at County Hall. The book discusses the difficulties involved in the co-operation of volunteer social workers with the salaried professionals, such co-operation being an integral part of the LCC's care committee procedure. Thinking of the London children of 1912, the author dreams of the time 'when work shall be once more of the nature of a sacrament, a pledge given by man and a token received from God, the outward and visible sign of inward and spiritual grace. Joy might then be known to the people in all the compass of their life. . . Those of us who go down the back ways of this city, who see the children at school or playing in the street, who know the misery of the single furnished room and the sights and sounds in the land of darkness, know the need for strong men and women with power to face these things and to overcome them.'

Eventually, finding the methods and ethos of Hampshire House and County Hall to be irreconcilable, Pepler resigned from the service of the LCC. After he had done so, in 1915, he published a second book, *Justice and the Child*, which dealt with problems of probationary and after-care work. Its principal theme is that 'procedure in the treatment of juvenile offenders is a means to an end, not an end in itself. The object we have in view is the healthy independence of men and women. To accomplish this we must somehow demonstrate to the delinquent youth, as to the neglectful parent, that the course of a man's life need not be set for destruction, that even the narrow way has its illumination, that truth is more than a statement that satisfies the Bench, and that life is something other than conduct approved by the police. The youth has to learn that life cannot be lived unto himself, and, in order that he may learn this, we should seek to develop rightly those links which bind the lad to his family and to his "set" rather than to ingraft some theoretical system of right living only possible of practice apart from his natural associates. . . There can be no departure from the law that it is only one man, by the grace of God, who can help another; and, though our organisations are doubled in number and every other citizen were an official, it would still only be possible for the most beneficent of schemes to be of use according to the personality and capacity of the men by whom it was represented.' Words as true today as when they were written.

At the outbreak of war in 1914 Pepler was exempt from military service for reasons of health. As a Quaker he would probably, in any case, have claimed exemption as a conscientious objector. But he could not remain indifferent to the situation.

With the approval of his fellow directors he offered Hampshire House as a hostel to accommodate some of the first refugees to arrive from German-occupied Belgium, the activities of the Club being mostly suspended for the duration.

Among the refugees who arrived at Hampshire House were a number of craftsmen, men and women, and these were helped to set up workshops of their own, and carry on their trades. Facilities were established for dress-making and embroidery, boot and shoe making and repairing, and woodwork. These three enterprises did well, and were of great benefit to the locality. After two years the Belgian refugees were transferred to other wartime relief centres, and the hostel and workshops were closed. But two of the workshops were soon reopened: the dressmaking and embroidery were continued by English girls who had been apprenticed to the Belgians; local woodworkers took over the joinery shop. No one could be found to succeed the master-cobbler and bootmaker from Brussels, but instead a bakery was opened. These workshops were jointly registered as a company under the name 'Hampshire House Workshops Ltd,' with offices at 6 Upper Mall, Hammersmith. The company was registered under the Industrial and Provident Societies Acts, and shares were offered to the public. The directors had invested £2000; another £800 was needed. An advertisement in the Quaker magazine *The Friend* said that the directors would 'be glad if this sum could be raised among Friends, for we have refused war contracts and believe our work is more likely to retain its original character if its chief supporters come from the Society.' This appeal was signed by Douglas Pepler, Fred Rowntree, and W. G. Cruickshank (secretary).

The same announcement said that 'The training we offer men, women, and apprentices is designed to lead to the mastery of craft and to independence of character and position; in other words we hope that our workshops will be a training ground for Master Craftsmen and a starting point for the formation of Trade Guilds. We want to see the majority of men earning their own livings in their own workshops rather than being employed to earn somebody else's living in his workshop.' This was Distributism in practice; its debt to the earlier thinking of Cobbett, Ruskin, and Morris is evident.

It was intended that as soon as it became financially possible the craftsmen should take over from the company the ownership of the workshops; for the time being each shop had its representative on a Committee of Management. By the end of 1919 the results were encouraging. The woodwork shop now employed forty-four men and four apprentices, and was branching out into house-building and decorating. The dressmakers were nearly ready to become an independent business on their own. The bakery was, in respect of quality, the best in the borough; but unfortunately its wholemeal bread and other products did not find sufficient favour among an urban population brought up on a nutritionally worthless 'commercial' white bread, made from flour from which the germ of the wheat had been removed; so there was little hope of this business being able to expand.

The Committee of Management remained optimistic, and noted, in a published statement, that the secret of success seemed to be 'in co-operation between the designing, the manufacturing, and the shopkeeping elements of the Society'. But the odds were against them. The workshops had thriven under wartime conditions, when skilled labour and its products were in short supply; but after the war, when mass-production industry got into gear again to meet the urgent demand for goods in large quantities and at cheap prices, things became more difficult. The Company struggled on until 1924, but then had to wind itself up to avoid insolvency.

In an article in the Dominican monthly *Blackfriars* in 1950,[4] Pepler said:

A quarter of a century later it is easy to see that the Workshops failed because of two fundamental errors: (i) The industries were set up and organised not for ourselves but for other people; (ii) we were insufficiently explicit in what was to be understood by 'good will' and 'working for the glory of God'! *We* were not Christian carpenters, bakers, and dressmakers—but Christian architects, social workers, and somewhat vague idealists who were employing such craftsmen to work and combine as directed! When later on Edward Johnston, Eric Gill, and I set about forming ourselves into a kind of self-sufficient group, we avoided, like the Guild which grew out of our beginning, those two errors; in Ditchling each member was to stand on his own feet, follow his own trade, and work in his own shop—all primarily at one only in the same Faith.

The Hampshire House Club, however, continued in being at least down to 1939, perhaps beyond. Pepler had left Hammersmith in 1916, but he was not forgotten by the Club's older members. One, a working man called Woolfrey, took a day-trip from Hammersmith to Ditchling every year in order to see him; and another, named Sanders, wrote to him not long before the war to tell him that his work for Hammersmith working people was still going on, and that they were grateful for it.

On leaving the employment of the LCC in 1915 Pepler started a small publishing business, with the imprint 'Hampshire House Workshops/ Hammersmith'. The first book to be issued was *The Devil's Devices* by Douglas Pepler, a kind of allegorical satire on bureaucracy and its minions, such as Health Visitors, School Attendance Officers, and a certain type of clergyman. This amusing squib, which cannot have been read with much delight at County Hall, was printed by Gerard T. Meynell at the Westminster Press. The dedication, to G. K. Chesterton, was reproduced from the calligraphy of Edward Johnston, and the book was illustrated from wood-engravings by Eric Gill. This was the beginning of nine years of close collaboration between Hilary and Eric.

In this same year, 1915, Hilary wound up his Hammersmith enterprises, and moved, with his family, to Ditchling, in his native Sussex. Eric, also a Sussex-born man, had left London for Ditchling two years earlier; Edward Johnston had settled there about the same time. They all had the same basic motive: to get their children out of London and give them a country upbringing. As a result of his experience with the Hampshire House workshops Hilary had decided that he wanted to be a maker, a craftsman, not just a man of business and entrepreneur, which is what a publisher is. He resolved that he would himself print the books that he intended to publish, and that he would print them by hand. He chose to use the hand-press—an already 'obsolete' instrument, relegated, in such printing-offices as still had such a thing, to the lowly use of a proofing-press—because he felt, and rightly, that it gave the printer a more direct control over his product and saved him bills for electric power. In his innocence he thought that 'any fool can print'; but he was soon disabused of this notion.

Of course, he had to learn to print; but he decided to learn 'on the job', so to say, not in a school of arts and crafts, nor in somebody else's workshop. He was lucky in obtaining the services of a veteran printer who had himself learned the craft some fifty years previously at a Shropshire printer's where everything was still done by hand. Mr Dawes—or 'Old Dawes' as he was spoken of in the Press long after he had vanished from the scene— was seventy when he was taken on, and had spent most of his working life in the printing works of the *Cape Argus*, in Cape Town.

T. J. Cobden-Sanderson, of the Doves Press, gave the project his blessing. Pepler was a printer in the Doves and Kelmscott tradition, but, as his friend Edward Walters, a younger private press printer, said, 'with a difference'. The difference was that he did not want to print 'fine' books for collectors. He probably would not have put it quite like that, but his attitude seems to have been that the essence of good printing is found in popular works like the Augsburg Calendar and the *Ars Moriendi*, rather than in the noble volumes of the Italian humanist printers. As Walters had commented,[5] he perhaps extended this belief a little too far when it came to such matters as perfection of impression and 'register', and misprints. In 1947 Pepler received a letter from a London bookseller who said: 'There are a few more of your St Dominic's books coming up for sale at Sotheby's tomorrow, and I shall certainly make a bid for them. I think those you sent me are really lovely, each in its kind. No one has printed better than you within the scope which you set yourself!' Which seems to me a just verdict.

At the beginning Pepler was especially anxious to print and publish books on crafts that looked as if they might be in danger of dying out. Hence Ethel Mairet's *Vegetable Dyes*, *Sculpture* by Eric Gill, Romney Green's *Woodwork in Principle and Practice*, R. J. Beedham's *Wood Engraving*, Dunstan Pruden's *Silversmithing for Small Workshops*, Pepler's *The Hand-Press*, and Jan Bussell and Ann Hogarth's *Marionettes: How to Make Them*. It was also his intention to do 'general printing', that is, to look after the printing needs of his neighbours. (His first commission was for a beer-bottle label for one of the Ditchling public houses.)

When the Press was set up almost everything was printed on

handmade paper from the Kentish mill of Joseph Batchelor and Son, the finest paper then obtainable in Great Britain. All type was set by hand, and the type exclusively in use was William Caslon's Old Face, from the London foundry of Messrs Stephenson, Blake and Company. The printer's ink was home-made—from linseed oil and lamp-black—and was applied to the type by means of home-made 'dabbers', such as may be seen in old prints of Gutenberg's and Caxton's workshops. But the manufacture of ink took too long; it was soon abandoned in favour of the products, supplied in handy tins or tubes, of Messrs Lorilleux and Bolton or Mander Brothers. Next, the dabbers gave way to home-made 'composition' rollers; but these too being found not entirely satisfactory gave way to rubber rollers supplied by Messrs Braddick, of Fetter Lane, London.

The history of St Dominic's Press is in part a story of the supersession of 'primitive' methods and tools by more modern techniques and machines. The process was very gradual, for Pepler was deeply attached to the old ways; but he was no rigid doctrinaire in such matters.

In 1916 he left the Society of Friends and joined the Catholic and Roman church. His friend Eric Gill was already a Catholic, but they had never discussed religion. Some time in 1916 Gill had taken Pepler with him on a visit to the Dominican priory and house of studies at Hawkesyard, in Staffordshire, where Gill was to lecture to the Fathers and Students. Gill had been introduced to the Dominicans (Black Friars) by his wealthy friend and patron André Raffalovich, who was a tertiary of the Order.[6] Writing about this visit to Hawkesyard, in some unpublished recollections, Pepler says: 'En route I thought: "Here is a chance to discuss religion without bitterness. The Quaker believes that the Holy Spirit gives man all the light he needs direct; i.e. without the priestly intervention conceived to be essential by the R.C." I was immediately impressed by the manner of discussion which followed E. G.'s paper—there was much difference of opinion, but all speakers supported their opinion by reference either to the Gospels or to St Thomas Aquinas. [The subject under discussion was industrialism.] Objective Truth was seen to be primary, and was sought for in order to form a right opinion. Next day I went for a long walk with Father Vincent;[7] at the end I capitulated without a shot!' On Rosary Sunday 1916 (the first Sunday in October) Pepler was baptised by Father McNabb, his sponsors being Wilfrid and Alice Meynell. It was then that he took the name Hilary, because he had been born on that saint's feast day, 14th January. Soon afterwards he was admitted to the Dominican Third Order, and renamed his printing office St Dominic's Press.

When Pepler, Gill, and Johnston were all settled in Ditchling they discussed the notion of setting up some kind of association of craftsmen, for purposes of mutual aid, whose members should subscribe to a common statement of aim based on a common philosophy of work. This shared philosophy of work would emphasise the idea of the artist and craftsman as a free and responsible maker, owning and controlling his own workshop and tools, and would correspondingly reject the methods of industrialism involving mechanisation and mass production. These ideas were discussed in a magazine called *The Game*, printed by Pepler. The first number appeared in 1916. But after Pepler's conversion Edward Johnston, finding himself out-numbered two to one by Catholics who were for ever talking of the philosophy of St Thomas Aquinas and Pope Leo XIII's encyclical *Rerum Novarum* (on the condition of the working classes), withdrew from the group. No damage was done, however, to the triple friendship. *The Game* was at first described as 'an occasional magazine', but after a time it appeared monthly. The principal contributors were Pepler and Gill, and there were wood-engravings by Desmond Chute[8] and David Jones. The 34th and last number was published in January 1923.

By 1920, perhaps earlier, Gill had moved from Ditchling village to Ditchling Common, a little over two miles to the north, in the Haywards Heath direction. Pepler followed him, and settled at Halletts, a farmhouse with outbuildings at the south end of the Common. Gill now had three or four assistants in his work-shop, Desmond Chute being one of them; and David Jones, demobilised from the Army, was learning engraving from Chute. A new development was the arrival of other independent master craftsmen eager to associate themselves with Gill and Pepler. The first of these was Valentine KilBride, a young weaver from Bradford, who was soon followed by George Maxwell, a carpenter from Birmingham. There were now enough men in the Group to make possible their formation into an organised fellowship, with common aims and a constitution. The joint founders of the association were Hilary and Eric, and the name chosen for it was The Guild of SS. Joseph and Dominic. The two founders put money into it, for the purchase of land and the erection of workshops and other buildings, which included houses and a chapel. For business purposes the Guild was registered as The Spoil Bank Association Ltd. Shares were taken up by various friends, and a published statement of aim explained that the Guild was primarily a religious fraternity of men who made things with their hands, and that its members held that 'the principle of individual human responsibility being a fundamental of Catholic doctrine, and this principle involving the principles of ownership, workmen should own their tools, their workshops, and the product of their work.'

However, the idea that workmen should own their workshops—at least if that meant that they should own them individually—was not strictly kept to by the Guild, whose members paid rent for their workshops, which were owned by the Guild collectively. Pepler and Maxwell owned their own houses—Maxwell's was actually built by himself—but the others paid rent for their houses to the Guild.

The workshops as seen from their Folders Lane side were not impressive. Except for the Press building on the far side of the grass plot they were a rather untidy collection of wooden hutments; but the Press building and the chapel, seen from the south side, as in a drawing made by Peter Anson in 1935, made a very pleasant grouping. From there could be seen also Eric Gill's great wooden Calvary, put up on a small wooded hill made from the excavations (spoil) when the London to Newhaven railway line was being laid down. This huge wayside crucifix of painted wood was erected as a war memorial to the Catholic soldiers and sailors of Sussex who had lost their lives in the 1914-1918 war. Unhappily, many years after the 1930s it succumbed to the ravages of wind and rain, which had not been detected in time.

The Guild chapel was of brick, with a temporary west wall of wood, that seemed to hint at possible future enlargement: which was never realised. On the outside of the west wall, on either side of the door, were large painted wooden figures, from the designs of David Jones, of St Dominic and St Francis. Alas, these too have now vanished; possibly for the same reason that the Calvary is no more.

The Guild got off to quite a good start. It had the enthusiastic backing of a number of Dominicans, especially Father McNabb; there could be no mistaking the quality of the things made in the workshops, and there was no lack of orders. But the course of attempts to·reverse the spirit of the age and get back to a simpler, more humane, way of living and working never did run smooth. Up and down the country today one may see the remains, or former sites, of numerous simple-life, back to nature, colonies or settlements. In the Cotswolds, near Stroud, there is Whiteways, and at Chipping Camden there are memories of C. R. Ashbee's 'Guild of Handicraft'; in Sussex, near Steyning, is 'The Sanctuary', with which Victor B. Neuburg ('Vickybird'), of The Vines Press, had some connection, while the neighbouring county of Surrey, in the 1930s, was the scene of the disastrous Catholic 'Marydown' farming settlement, at Elsted. In the Cotswolds, again in the Thirties, there was the oddly name Kibbo Kift. It is an old, and seemingly perennial story. But the Ditchling Guild was more realistically based than most of such enterprises, and in fact it still survives today. It has had its tensions and schisms; the first of these occurred in 1924, when the two founders fell out, and Gill left Ditchling for a disused monastery in the Black Mountains of Brecknockshire.

The marvel really was that they had worked together harmoniously for so long. As another Dominican friend of theirs, Father Reginald Ginns, was to put it later on: 'Anyone who really knew them both could see how different they were in fundamental character—Eric a firebrand and Hilary like a steam-roller; in many ways an excellent combination for the beginning of a movement like theirs.'

One result of this upheaval was that when the necessary settlements and adjustments had been made Hilary sold Halletts and took over Eric's house, Hopkins Crank, an old purple-red brick farmhouse set in an orchard, with an annexe built on by Gill. The Crank stood close to the main road crossing the Common, about five minutes' walk from the workshops. In his autobiography, *A Roving Recluse*, published in 1946, Peter Anson says: 'On looking back after a quarter of a century I find that . . . what I remember best is the "atmosphere" of the place. I fell in love with the setting—the people whom I met there, the kindly welcome, and the homeliness of everything. . . There was a certain spartan simplicity about the domestic arrangements, and a complete lack of what are known as "modern conveniences". Water was drawn from a pump. Meals, though the food was abundant, were somewhat erratic, because all cooking was done on an open fire which burned logs.' That was in 1920, under the Gill occupation; it was much the same when I first stayed with Hilary and Clare at Hopkins Crank in 1928. The water was still being pumped up by hand, and oil lamps, supplemented by candles, were still used for lighting. In the winter the big, lofty living room, with a large round dining table in the middle, was still heated, if you could call it that, from a great open fireplace with ingle-nooks. Most of the heat went up the chimney, so that on really cold days we took our meals in full equipment of greatcoats, scarves, and even hats. This was regarded as quite normal, and no one complained. The unheated bedrooms were icy; one went to bed with a candle in one hand and a hot brick wrapped in newspaper in the other.

Hilary was a hospitable man. Visitors were always made welcome, even if they arrived without previous notice. Usually they were offered beer, which was drunk from pewter tankards. Hilary always began the day with a bowl of sour cream, which seemed to constitute his breakfast. He took this for its health-giving properties. He held the ancient and Chaucerian office of Reeve of Ditchling Common, of which he was very proud. It was the Reeve's duty to look after the fencing and ditching on certain parts of the Common on which the local farmers held grazing rights; he was responsible also for 'moving on' the wrong kind of gypsies—usually not true gypsies at all—and also people committing litter offences and other nuisances. Every morning, before he went to the Press, he could be seen setting out, thistle-grubber in hand, on his tour of inspection, accompanied always by his faithful 'looker'—I believe his official title was Ranger—Alge Leaney, with his dog. Leaney, broad of speech and sharp of eye, was the last local representative of the old generation of Sussex countrymen.

After lunch Hilary usually read aloud to his household for twenty minutes or so from a book by Hilaire Belloc, P. G.

Wodehouse, or some other favoured author; after which he took a short nap in his little study at the front of the house. He was one of those people who can recharge their energies at any time by dropping off to sleep, and waking up again after a predetermined interval.

In the 1930s his son Mark, who worked in the Press, was living at home, and his three daughters, Susan, Janet, and Margaret. The household included two *familiares*—you could not really have called them servants, so much were they part of the family: a young man always addressed and referred to as Hopkins, who seemed to have no Christian name, and Hattie, a young girl who later went to America, married, and settled there. A good deal of the domestic work, including the preparation of meals, was a co-operative effort, so that the running of so primitive an establishment, as it would seem to us today, imposed relatively little strain on Clare, who was able to keep up her painting and other interests. At the end of each day the grave goodnight of the children, who knelt for their father's blessing, was reminiscent of Sir Thomas More's household at Chelsea.

At Christmas and Twelfth Night, on St Dominic's Day (4th August), and certain other high festivals, there would be splendid parties at The Crank, with music and dancing. The house would be thronged with guests, and something stronger than beer would be drunk. Hilary himself made an extraordinarily, even dangerously, strong rough cider from apples from his orchard; and for a short time there were three illicit stills operating within a range of half a mile. (These moonshiners—actually Dunstan Pruden, one of the workers in George Maxwell's shop, and a certain Commander Herbert Shove (RN ret.)⁹—did not flourish for long. News of their activities got abroad, and it was thought wise to bury the stills at dead of night beneath the bracken of the Common.)

The Press had a staff of six or seven workers. Hilary—always spoken of by his staff as 'The Boss'—was there on most days, unless he was away from home. In his absence his partner, Cyril Costick, a local man who had been his second apprentice, took charge. Mark Pepler, then in his early twenties, was the next in command. Mark and Cyril were both fully qualified printers. There was usually an apprentice, and often one or two trainees

who were not formally apprenticed. In my time there was a
retired naval officer—not Commander Shove—but he did not stay
long, and a young man, Arthur Fressanges, who had recently left
the Dominican novitiate at Woodchester. He too did not stay
long, but left to resume his clerical vocation. Eventually he was
ordained as a secular priest for the diocese of Northampton.
Hilary was very generous in offering temporary employment to
Dominican ex-novices, and helping them to adjust again to life 'in
the world'.

The secretary to the Press was another young local man,
Truscott Hargrave, who looked after the accounts, packed up
parcels for the post, and dealt with correspondence. Finally, there
was a general factotum, or odd-job man, Augustine Linehan, a
small elderly Irishman. 'Mr L.', as we used to call him, kept the
workshop tidy, made tea at the appropriate times, and sometimes,
when printing was going on, acted as 'taker-off'. (The taker-off
removed each printed sheet from the press, and with a long
T-shaped stick elevated it onto a clothes-line stretched across the
press room at just short of ceiling height. Hot air, as is well
known, rises, and this is the best method of getting freshly-
printed sheets of damp hand-made paper to dry off quickly.)

We enjoyed our work in the Press. The working hours were 9
a.m. to 5 p.m., with an appropriate lunch interval, and Saturdays
and Sundays off. The actual business of printing was an
exhilarating affair, with one man inking the type—often the Boss
would see to this delicate task himself—a second man 'running in'
the bed of the press, below the platen, a third taking the
impression, being careful to allow the platen to 'dwell' for a
moment or two on the type. The second man then ran the type
out from under the platen, and opened the frisket—a thin iron
frame which held the paper firmly in position while printing—and
removed the printed sheet (unless Mr L was present to act as
taker-off). In the workshop Pepler liked to 'get a move on', and
printing was conducted briskly. It is said that the old printers,
such as those who once printed the *Times* newspaper on hand-
presses, could attain a speed of 160 sheets an hour; but I doubt if
such a speed was ever reached at St Dominic's Press. The old
compositors could set an astonishing number of lines of text in an
hour, and I remember Pepler saying that when these ancients

distributed type back into the cases, after printing, it was like liquid pouring from the spout of a tea-pot. These were examples that we were supposed to emulate. But on the whole we had to recognise that the feats of the legendary printers of old were a little beyond us. In 'dissing', or distributing type, a particular degree of care was necessary if one was to avoid the horror of getting the letters mixed up through dropping them into the wrong 'boxes'.

For bookwork, the press mostly used was the Stanhope. The Albion press, patented a few years later than the Stanhope, was supposed to be an improvement on it; such was not Pepler's view. But the Albions were used quite a lot. The press that was never used was the picturesque Columbian, an American invention that was supposed to be an improvement on both the Stanhope and the Albion. The St Dominic's Columbian was used only, and then infrequently, for taking proofs; mostly its bed was used as a place for depositing odd formes and galleys. It never seemed to work properly; yet that famous Victorian printer's manual Johnson's *Typographia* records that when attempts to print an enormous wood-engraving, *The Death of L. Dentatus*, had failed, breaking both an Albion and a Stanhope press in the process, a Columbian had taken a perfect impression with no difficulty at all!

Handmade paper needs to be damped before printing; otherwise it will not take the ink properly. Pepler always saw to this himself. The day before printing, the paper had to be cut to size in the guillotine, and stacked up, every seventh sheet being run quickly through a sink of cold water. The paper was then left to stand all night, weighted down by a caseful of type. During the night the water from the damp sheets permeates the whole pile. The next day the printer has to judge the exact moment when the paper is neither wet nor dry, but has just the right degree of dampness to take a good impression from the type. At this Pepler was expert.

He had a remarkable sense of design, and could create a beautiful title-page or a striking poster extempore, standing at the composing frame and improvising; he never used any preparatory designs or layouts. He thought that the best title-page he had ever created was that of the first edition of Ethel Mairet's *Vegetable Dyes*; but the title-page of Frances Cornford's poems *Autumn*

Midnight is quite as good, and one might cite several others.

Stanley Morison, that great authority, thought that the best work of the St Dominic's Press was its liturgical printing. This began in 1917 with *The Order of the Burial of the Dead*, a neat little book with the Latin and English texts of the Roman-rite service on facing pages. This was followed, in the same year, by the Greek Orthodox *Order of the Burial of the Dead*, printed in Greek, with the rubrics in red. In 1923 came the beautiful *Horae Beatae Mariae Virginis*. In 1926 this was outshone by *Cantica Natalia*, a magnificent folio containing twenty Christmas carols, in Latin and English, with plainsong musical notation printed between red staves. Ten hand-coloured wood-engravings, by David Jones, Desmond Chute, and Philip Hagreen, adorn the handsome pages. Ninety-five copies only were printed, and bound in brown sailcloth. The book was intended for use by groups of singers standing at a lectern, and was first so used by the choir of St Wilfrid's church, Burgess Hill.

The most 'important' book—from one point of view at any rate—printed and published by Pepler was *The Philosophy of Art* by Jacques Maritain, a translation into English by the Reverend John O'Connor of Maritain's *Art et Scolastique*. This was the first work by the distinguished French philosopher to be published in England, and so is something of a landmark. It is an exposition of the thought of the medieval Scholastics, especially St Thomas, on the matter of art, defined by Aquinas as 'recta ratio factibilium'. This key phrase was rendered by O'Connor as 'the right making of what needs making'. Whether 'right making' brings out the full meaning of 'recta ratio' seems questionable; and yet, what a brilliant rendering it is. At Ditchling the book became a kind of guildsmen's bible; and indeed it was widely appreciated elsewhere; but later, when the London firm of Sheed and Ward began publishing Maritain's books, a new translation was commissioned, Father O'Connor's having been said to lack accuracy. However that may be, the new version certainly lacked the readability and verve of O'Connor's.

The Philosophy of Art was published in an edition of 400 copies, some in paper covers, some in boards. Eric Gill, in his *Autobiography*, speaks of its 'inexperienced' printing; but this judgement seems slightly captious. The 'register' of some of the pages may be a little out of focus, and certainly the type is well banged into the paper. But the charm of handmade paper is that it can stand such treatment, and possibly to some extent demands it. It seems pointless to seek to impose on a handpress the delicate impression—sometimes almost a non-impression—of a machine-printed book on machine-made paper; though one may admire the skill of any printer who achieves such effects while working with a hand press.

Pepler never quite approved of the splendid volumes printed at William Morris's Kelmscott Press, St John Hornby's Ashendene Press, and Robert Gibbings's Golden Cockerel Press. He thought that books should be for use, and not simply for admiration as *objets d'art*. From this point of view it is interesting to compare with Pepler's *Cantica Natalia* the folio Book of Common Prayer printed at C. R. Ashbee's Essex House Press in 1903. The large type of *Cantica Natalia*, Caslon Old Face 36-pt, does its work perfectly; it has an elegant solidity, perfect legibility, and a complete absence of fussiness. If the reader cares to pause to consider it, he or she is bound to admire the beauty of this typeface; but it will not distract the reader from the text. Ashbee's specially designed typeface for his Prayer Book is certainly interesting; but it is fussy and distracting. (The upper-case B and the ampersand sign, for instance, are very peculiar indeed.) *The Prayer Book of King Edward VII* was printed to commemorate the accession of that monarch; his portrait, from a wood-engraving, in the centre of the elaborate frontispiece page, seems a distinct error of judgement. One cannot imagine any clergyman using Ashbee's great Prayer Book with any degree of comfort; nor is it a book that any private person would want to use for their devotions.

Working conditions in St Dominic's Press were very pleasant; idling was not encouraged, but there was no sense of being under pressure. The morning break for 'elevenses' enabled those who wished to do so to share in the sociable gathering of craftsmen which took place daily in the workshop of Dunstan Pruden, silversmith. (Pruden was another Hammersmith man; he had actually been born in the borough, and had set up his first workshop there.) He was an expert coffee-maker, and a considerable connoisseur of the various kinds of coffee. Philip

Hagreen, engraver and ivory carver, was usually there. Hagreen
was a keen Dickensian, and often had an apt quotation from the
'Inimitable' with which to enliven, and add point to, discussion.
George Maxwell, carpenter and builder, was the 'professional'
philosopher of the group; it was fascinating to hear him
expounding, in the accents of Birmingham, pipe in hand, the
teachings of St Thomas Aquinas and Jacques Maritain. Pruden
himself, one of the finest silversmiths in the kingdom, was a man
of encyclopaedic knowledge; he was a frequent visitor to France,
where he had acquired a wonderful mastery of French cuisine;
and he was a considerable musician as well. KilBride the weaver,
and Joseph Cribb, stone-carver, were also valued contributors to
these mid-morning symposia. Pepler, however, tended to avoid
them. I think he preferred to take his philosophy direct from
Father McNabb or other Dominicans rather than from their
disciples. Maxwell, Pruden, and Hagreen would all have made
excellent contributors to the BBC's then celebrated 'Brains
Trust'—along with Professor Joad and Commander Campbell—
had anyone thought to ask them; but Hilary did not much enjoy
this kind of thing. Perhaps he was too conscious of his neighbours' foibles, on which, without being uncharitable, he could be
very amusing, and at times caustic.

One feature of life at St Dominic's Press seems to have been
unique; at least I have never come across any mention of a similar
custom in printing histories and biographies. If the Boss was away
from home, work in the Press was sometimes suspended in favour
of a 'Type Battle'. In these recreative contests the printer's staff
assailed each other, from behind composing frames, presses, and
other points of vantage, with handfuls of metal type. Of course,
the type was collected up afterwards and distributed back into the
cases; but such treatment cannot have been good for it. And it
seems extraordinary that no one was ever blinded or otherwise
injured.

By 1930 the best days, typographically speaking, of the St
Dominic's Press were over. Yet outstanding books were still
produced, notably G. K. Chesterton's mummers' play *The
Turkey and the Turk*, which was illustrated from drawings by
Thomas Derrick. This was produced in large quarto format, in a
limited edition of one hundred copies signed by the author and

artist. It has features which show that Pepler was being forced, by prevailing economic conditions, to come to terms with modern printing methods. Ramsay MacDonald's 'economic blizzard' was blowing, and the cost of type, as of paper, was rising steeply. Moreover, there were now too many people looking to the Press for a living. Mark Pepler had married Rosemary Meynell, Gerard's younger daughter, and Hilary's eldest daughter, Susan, had married Mark's schoolfriend Gerard Falkner, who was working in the Press. Something had to be done to increase the Press's income, and one way of doing so, in addition to raising prices, was to introduce modern methods that would reduce production costs.

Thus Thomas Derrick's fine drawings for *The Turkey and the Turk* were reproduced from zinc line blocks; something that would never have been tolerated in earlier days.

The next thing was to supplement the setting of type by hand with machine-set Monotype, hired from a firm of type-setters in Bristol, and sent back to them after printing. This was certainly useful for larger books, such as *The Natural Moral Law* by Father Walter Farrell, O.P. (1930), Percival Hinton's *Eden Phillpotts: A Bibliography of First Editions* (1930), and *Margaret Douglas: a selection from her writings* (1931). The introduction of Monotype made it easy to experiment with typefaces other than Caslon, as in the St Dominic's Press edition of Bishop Challenor's *A Catechism of Christian Doctrine* (known to Catholics in those days as the 'Penny Catechism', though in fact its price had risen to sixpence). This was set in Monotype Goudy Bold, a very good choice, for it combined perfectly with the woodcut borders made specially for this book by Philip Hagreen. Smaller books were still set by hand; for instance Father McNabb's *Geoffrey Chaucer: A Study in Genius and Ethics* (1934) and Bernard Kelly's *The Mind and Poetry and Gerard Manley Hopkins* (1935); but the handmade paper on which these were printed was not Batchelor's, the price of which had become prohibitive.

For general printing—letterheads, handbills, and the like—we were by now using good quality machine-made papers from the well known firm of Wiggins, Teape and Company. This firm had the charming custom of sending every spring a small box of primroses to all the printers who bought their paper. The

Wiggins Teape mill was in semi-rural Hertfordshire, so presumably primroses were at hand in plenty. Perhaps they even grew them? I should think it unlikely that this delightful gesture continues today.

In the mid-1930s Cyril Costick had persuaded Hilary to acquire for the Press a second-hand treadle-operated platen press of the 'Arab' type, which certainly speeded up the production of a lot of the jobbing work that was done: letterheads, handbills, bookplates, ordination and memorial cards, and so on. In 1933 Costick printed on this machine one of the nicest of the smaller St Dominic's books, a new edition, in red and black, of *The Jesus Psalter*, a favourite traditional devotion of English Catholics, attributed to Richard Whitford, a Brigittine monk of Sion Abbey, on the Thames, temp. Henry VIII. In the same year he printed, on the same machine, but on machine-made paper, quite a large book. A. M. Scarre's *An Introduction to Liturgical Latin*. Costick liked machinery, and had no distributist misgivings about it, so it was not long before he got Pepler to see how sensible it would be to install a small electric motor to power the 'Arab'. This was done; but these innovations in work-methods were not well received by the other members of the Guild of SS. Joseph and Dominic. Their criticisms, often voiced at Dunstan Pruden's morning coffee sessions, became more bitter when Hilary set himself up with a motor car. (He never learned to drive, probably because his sight was defective in one eye;—which is perhaps why he was never a very good proof-reader—his dazzlingly beautiful eldest daughter, Susan, acted as his chauffeur.) A crisis came in 1934, when Hilary was away in America, where he delivered to the Society of Typographic Arts in Chicago the lecture which forms the text of his book *The Hand-Press*. In addition to the above-mentioned 'modernisations', he had taken on a non-Catholic boy from the village—who eventually married his second daughter, Janet,—as an apprentice. This was alleged to be contrary to the Constitutions of the Guild—which I do not think it was—but it was certainly contrary to the prevailing Guild ethos.

These were provocative actions, no doubt, given the very rigid attitudes of the other Guildsmen; but while Hilary was in the United States the Guild put themselves in the wrong by publishing a Guild catalogue, listing the workshops and describing, with illustrations, the varied kinds of things that they could make—from church vestments, chalices and croziers, stone and wooden statues and carvings, to cloth for suitings, and all kinds of domestic furniture—without any mention at all of St Dominic's Press. The upshot of this was that on his return Hilary and the Guild parted company.

However, Pepler had already decided to retire from printing, and to hand over the Press to his son Mark and to Cyril Costick. So the logical thing to do, in view of the prevailing tensions, was to move the Press from the Common back to Ditchling village, where it had begun twenty years previously, and there to re-equip it, with a Monotype machine, and with Heidelberg and other automatic presses. The enterprise was renamed The Ditchling Press, and it continues in being today as a commercial printing firm of high repute.

In his 'retirement' Pepler was able to give rein to his other talents and interests, for he was very much of a polymath. He had never lost his interest in the theatre, and was the much-loved President of the Ditchling Players, a group which had produced, among much else, his nativity play *Bethlehem*, and his *Pilate: A Passion Play*, which had both been printed and published by St Dominic's Press. He was now able to give more time to his puppets and puppet theatre, in a small barn at Hopkins Crank. In 1929 the Press had published his *Plays for Puppets*, a delightful little book, with wood engravings by a very young and very talented artist whom he had recently discovered, Mary Dudley Short. In 1930 he had taken his puppets, which were made for him by Joseph Cribb, to the international marionette congress at Liège, where they were well received.

But now, during and after 1934, it was the art of mime on which he concentrated. On this he came to be recognised as an authority, and for a time he held classes in mime at the Royal Academy of Dramatic Art in London. In 1932 he had produced a mimed version of the Stations of the Cross in the church of the Sacred Heart, Pittsburgh, which was later repeated in the cathedral at St Paul, Minnesota, and, with Indian actors, at Santa Fé, New Mexico. Another notable achievement was the production of his mime *The Field Is Won* at the Victoria Palace theatre in London, in 1936, as part of the celebrations in honour of the canonisation of St John Fisher and St Thomas More. In the early days of television he produced for the BBC, at Alexandra Palace, mimed versions of *Pilgrim's Progress*, *Everyman*, *The Eve of St Agnes*, *The Ancient Mariner*, the story of Jacob and Esau, and Belloc's *My Lady Poltagrue*. During the second world war he presented mimed Stations of the Cross in a London Underground station which was being used as an all-night shelter and dormitory for people seeking refuge from the bombing. With his daughter Margaret, who had trained with the ballet Rambert and acted in repertory for some years, and a few friends, he presented several night-time entertainments for these refugees, and his Dominican son Stephen (Father Conrad) played to them on his violin.

Hilary's last public activity was the production of his mime *The Passion of our Lord*, which was presented, with the collaboration of the religious society The Grail, at the Albert Hall on Maundy Thursday of 1951. Hilary watched it from the audience, and when it was over forestalled the coming praise by saying: 'I hope they'll say their prayers.'

In 1936 Gilbert Chesterton died. Pepler at once persuaded Hilaire Belloc and Belloc's son-in-law, Reginald Jebb, to join him in a scheme for ensuring the continuance of Chesterton's paper, *G. K.'s Weekly*. The board of directors wanted to close the paper down, but somehow Hilary got them to change their minds and hand the paper over to a new board of directors. Just how he did this is not clear; but as Rex Jebb said later on: 'Where Hilary was set upon getting something done, opposition ran off him like water from a duck's back.' Belloc was appointed as the new editor, but he did not like this kind of work, and in fact did it only until the paper's continuity was assured. He then resigned; the paper was renamed *The Weekly Review*, and Jebb and Pepler were left in sole charge. Their collaboration kept the *Weekly* going for several years.

The *Weekly Review* benefited greatly from Pepler's journalistic gifts. (At the same time he was contributing to, and had a kind of advisory post on, the popular weekly magazine *Everybody's*, where he shared an office with the poet and biographer Charles Richard Cammell, who became his close friend.) To the *Weekly*

Review he contributed regularly a column of humorous comment on current affairs; especially popular with the readers were his Chaucerian poems commenting on events of the day. These poems approximated very closely in style to Chaucer, whose works he knew well. He had always had a gift for light verse; his poems 'Concerning Dragons' (for children) and 'The Law the Lawyers Know About' (which had first appeared in *The Devil's Devices*) have been continually reprinted in anthologies. One of his happiest pieces in this vein was printed in *G. K.'s Weekly* in 1936.

A PORTRAIT

His name was Doctor Something, I can't remember what;
He may have come from Ireland, I rather fancy not;
If I am not mistaken he stammered in his talk,
And limped, however slightly, or shuffled in his walk.
He wrote (or was that So-and-So?) under a pseudonym,
And published several poems—you must remember him—
His name was Doctor Something, he'd travelled quite a lot,
I'm sure you must have heard of him, quite famous as a shot.
His name was Doctor Something—or am I talking rot?

Round about 1950 the heart trouble which had bothered him, intermittently, for a good many years, became more severe, and he had to begin to take things more slowly; but at Hopkins Crank he was still quietly active in house and garden. On 20th September of 1951 he had a severe heart attack while he was raking mown grass, and died almost at once. It was a death such as he would have wished. The funeral took place on 24th September. A solemn Requiem Mass was sung in the chapel of the Guild that he had helped to found. The celebrant was his son Father Conrad, the deacon Father Reginald Ginns, both of them Dominicans, and the subdeacon was the Reverend Vincent Maxwell, eldest son of Hilary's old friend George Maxwell. The panegyric was preached by Father Kenneth Wykeham-George, the then Prior of Blackfriars, Oxford.

After the Mass a procession was formed, to accompany the coffin to Ditchling churchyard, over two miles away. While the procession was on its way all the shops in the village were closed, with the blinds drawn. On arrival at the parish church, St Margaret's, a halt was made at the church porch, where prayers were said by the Vicar of Ditchling. The burial, at which Father Conrad officiated, was in a grave next to that of Hilary's eldest son, David, who had married Elizabeth Gill, Eric's eldest daughter, and who had died in 1934.

To convey a living impression of this remarkable man, with his sense of beauty, his slow, deliberate utterance and his balanced judgement, his caustic wit, his piety and profanity, his tolerance of fools and nuisances, his love of his family, and his devotion to St Dominic and the Dominican Order, seems impossible. His memorial card, printed at the Ditchling Press, bears two appropriate lines from the Prologue to Chaucer's *Canterbury Tales,* in which the poet is speaking of the Reeve who was one of those immortal pilgrims:

> His woning was ful fair up-on an heeth,
> With grenë treës shadwed was his place.

NOTES

1. Pepler was never known by his first name Harry. At home and at school, and in his early manhood, he was always called Douglas. After he was baptised, in 1916, he adopted the name Hilary, and his wife Clare remained the only person to call him Douglas.

2. Published in *The Register*, a small magazine edited by Pepler in the 1940s.

3. Romney Green, mathematician, boat-builder, and furniture-maker, at Christchurch, Hampshire (now in Dorset).

4. H. D. C. Pepler, 'Hampshire House Workshops', in *Blackfriars,* February 1950.

5. Edward Walters, 'Hilary Pepler, Printer', in *The Aylesford Review*, vol. vii, no. 1, Spring 1965.

6. The Mendicant Orders of the Catholic Church—
(Franciscans, Dominicans, Carmelites, Austin Friars, etc.)
have a tripartite structure: First Order, friars (priests and
laybrothers); Second Order, cloistered contemplative nuns;
Third Order Regular, 'active', unenclosed Sisters: Third
Order Secular, lay men and women, and secular priests,
living in the spirit of the Rule of the First Order.

7. Father Vincent McNabb, of the Order of Preachers.

8. Desmond Chute: 1895-1962. Educated Downside School
and Slade School of Art. Ordained priest 1927, and thenceforward lived in Italy for reasons of health. Ezra Pound
attended his funeral at Rapallo. Cf. Walter Shewring,
'Desmond Chute', in *Blackfriars*, January 1963.

9. For Herbert Shove, brother of the 'Bloomsbury' and
Cambridge economist Gerald Shove, cf. Brocard Sewell, *My
Dear Time's Waste* (Aylesford, 1966).

THE MYSTERY OF
MONTAGUE SUMMERS

PROBABLY I first heard of Montague Summers in 1931, when his collection of ghostly and arcane stories, *The Supernatural Omnibus*, was published by Victor Gollancz, and was received with great *réclame*. Since then it has gone through edition after edition, and has never been out of print for long. In 1933 *The Supernatural Omnibus* was followed by *Victorian Ghost Stories*, 'edited by Montague Summers', and in 1936 by *The Grimoire and Other Supernatural Stories*,[1] 'collected by Montague Summers'. Each of these three books has a scholarly introduction by its editor.

In 1932 I was learning the trade of compositor at St Dominic's Press, Ditchling. This Press was one of a group of workshops that collectively constituted the Guild of St Joseph and St Dominic, a fellowship of Catholic craftsmen which looked to the Dominican Order for spiritual direction, and for guidance in formulating its philosophy of work. In Dominican circles Montague Summers was well known, if somewhat *mal vu*. He was a prominent but mysterious figure in Oxford, where he lived, with his secretary and companion, Hector Stuart-Forbes, at Number 43, The Broad: since demolished, to make way for the New Bodleian Library. (Summers was an alumnus of Trinity College, where he had graduated early in the century.) Although he had his own private oratory at No. 43, he would often on Sunday mornings make his way to High Mass at Blackfriars, the Dominican priory in St Giles's, or at St Aloysius's, the church of the Jesuit Fathers, walking in the gutter, as was his curious wont, and carrying an altar-size missal, with its coloured markers gaily fluttering in the breeze. A good deal of comment on the Reverend Montague Summers was to be heard in Oxford in those days; and 'comment' in this world is more likely to be unfavourable than favourable. Many strange stories about him circulated in the City of Dreaming Spires; some of them amusing, others of a sinister cast.

Since Dominicans were frequent visitors at Ditchling, some of these stories were in circulation there too. It was said that Summers had obtained his priesthood surreptitiously and irregularly; which was probably true. That he was in holy orders was not doubted by anyone who knew anything of his history; but some people put it about that he was either an unfrocked parson or had never been ordained at all: neither of which was true.

In 1932 the Ditchling Guild gained a recruit, Dunstan Pruden, a young silversmith from Hammersmith. From him I heard a first-hand account of Montague Summers during the years 1919-1921, when Pruden had been taught by him at the Junior School of the Central School of Arts and Crafts (now the Central School of Art and Design) in Holborn, London. In the school's prospectus he was listed as 'The Rev. Michael Summers, M.A.', for which reason he was known among the boys as 'Old Mick'. Summers was rather given to assuming new Christian names; his first name, Augustus, he replaced quite early with Alphonsus, which was at once more Christian and more euphonious. One wonders whether 'Michael' was simply an editor's or printer's error, or whether it was an attempt by Summers to conceal his identity. There were people at that time, and indeed all through his life, who assumed that he was some kind of clergyman who had got himself into trouble with his superiors: which was not far short of the truth.

Between 1911 and 1926—by which time he was earning a good income from his pen—Summers taught in a number of schools, both in and outside London, and his surviving pupils all agree that in spite of his eccentricities he was a very good teacher. At the Central School, as elsewhere, his instruction was not always according to the Ministry of Education syllabus. His history, for example, was Catholic history, very much in the vein of Hilaire Belloc; and the English was carefully selected, Dryden, a notorious papist, being given highly preferential treatment. On the Stuart period his views were frankly, and strongly, Jacobite. He wore clerical dress, and said his Office, from the Roman breviary, in the classroom, after he had got his class going on their written work.

In the 1930s Montague Summers was chiefly known as the author of *The History of Witchcraft and Demonology*, and works on kindred subjects. Availing myself of the Sussex County Travelling Library, whose van, full of books, appeared in the Ditchling area every week, I applied for the loan of the *History of Witchcraft and Demonology*, and of Summers's translation of the *Malleus Maleficarum*. This latter work, which John Rodker had published in 1928, is a magnificent folio, printed in Baskerville type on a Dutch handmade paper, with a stately portrait of Pope Innocent VIII for frontispiece, facing a noble title-page printed in red and black. Summers's long introduction to this classic treatise on witchcraft by two medieval German Dominicans precedes the text of Pope Innocent's famous bull *Summis desiderantes affectibus*, 'Desiring with the most heartfelt anxiety. . .', which Summers describes as 'a clarion sounding at the gates of trembling hell'.[2]

I do not think I can have made much of the elaborate and lengthy manual for inquisitors written by the Fathers Sprenger and Kramer. Truth to tell, it is not the easiest of reading, even in Summers's vigorous if slightly archaic English. But *The History of Witchcraft and Demonology* was another matter, and I was soon studying its sequels, *The Geography of Witchcraft*, *The Vampire, his Kith and Kin*, *The Vampire in Europe*, and *The Werewolf*.

At that time, the early 1930s, Summers was living in Hove, where he officiated as chaplain (unlicensed) to the Hon. Mrs Ermyntrude Greville-Nugent, a lady of strong Jacobite sympathies, who had a private oratory in her house. When news of this reached the ears of the Bishop of Southwark, Dr Peter Emmanuel Amigo, he threatened to put the oratory under an interdict unless these unauthorised ministrations ceased. Mrs Greville-Nugent was greatly aggrieved, and to the end of her days believed that her erstwhile chaplain had been much wronged.

Looking back, nearly fifty years later, it seems to me a pity that Dunstan Pruden never invited Summers over to Ditchling; but as a priest of doubtful repute, whose name was not to be found in the *Catholic Directory*, he would hardly have been a welcome visitor at the Guild. However, Pruden used to meet him quite frequently at the monthly meetings of an informal luncheon club in Hove, whose other members included Lord Alfred Douglas and his wife Olive Custance.

I did once myself see Summers in Hove, one sunny summer afternoon. He was an unmistakable figure, in clerical dress and broad-brimmed black hat, sitting on a seat on The Lawns, looking out to sea. Beside him, on the ground, was his little dachshund dog, Cornelius Agrippa, named after the famous warlock Cornelius Agrippa von Nettesheim. Unfortunately, I was a nervous and timid young man, and hesitated to approach him. A moment or two later he rose, turned round, and crossed the road. I followed, quite close behind, meaning, after all, to introduce myself; but suddenly he had turned a corner. When I rounded it, only a few seconds later, he was gone. Either he must have moved with an extraordinary rapidity or else he must have made himself invisible, so it seemed to me at the time. But no doubt the road into which he had turned was Montefiore Road, and his house, No. 47, must have been on the corner. I never saw him again.

In 1938 I was working with the late Edward Walters at his private press in the attic of his parents' house, No. 36, Oppidans Road, Primrose Hill, London. As part of our typographical programme we had announced the impending publication of a new magazine, *The Thing*. Only one number ever appeared; soon afterwards the approach of war put an end to the Press's operations. But we had approached a number of possible future contributors to the magazine, and we received promises of articles from, among others, Arthur Machen,—the author of *The Great God Pan*, *The Inmost Light*, and other macabre tales—and the Reverend Montague Summers. Summers replied quickly and favourably to the letter I had sent him soliciting a contribution; perhaps because our address in Oppidans Road was close to Eton Road, where he had lived during the first war and for some time afterwards. But in fact, he was always generous in giving help to young and aspiring writers and editors, as long as he was satisfied that they were working along the right lines, and not attempting things that were beyond them.

During the war of 1939-1945 Montague Summers was not much in my mind; but in 1948, when I was pursuing my theological studies at a house of Austin Canons in Hertfordshire, what was my astonishment one August day to read in our daily paper of the sudden death of the Reverend Montague Summers, at his home in Richmond, Surrey. At the time I was living under a very strict discipline; asking permission to attend the funeral of anyone but a close relative was not to be thought of. But I rather wish now that I had gone to Summers's funeral, with or without permission. It was attended only by Hector Stuart-Forbes, and four other friends. Had I gone I would have met Stuart-Forbes, and so might have been able later to ask him certain questions which remain unanswered to this day.

At the time of Summers's death I was aware that the London publishing firm of Rider and Company Ltd had commissioned from him an autobiography, which had been announced for publication under the title *The Galanty Show*. The book had been advertised as being 'in the press'; but time went by and it did not appear. Studies, some of them pursued on the continent, kept me fully occupied, and it was not until 1954 that I began to think again about Summers and his autobiography. Not only had *The Galanty Show* not appeared, but there was no sign of it; and there was no sign of anyone attempting a memoir or biography of its author. Should I try to remedy this state of things? I wondered. At least there could be no harm, I thought, in writing to the *Times Literary Supplement*, and a few other papers, asking anyone who had known Summers, or corresponded with him, to get in touch with me. I received a surprisingly large number of replies; but it was disappointing to learn that a number of those who had been closest to him, such as Hector Stuart-Forbes and the young poet Wrenne Jarman, were already dead.

The next thing to do was to try to find out what had happened to the manuscript of *The Galanty Show*. I knew that it existed, or had existed, because Iona Cammell, the wife of the poet and scholar Charles Richard Cammell, had told me that three weeks before his death Summers had telephoned to tell her that he had finished his autobiography. On inquiry of them, Rider and Company said that they did not know what had become of the manuscript. The people who had dealt with the book were no longer with the firm; but it was thought that after Summers's death they had decided not to publish it; partly because it had not been revised by the author and so would need a great deal of editorial attention, but also because they felt some doubt as to whether the book had really been written by Summers himself.

In the mean time I had discovered that it was not only the

manuscript of *The Galanty Show* that was missing. Summers had left all his property—his house, No. 4, Dynevor Road, Richmond, his valuable library, and the sum of £10,000 in the bank—to Hector Stuart-Forbes. After the funeral Forbes remained in the house; but he was unwell, and in a very nervous condition. He told Wrenne Jarman and other friends that there were 'manifestations' in the house; for instance, the electric lights kept switching on and off all night of their own accord. When he cut all the flexes off at ceiling height, thus reducing the house to darkness at night, there were still uncomfortable phenomena. He became so disturbed that he left the house and went into lodgings, taking with him, in several tea-chests, all his late employer's private papers and literary remains. Among the latter were the manuscripts of about twelve books, in varying stages of completion: among them *The Gothic Achievement*, the third volume of Summers's trilogy on the Gothic Novel. Unfortunately, the will had not yet been proven, and Forbes, who had no independent income of his own, got behind with his rent. One day, when he was out, so it was reliably said, his landlady had piled the tea-chests onto a barrow or barrows, and had taken them down to Twickenham, where she disposed of their contents to a general dealer. Apart from the manuscript of *The Galanty Show*, and a small bundle of letters to Montague Summers from various correspondents, no trace of any of this property has yet been discovered.

Among the letters concerning Summers that I received in 1954 was one from Leslie C. Staples, the Dickens scholar, who had known Summers since the days of The Phoenix, a society for the production of old plays, of which Summers had been the principal founder. (The first meeting of the society was held at his house in Eton Road, Primrose Hill, in 1919.) The Phoenix's productions had begun in 1919 with Webster's *The Duchess of Malfi*, had reached their zenith, possibly, with Wycherley's *The Country-Wife* in 1924, and ended, with the same playwright's *The Gentleman Dancing-Master*, in 1925. Summers, who had loved old plays, and had been fascinated by the history of the stage, since his childhood, had amassed an unrivalled knowledge of these subjects, which enabled him to write the Theatrical History notes for all the programmes of Phoenix productions. He was present at all rehearsals, where his knowledge of the details of the original productions of the plays was of great assistance. It was at his urging that *The Country-Wife* was presented. It had not been seen in the London theatre within living memory. The critic William Archer had said that it was too bawdy ever to be revived, as well as being so clumsy in construction as to be virtually unstageable. Even Sir Edmund Gosse and George Moore, two of The Phoenix's keenest supporters, had expressed their doubts. But the first night was a triumphant success, a complete vindication of Montague Summers's critical judgement.

Leslie Staples saw all the Phoenix productions; round about 1920 he had become the owner of the famous George Inn at Southwark, where he would often dine with Summers. It was Mr Staples who gave me the clue that led to the discovery of the missing manuscript of *The Galanty Show*. 'Try Montie's solicitors,' he said, 'Messrs So-and-So, of Bedford Row, WC1.'

A letter to the solicitors brought a prompt reply which said, Yes, they knew all about *The Galanty Show*, and that the manuscript, wrapped up as a brown-paper parcel, was in their cellars. A further letter was sent: Might I be allowed to see it? Yes, certainly. A day and hour were appointed, and the manuscript was produced for my inspection. It was with some anxiety that I opened the package, but it took very little time to see that here was a literary treasure, written, unmistakably, from beginning to end, by Montague Summers. There was no mistaking his orotund and yet most lively prose style, which defies imitation, though it is susceptible of parody. The manuscript (mostly typewritten) consists of 155 folio leaves of single-spaced typing—enough to put off any prospective editor or printer—with numerous additions, corrections, deletions, and emendations in Summers's unmistakable handwriting, in the blackest of black ink. It is impossible to understand how anyone could have got the idea that the book had not been written by Summers himself. (The not very expert typing must have been done by Stuart-Forbes, since Summers detested the machine. So probably he had dictated the book, which would account for the diffuseness of some of the unrevised text.) A more likely reason for the book's rejection by Rider's, who specialised in books on occult and esoteric subjects, is that it contained little or nothing about Summers's arcane interests or his abortive career as a churchman.

At the time of the discovery of *The Galanty Show* I was living at Aylesford Priory, in Kent. A friend and neighbour of ours in those parts was Erica Marx, poet and publisher, founder and proprietor of the Hand and Flower Press at Aldington.[3] Miss Marx was interested in Summers because she had published—though it did not appear until after his death—his last book, a new edition, with introduction and notes, of *Pandaemonium, or The Devil's Cloyster, Being a further Blow to Modern Sadduceism, Proving the Existence of Witches and Spirits*, by Richard Bovet, Gent: London, 1684. Miss Marx, who had never met Summers, but had often spoken to him on the telephone, was greatly interested to hear that his autobiography had come to light, and asked me to find out whether the manuscript, and the copyright in it, might be for sale. Inquiry brought the information that the ownership was now vested, since Stuart-Forbes had died intestate, in two cousins of his, one living in Canada, the other in the Antipodes. The effort to get in touch with them took a long time, but eventually the lawyers wrote to say that neither of Forbes's relatives was interested in this piece of literary property, and that both the manuscript and the copyright could be purchased for £25, plus solicitors' fees not to exceed ten guineas. Miss Marx sent them a cheque for the full sum, and then most generously made me a present of the manuscript and the copyright.

When I acquired the manuscript Muriel Spark, who was just beginning to make her name as a novelist, was living in a cottage in the grounds of Allington Castle, only two miles from Aylesford. Mrs Spark, a friend of Erica Marx, was interested in the history of *The Galanty Show*, and asked me if I would let her read the manuscript, which I was happy to do. A day or two later she told me that she had been reading it before going to sleep the previous night. Before putting the light out she had placed the manuscript on her bedside table. During the night she had woken up, as it seemed to her, and had sensed a strange, yet benign, masculine presence, clothed in black, standing by her table and poring over the manuscript. Montague Summers, one can scarcely doubt.

Miss Marx was not in a position to publish the book herself; but Mr Cecil Woolf, who had just published 'Joseph Jerome's'

Montague Summers: A Memoir, was anxious to do so. The first
step was to begin the revision of the text that its author had not
been able to make. To start with, Mr Timothy d'Arch Smith,
Summer's bibliographer, took in hand the work of checking the
titles and dates of publication of the many books and magazines
cited by Summers, and of the many stage productions mentioned
or described by him. Writing in old age, and in indifferent health,
and in part from memory, many of these references were inexact.
Then the whole work had to be retyped, in a form that a printer
could deal with without trouble. In the course of this retyping I
took the opportunity to make occasional small adjustments to the
grammar and syntax, to eliminate repetitious matter, and to excise
a few passages that seemed to be, if not libellous at least
injudicious. The aim was to revise the text along lines that one
hoped the author would have approved, and so to produce a
smoothly-reading book.

All this took time, for the work had to be done in intervals
between more urgent tasks and duties. Then the publisher
developed problems of his own, and the book's editor had to take
up a new post in Canada, which slowed things up even more.
However, at last it was published; but not until 1980, the year
which saw the centenary of the birth of Montague Summers. This
timing, unplanned though it was, was fortunate. After
completion by its author *The Galanty Show* had remained
unpublished for thirty-two years. When at last it appeared it was
very favourably received, being recognised not only as a delightful
book, full of memorable anecdote and pithy comment, a grateful
reminiscence of bygone days, but also as a work of scholarship
and the literary testament of a remarkable personality.

With the publication of *The Galanty Show* my biographical
work for Montague Summers was finished.

What sort of man was Montague Summers? By his friends of
later years he was remembered as a kindly and much missed
companion, a charming and generous host, a racy con-
versationalist of rare brilliance, humour, and learning, and, in his
own way, a clergyman of faith and piety. Of course, there was a
mystery about his life. Even today the source of his holy orders is
not entirely clear. But it is clear that there was reason for the

shrugged shoulders and quizzical looks that used to greet the mention of his name in some circles. There had been dark passages in his early life. Yet a contemporary of his at Lichfield Theological College early in the century has testified that at that time he had sincere piety. 'At my college', this writer says, 'he attracted around himself the best elements and the finest minds.' [4] But only a year or two later, when Summers was in Anglican deacon's orders, and was serving a curacy in a Bristol suburban parish, he was in a thoroughly neurotic state, and was manifesting a morbid preoccupation with evil. When his friend the poet John Redwood-Anderson, who had been up at Oxford with him, went to visit him he found him behaving very strangely.[5]

That Summers was abnormal beyond the average, and that he was a deeply divided personality, is evident. Mr Redwood-Anderson said that as a young man he seemed to be 'wearing a mask'. In this respect he reminds me of William Beckford of Fonthill. No one ever knew what was really behind Beckford's mask, nor Summers's. They were both romantics, and Summers's love of Italy is paralleled by Beckford's enthusiasm for Spain and Portugal. Like Summers, Beckford had a great sense of theatre, which he expressed in the building of Fonthill Abbey, and the great entertainment—never repeated, alas—that he put on there for Lord Nelson and Lady Hamilton. Both men were ardent ritualists (Beckford speaks of 'the Vathek-like ceremonial of my establishment'); and both were interested, at least for a time, in the black arts. Summers's decidedly 'baroque' Catholicism, and his detestation of Protestantism, are reminiscent of Beckford's enthusiasm for 'the true Church'—which he never joined—and his contemptuous attitude towards the Established church and the sects. Similarly, Summers's somewhat enthusiastic attitude towards the Blessed Virgin and the saints is paralleled by Beckford's cult of St Anthony of Padua. The split in Summers's personality is reflected in the different views that different people took of him. His friends thought him a delightful personality, kindly, helpful, urbane. Others found him in some undefinable way sinister.

Mr Timothy d'Arch Smith has suggested, and he may well be right, that round about 1913 Summers underwent some very terrifying experience while performing a satanist rite, and that this so frightened him that he was converted to an almost fanatical religious orthodoxy, so that thenceforward he denounced, and with a passionate sincerity, every kind of satanism, witchcraft, and necromancy, with modern Spiritualism thrown in for good measure. His proclaimed views on witchcraft were exactly those of the authors of the *Malleus Maleficarum*, and of Ludovico Maria Sinistrari, Henry Boguet, Francesco Maria Guazzo, Nicolas Rémy, and the other medieval writers on these subjects whose works he edited. In 1927 three of Summers's witchcraft books drew down on him a severe attack from the pen of Father Herbert Thurston, S.J., a Jesuit scholar who was a specialist in this field.[6] In so many words, Thurston challenged Summers to declare the source of his holy orders; but no reply was forthcoming.

Summers's books on the occult keep their value as a storehouse of recondite information, but his judgements and interpretations are not to be relied on. The books are still readable since they are written in a vigorous prose which is heightened by an effective use of archaisms; but it must be admitted that occasionally his style gets badly out of hand, as in this quaint passage from *The Werewolf* (1933):

Whereon mine host, little minded to be made a meal of, in a sad fright bolted rous through the door, which he took good care to double lock and bar behind him, leaving his cloak to shift for itself. So the budge nims the togeman, and Prince Prig is off on his way to see more of the world. Moral: We must not believe everything we hear.

Of fuller and more lasting and solid value are Montague Summers's writings on the Restoration Drama; notably his classic works *The Restoration Theatre* (1934) and *The Playhouse of Pepys* (1935), and the splendid editions of Congreve, Otway, Wycherley, and Dryden that he edited for the Nonesuch Press; the Shakespeare Head Press five-volume *The Works of Mrs Aphra Behn*; and the five-volume Fortune Press *The Complete Works of Thomas Shadwell*. Summers cannot be held free from faults of editing, which later editors have corrected, but in the range of his achievement, and the learning and enthusiasm that he brought to it, he must surely be held the Prince of Restoration Scholars. As he himself stated, he might not have said the last word about the Restoration Theatre, but his books would have to be read for a long time to come.

His third field of study was the Gothic Novel; here again he was both pioneer and master. Recent reprintings of *The Gothic Quest: A History of the Gothic Novel* and the massive *A Gothic Bibliography*, first published in 1938 and 1940 respectively, show that here too his work is not yet superseded. The loss of the manuscript of the concluding volume, *The Gothic Achievement*, is matter for deep regret.

Summers's romantic enthusiasm for the Gothic is finely expressed in his introduction to the sumptuous edition, of five hundred copies only, of Horace Walpole's *The Castle of Otranto* which was published by Constable and Company in 1924. There he tells us that

There is in the Romantic revival a certain disquietude and a certain aspiration. It is this disquietude with earth and aspiration for heaven which informs the greatest Romance of all, Mysticism, the Romance of the Saints. The Classical writer set down fixed rules and precisely determined his boundaries. The Romantic spirit reaches out beyond these with an indefinite but very real longing to new and dimly guessed spheres of beauty. The Romantic writer fell in love with the Middle Ages, the vague years of long ago, the days of chivalry and strange adventure. He imagined and elaborated a mediaevalism for himself, he created a fresh world, a world which never was and never could have been, a domain which fancy built and fancy ruled. And in this land there will be mystery, because where there is mystery beauty may always lie hid. There will be wonder, because wonder always lurks where there is the unknown. And it is this longing for beauty intermingling with wonder that will express itself, perhaps exquisitely and passionately in the twilight moods of the romantic poets, in the picturesque description of Italian landscapes and far-off mountain scenes, perhaps a little crudely and even a little vulgarly in tales of horror and blood.

In the great field of Gothic literature Montague Summers's strongest love was reserved for Mrs Ann Radcliffe, 'the mighty mistress of romance', who was the subject of his inaugural lecture, in 1916, on the occasion of his admission as a Fellow of the Royal Society of Literature: an honour, as Summers wrote in 1948, worth a great deal more then than it had become.

In *The Gothic Achievement*, almost completed at the time of his death, he had intended to treat of Mrs Radcliffe's work in detail; also of the work of Mrs Parsons, Mrs Charlotte Smith, Charlotte Dacre (whose *Zofloya, or The Moor* he had edited for the Fortune Press), as well as Mary Wollstonecraft Shelley and *Frankenstein*, Charles Robert Maturin, author of *Melmoth the Wanderer*, and many others.

After Summers's death his library was sold off in two stages. Some of his books were acquired by the antiquarian booksellers Harold Mortlake and Company, of Cecil Court, Charing Cross Road. Among them I remember seeing the first volume (but not the second) of Summers's own copy of Matthew Gregory Lewis's *The Monk*, which Mr Mortlake transferred to his own private library. From another source Mortlake's had acquired a copy of *The Gothic Quest* inscribed by Summers to that other great Gothic scholar Michael Sadleir. It was always a pleasure to drop in on Harold and Lily Mortlake and share their reminiscences of their distinguished customer Montague Summers. It was Harold Mortlake, I think—but if not it was another London book-seller—who received a cheque in settlement of Summers's account written and signed a week after his death. It could have been postdated, of course; but one wonders.

The Mortlakes had as assistant, and manager in their absence, an Indian lady, always spoken to and of as 'Alix', who once told me that after Summers's death she had had a dream in which she was walking down a London street, when she saw on the other side of the street a building whose doors stood wide open, with people going in and out. Out of curiosity she entered, and found that she was in an auctioneer's premises. In the middle of the floor there were several tea-chests, which on inspection proved to be full of books from the library of the Reverend Montague Summers, each one bearing one or other of his two bookplates. At that point the dream ended. For years Alix had been hoping to come upon this auctioneer's premises in some London street; but she never did. And now, the Mortlakes' shop has been sold, to new proprietors who know not Joseph.

Montague Summers died suddenly at his home in Richmond on 10th August, 1948, and was buried three days later in Richmond Cemetery. In his will he commended his soul to Almighty God through the prayers of the Blessed Virgin and his patron saints, affirming that he died in the Holy Roman Catholic Faith. May he rest in peace.

NOTES

1. The anonymous story in *The Grimoire*, 'The Man on the Stairs', is by Montague Summers.

2. Summers's long introduction to the *Malleus Maleficarum*, which contains a scathing and amusing attack on his old enemy Father Thurston, is unfortunately much abridged in the later small-format edition published by the Pushkin Press.

3. For Erica Marx, see Barry Newport, 'Erica Marx and the Hand and Flower Press', in *Antiquarian Book Monthly Review,* vol. vi, no. 12, issue 68: December 1979.

4. The Reverend Arthur Valentin, priest of the diocese of Westminster. Private letter.

5. John Redwood-Anderson, *Recollections of Montague Summers* (unpublished). This manuscript is now in the Leslie C. Staples Montague Summers Collection, recently acquired by Professor Devendra P. Varma, of Dalhousie University, Halifax, N.S.

6. Father Thurston's article was published in the Irish monthly *Studies*, in 1927. It was entitled 'Diabolism', and purported to be a review of Summers's *History* and *Geography* of *Witchcraft*, and of his translation of Sinistrari's *Demoniality*. This latter book, together with Summers's translation of *The Confessions of Madeleine Bavent, the Possessed Nun of Louviers*, was confiscated by the police soon after publication, and was suppressed by order of the magistrate. It would excite no particular remark today. A disagreeable book, certainly, it has a certain value for historians or students of the paranormal.

Henry Williamson

HENRY WILLIAMSON

I CANNOT REMEMBER when I first read a book by Henry Williamson. It was not when I was at school. At Weymouth College in the 1920s we had an English teacher of genius (I mean with a genius for teaching English), Lionel Gough, who went on from Weymouth to Haileybury, and then to Marlborough. Gough introduced us to Surtees;—from whose works he later published an anthology—I do not think he ever mentioned Williamson. But then, Williamson's most famous book, *Tarka the Otter*, was not published until the year I left school. Working in the offices of *G. K.'s Weekly*, I was aware of the excitement caused by the publication of *Tarka*, and of the award to its author of the Hawthornden Prize. I do not think the book was reviewed in *G. K.'s*, and I made no effort to obtain a copy. Animal books are not my favourite reading, and I am quite happy to disclaim any relationship, save the most distant, with the author of *Black Beauty*. And yet towards the end of the 1930s I was reading everything by Henry Williamson that I could get hold of. It was then that I acquired, for ten shillings each, at Foyle's second-hand department, the rare first editions (Collins, 1921 and 1922) of *The Beautiful Years* and *Dandelion Days,* Williamson's first and second novels, which were almost completely rewritten for the later editions published by Faber and Faber.

Henry Williamson was my preferred reading during the war years 1939-1945. Ten years after the war, as a newly-ordained priest at Aylesford Priory, in Kent, I was instructed by the then Prior-General of the Carmelite Order to start a magazine to be read primarily by our Tertiaries (lay associates of the Order), of whom there were about a thousand in the country. The first number of *The Aylesford Review* appeared in the autumn of 1955, and contained articles on Pilgrimages, the Blind Mystic of Rennes (a 16th century Carmelite laybrother, the Ven. John of St Samson), and St Teresa of Lisieux, a late 19th century Carmelite nun. The expected readers and subscribers showed little interest;

172

and the second number met with a similar reception, or non-reception. At that point the editor, presuming the consent of his superiors, began to point the magazine in a more literary direction: a policy that was to prove reasonably successful. Through a variety of expedients the magazine, a quarterly, survived for thirteen years, succumbing eventually to financial and other difficulties. Its circulation never rose above the five hundred mark, and was usually nearer four hundred.

Advice was sought and taken from various quarters, and quite early on it was decided that from time to time we would devote an issue of the *Aylesford Review* to articles on some writer whose work seemed to be either too little known or not sufficiently appreciated. The first of these special numbers appeared in 1956, and was concerned with the novelist Elizabeth Myers, who had died at the age of thirty-five in 1947. It was well received, and we decided to follow it with a number on Henry Williamson. Williamson was, of course, a famous writer; but famous really because of one book, or perhaps two: *Tarka the Otter* and *Salar the Salmon*. His many other books were relatively little known. The tetralogy of novels, *The Beautiful Years*, *Dandelion Days*, *A Dream of Fair Women*, and *The Pathway*, known collectively as *The Flax of Dream*, had achieved considerable popularity, but it was not a best-seller. By 1957 Williamson had published the first four volumes of his second novel-series, *A Chronicle of Ancient Sunlight*.

Williamson's approval had to be sought for this project, and he invited me to meet him in London to discuss the idea. So in the summer of 1957 I met him at his daughter Margaret's house in Redcliffe Road, Fulham. For the next twenty years, until his death in 1977, I saw a great deal of him, remaining in touch during five years that I spent in Canada. He was often at our priory at Aylesford, where he shared weekends with a group of younger writers and artists whose company he enjoyed. Sometimes we would meet in London, sometimes I would visit him at his home in Devon. I got to know him well. He was a great letter-writer; often his letters were very long, sometimes hand-written, sometimes typescript, sometimes a mixture of both. Meeting, as we did, fairly often, there were periods when no correspondence passed between us; but I received about a hundred letters from him, which have now passed into the ownership of the recently-founded Henry Williamson Society, with an embargo on their publication, in whole or in part, until the year 2028.

Everyone who met Henry Williamson acknowledged his charm, and most people succumbed to it. He was a wonderful friend, and the best of company. One knew that any gathering at which he was to be present would be a lively and exhilarating affair. But on occasion he could be 'difficult', and the reverse side of his temperament lost him a number of friends. He lived on his nerves; as so many of the greatest writers have done. I am sometimes asked if I ever had any experience of this side of his personality. The answer is no. Occasionally I was made aware, though very gently, that I had said or done something lacking in tact; but Henry had a great respect for the cloth, and I think that more than once this saved me from a dusty answer.

He was a perfectionist; his own work rarely satisfied him, and it would be revised time after time. His later publishers, Macdonald and Co., were understanding and indulgent to an astonishing degree, permitting wholesale revision of a book even at the proof stage. They once pulped a whole first printing in order to allow yet further rewriting. For him, there was only one way to do anything, and that was the right way: whether it was writing a book, pruning a fruit-tree, or rebuilding a faulty fireplace to stop it from smoking. He once spent twenty minutes teaching me how to shut the door of his car. It was a worthwhile lesson, but a little trying while it lasted.

The formal notice of Henry's death which appeared on the back page of *The Times* on 14th August, 1977 recorded him as (I quote from memory) 'WILLIAMSON, Henry, Old Soldier, writer, farmer, and friend'. This happily sums him up in his principal aspects. 'Old Soldier' is appropriately placed first, since the war of 1914-1918 was the central and most formative experience of his life. By a kind of psychological compulsion most ex-combatants either forget or romanticise their experience of war. Williamson remembered.

On the whole it is easy to forget: the life-eager animal in us all wants it that way . . . Yet here and there a man of more than ordinary sensibility arises for whom to forget is an impossibility. The experience of war becomes a festering wound in his psyche for which the rest of his life is a

quest for healing: he is conscious of bearing a burden of guilt and responsibility for a lost generation. He must remember and not forget; and in
order to remember without indignation or self-pity or agitation, he has to
await a slow and gradual clarification of his soul.[1]

It was his custom to spend part of every Christmas alone,
remembering Christmas Eve 1914, when the British and German
soldiers in opposing trenches ceased firing, sang their national
Christmas carols to each other, and then met to fraternize in No
Man's Land. Each Christmas he was there again; the experience
had affected him for the rest of his life. He never tired of recalling
it, whether in reminiscence with friends or in his writings.
Perhaps his finest account of this almost miraculous happening is
in his volume of autobiography *The Story of a Norfolk Farm*,
published in 1938.

Francis Thompson's poetry had become Williamson's companion long before the war. Soon after the war, early in 1919, he
picked up in a secondhand bookshop in Folkestone a copy of
Richard Jefferies's *The Story of my Heart*. Here, and in Jefferies's
other books, he found a new source of inspiration. His view of
life, and his conviction of his own mission in life, were now
formed. Twenty years later he summed it up in another
autobiographical book, *The Children of Shallowford*:

In the light of nature I knew that only the country could give a man
knowledge; that the townsman could only have that secondary thing,
learning. I knew that true knowledge, apart from research, was that
learnt by the body used in harmony with the mind: that the brain was
only a control-tower and reference library. Intuition was a living thing,
and the source of intuition was the land. A man cutting and laying a
hedge, a man driving a furrow, a man observing how a bullock tears
away its bite with its tongue wrapped round grass, while a sheep nibbles
close and thereby ruins a balanced pasture if allowed too long on it; or a
man singing on a windy, cloud-and-sunshine rushing day of spring as he
harrows clover in the barley stubble—that man lived naturally, his
knowledge was part of his spirit; not apart from his life.
Once I was a little boy being perplexed and (because my nervous
reactions were quicker than the normal) mentally torn by lessons which
my mind could not understand, or be interested in. The mental barbed
wire became, at seventeen, material barbed wire; and after four years of
human desolation and dereliction it was borne in on me that the cast of
thought which had directed the education of my generation in Europe
arose directly from the internecine financial system. The natural
intelligences of the children of Europe were broken in, enslaved: and the

Great War was the result. When I tried to stammer this discovery, everywhere blank faces were turned to or away from me. Everywhere the mass mind-sterility called the educated point of view seemed to be in deadly negation of the truth. Countrymen, peasants, contented men, went to the war which the sterilized town-mind, enslaved to the international-trading, price-cutting, market-grabbling, money-lending system had, by its very existence, prepared and created. Ten million men died in that apotheosis of mind-sterility.[2]

Even before the war had ended Williamson had begun writing his *Flax of Dream* novels, through which he hoped to extend Richard Jefferies's gospel of redemption through Nature as the way to unite men and end wars. But when the whole four-volume series was complete he was not sure that the work was fundamentally true to its theme. At the end of *The Pathway*, which had been recognised as an outstanding, and almost a great novel, its hero, the ex-officer William Maddison, is accidentally drowned, before he has been able to complete his life-work, to tell the truth about the war, and propagate a new policy of social reconstruction.

Williamson was still under thirty when he completed *The Flax of Dream*. In spite of its hero being an ex-officer from the 1914-1918 war, there are no scenes from the war in the book. Its author was still too near to his war experiences to be able to write about them. Conscious of the book's limitations, he now imagined a new series of novels in which William Maddison's London cousin Phillip would take up and continue Willie's mission. 'I had thought', Williamson says, 'of the *Flax* as the subjective or romantic treatment of the theme of redemption, while the story of Phillip, the poor London cousin, would be built on the classic or objective pattern.'[3] But twenty years were to elapse before the first of these new novels was begun; years that were filled with a great quantity of other writing. *The Dark Lantern*, the opening novel of *A Chronicle of Ancient Sunlight*, was not published until 1951; the final volume, *The Gale of the World*, appeared in 1969.

Writing ten years earlier, George D. Painter had affirmed his conviction that 'it will be among the accepted facts of English literary history that our only two great novelists writing in the second quarter of the twentieth century, after the deaths of Lawrence and Joyce, were John Cowper Powys and Henry

Williamson.'⁴ In the same article Painter remarked that Powys and Williamson were recognized for what they were during the dark period of the treason of the critics 'by an underground army of unknown readers'. He believed that ultimately *A Chronicle of Ancient Sunlight* would be recognized as 'the great historical novel of our time, its subject as the total experience of twentieth-century man.'

Old soldiers place a high value on loyalty. Henry's loyalty to his friend, a fellow front-line soldier of the 'Great' war, Sir Oswald Mosley, won him much unpopularity and misunderstanding. This was the principal reason why for years his books were either ignored or else reviewed dismissively by many critics; and it was the reason for his lack of public recognition from the university of which he was an outstanding benefactor. In spite of the good will of two successive Vice-Chancellors, and the endeavours of the Professor of English Language and Literature and other sympathisers, the committee for the bestowal of honorary degrees twice vetoed the proposal—of which Williamson knew nothing—to confer on him an honorary doctorate. In the 1960s he received some kind of unofficial notification that he could expect to find his name in the next Honours List to be promulgated by the Sovereign; but when the time came his name was not there. At least twice a Prime Minister was approached on his behalf; but it was probably unrealistic to expect anything from that quarter. However, had he known, he would not have worried. One of the characters in his last novel, *The Gale of the World,* fails to receive a promised award of the OBE, and when asked about it wryly replies: 'Well, I believe the British Empire no longer exists, so perhaps I've escaped being given *nothing!*' A typical good-humoured Williamson joke. All the same, some public recognition of his status as a senior and major writer, and of his love of country, would have pleased him, and it is sad that such bitter narrowness of spirit should have denied it to him.

Williamson's 'Fascism' continues to be matter for discussion even among admirers of his work, many of whom seem to find it hard to understand. Discussion is not made easier by the current devaluation of the word Fascism, which has become a term of abuse covering almost any kind of social order that incorporates traditional values. Not that it is easy to define Fascism, except as it was first adumbrated by Benito Mussolini. Since this was based on an intense nationalism it took many different forms as it appeared in other countries than Italy: National Socialism in Germany, the Catholic Corporate State in Portugal, Rexism in Belgium, the Iron Guard in Romania, the Arrow Cross in Hungary, the Phalange in Spain, General O'Duffy's Blueshirts in Ireland, and Sir Oswald Mosley's British Union in Britain. But whatever form it took, its adherents always saw it as a 'modern' movement, which would get rid of the old morally and politically bankrupt political parties of Europe, put an end to the power of international finance, and inaugurate a dynamic policy of social reconstruction, which would regenerate and rebuild nations reduced to chaos or near-chaos by war, corruption, and incompetence.

Everywhere, Fascism seems to have attracted large numbers of ex-soldiers from the 1914-1918 war, determined that neither themselves nor their children should have to go through another such ordeal. In England a high proportion of Sir Oswald Mosley's followers were ex-service men (and women). Mosley himself was a professional soldier, who had served during the war as a pilot in the Royal Flying Corps, and then as an officer in the Army. One of his principal aims during the 1930s was to keep Britain out of foreign quarrels that did not concern her, and this had a strong appeal for the ex-officer Henry Williamson. Another of Mosley's aims was the restoration of British agriculture, then in ruins as a result of the policy of successive governments which allowed the importing of cheap foreign food by way of interest on the huge financial loans advanced by the City of London to far-off foreign countries. Williamson the countryman was attracted by this too.

Who can be surprised that thousands of ex-soldiers, and thousands of the younger generation, were attracted by a leader who declared: 'We count it a privilege to live in an age when England demands that great things should be done, a privilege to be of the generation which learns to say what can we give instead of what can we take. For thus our generation learns that there are greater things than slothful ease; greater things than safety; more terrible things than death.'

Ezra Pound's economic thinking was along similar lines; but now goes unstudied because of his rabid anti-semitism—a fault from which Mosley himself was free; though his failure to deal firmly with the 'lunatic fringe' of his followers may reasonably be held against him in this matter.

Williamson's study of Mosley in two of the *Chronicle* novels, *The Phoenix Generation* and *Lucifer Before Sunrise*, where he appears as Sir Hereward Birkin, is a well-drawn portrait. Williamson also expressed his admiration for Mosley in another novel, *The Phasian Bird*, a powerful allegory which records with passion and precision the temper of those now distant days of 1939-1945.

Some of Williamson's defenders have tried to dismiss his Fascism—if such it really was, for the word was never in his vocabulary—as being due to his naiveté in political matters. I doubt if this kind of defence does him much service. In 1935 Williamson attempted to bring about a peaceful revolution in European and British politics which would have affected our history as a nation, and very possibly have prevented the second world war. If he had succeeded, no one would today be able to think of him as politically naif; on the contrary, he would have gone down to history as a master of political realism.

In 1928 Williamson received an appreciative letter about *Tarka the Otter* from T. E. Lawrence (Lawrence of Arabia), which was the beginning of a friendship between the two men. In 1935 Williamson conceived the idea that if Aircraftman Shaw (as Lawrence now was) and the former corporal Adolf Hitler, now the Chancellor of the Third Reich, could meet, they might be able to halt the drift to war. And, 'With Lawrence of Arabia's name to gather a meeting of ex-Service men in the Albert Hall, with his presence and stimulation to cohere into unassailable logic the authentic mind of the war generation come to power of truth and amity, a whirlwind campaign [which] would end the old fearful thought of Europe (usury-based) for ever.'[5]

Williamson was to have met Lawrence at Clouds Hill to have discussed this idea with him on a day in May 1935. Lawrence was killed in a motor-cycle accident on his way back from sending Williamson a telegram fixing the day and time of their meeting.

Of course, we cannot be certain that Lawrence would have accepted the proposal; but it seems probable that he would.[6] Possibly we shall know more if one day all Williamson's letters from Lawrence are published.

Henry Williamson was an exceptionally fit and active man up to the age of 79; but a little before his 80th birthday, in December 1975, his health began to decline. He died on 13th August, 1977 at Twyford Abbey, the hospital of the Alexian Brothers at Park Royal, in North London. He was buried on Thursday, 18th August, at Georgeham (Ham St George), the North Devon parish where he had lived since 1928, except for his short interlude in Norfolk. His grave is close to the churchyard hedge a few yards west of the church tower. What that tower meant to him you can read in his foreword and afterword to *The Wet Flanders Plain*, an account published in 1929 of a visit that he made in that year to the battlefields of 1914-1918.

The Flax of Dream was dedicated 'To all who fought for freedom in the World War, and who are still fighting'. To all: that is, to the surviving combatants from both sides; for the German soldiers, sailors, and airmen also believed in the justice of their cause. When that war was over Henry Williamson kept up the fight for freedom in his writings, and through the support of policies which, to his eyes, seemed to offer hope that a second fratricidal war could be averted. This hope was not realised; the suffering that this brought on him was perhaps a necessary factor in preparing him for the tremendous task of writing *A Chronicle of Ancient Sunlight*, the great novel in fifteen volumes in which he has told, with unparalleled effect, the truth about the war: and, indeed, about most wars.

NOTES

1. John Middleton Murry, 'The Novels of Henry Williamson', in *The Aylesford Review*, vol. ii, no. 2, Winter 1957-58.

2. Henry Williamson, *The Children of Shallowford*: London, Faber and Faber, 1939.

3. Henry Williamson, 'Some Notes on *The Flax of Dream* and *A Chronicle of Ancient Sunlight*', in *The Aylesford Review*, vol. ii, no. 2, Winter 1957-58.

4. George D. Painter, 'The Two Maddisons', in *The Aylesford Review*, vol. ii, no. 6, Spring 1959.

5. Henry Williamson, *Genius of Friendship, 'T. E. Lawrence'*: London, 1941.

6. Cf. Desmond Stewart, *T. E. Lawrence*: London, 1977, chapter 27, 'The Partitioned Soul'. (Lawrence's death may not have been an accident; and it certainly was not suicide.)

Ann Quin

ANN QUIN: IN MEMORY

ANN QUIN first came to our priory in Kent in April 1964. She had been introduced to me by Henry Williamson, who had recognised her as a gifted writer when he read her first book, *Berg,* which had just been published. A few days after she had gone home I received my first letter from her. She wrote to me, from 96 Lansdowne Road W11, to say that she had had a peaceful time at the priory, and would have liked to have stayed longer. 'I seek stillness, as that is the vital reservoir needed for creating, and only by living on my own am I able to achieve that—it is possible that I have not learned to really give, and basically fear a permanent relationship having in my childhood never known family life as such. . . I am not prepared to make a sacrifice, and this above all bothers me into overwhelming depression. . . I am glad (though apprehensive!) that you have a copy of Berg—the best part of which, at the moment anyway, for me seems the cover! The rest is dead. The book was a necessary struggle to free myself from inhibiting constrictions. . . Once again I thank you for that lovely memorable day, and I am looking forward to seeing you again at Hawkesyard in June.'

A month later she wrote to me about her second novel, *Three.* 'I don't know about the book I'm on at the moment as being in another vein, expressing more truly myself. I think it will take many years before I strip off the layers of "spectres" in my own nightmarish way. In the present work I am still dealing with three people, this time a girl who lives with a couple. The relationships between three has always fascinated me, being I suppose partly because I have never known the family unit, and partly the influence of the Roman Catholic convent I spent my childhood in (the trinity etc.). In reality I have often found myself at my best, a kind of security when with two other people, most of my friends are couples, and I suppose automatically I play the role of the child. Does all this sound too Freudian for words?!'

In June Ann came to a literary conference at Spode House, in

183

the grounds of Hawkesyard Priory, in Staffordshire. About fifty people were present, among them Henry Williamson, Colin Wilson, Alan Neame, Dom Sylvester Houédard, and Ann's neighbours Michael Hastings and Jane Percival. After the conference she left to visit friends on the remote island of Paxos, near Corfù. Letters arrived from her written from Ithaca. The first three weeks' travels, which included a fruitless journey from Athens to Turkey, had been 'pretty well worse than a nightmare . . ., having to turn back because of the riots in Istanbul, and more or less had to bribe our way back to Greece . . . Frankly I don't think I could stay longer than a few more weeks—I find that because of the heat I spend most of my time SLEEPING, and in fact feel as tho' I'm convalescing! I'm always intending to get up early tomorrow, but never make it before eight o'clock! The room I have is good tho'—white walls, green shutters, a balcony overlooking bay and mountains, for which I pay about 7/6 a day—the water is so clear, so green, so clear in fact that one has no need to swim underwater to see that strange silent world of the sea kingdom. It has been marvellous to relax here after those weeks of travelling, but it is almost too cosy, too safe—if you can understand this—I miss a certain atmosphere of England, London—books, films, friends, and then the occasional contrast of the stillness of the countryside.'

By September Ann was back in England. At that time the financial difficulties to which the *Aylesford Review* eventually succumbed were making themselves felt. She refers to this in her next letter.

96 Lansdowne Road, London, W.11
September 16th,—'64.

Dear Father Brocard,
Good to hear from thee—tho' I don't like the sound of you're feeling like retiring into the monastery at Aylesford and packing up the Review, at the same time I can appreciate how you must feel about it all at such times; I go through exactly the same reactions with regard to writing, on such occasions I say: oh I'm deluding myself with this writing lark, why don't I get down to having a normal life, be a woman, get settled, have children, and lead a quite ordinary time. Of course, fortunately (but for who—only myself I suppose?!) these moments don't last all that long. So I hope by now you are feeling less 'retiring' and have a renewed faith in the Review—anyway I think its a super review, the only one I can really

ever enjoy from beginning to end!

. . . for the next three months I won't have to worry too much, and after December I might get other foreign advances. I can't tell you how relieved I am at the prospect of not having to go out and earn something to exist, for the first time in ten years I feel a REAL WRITER—it makes such a difference to me as a person as well as a writer to have this security. When I think back at the time while writing Berg I wonder how on earth I managed—especially as for nearly two years I was suffering with glandular T.B. (No doubt that alone 'inspired' THOSE PARTS that seem to nauseate many people in Berg!) and trying to exist on less than £7 a week! In comparison I feel a millionairess now. . .

Have got really immersed in new book, which I'm calling THE CHAMELEON (had my doubts about this title as it seems such an obvious one that I was so sure it must have been used—but Calder's say they haven't heard of any novel by that title. So.) and am terribly excited about it—theme and style, the merging of the two. It will be longer than Berg and BETTER in every way of course!

Ann had recently won a Harkness scholarship, and in the summer she left for the United States. In May she sent a postcard from the Lawrence Ranch at San Cristobal, New Mexico:

Just arrived here—it really is a lovely lovely place, with pine trees just outside, & so much space before & beyond, giving for the first time a real sense of place since arriving over. Loathed New York—like being in a whale's mouth: people so loud & rude ugh!

Strange atmosphere of this ranch Inside being v. English—can just imagine Lawrence & Frieda here—so far not haunted by them—probably frightened them away! Will be here for 2 months—hope to get started on another book. . .

Another postcard, sent in June:

Lovely lovely country—mountains all around, change from cobalt to magenta. Stars at night so near almost seem touchable. Any number of birds: lovely blue, scarlet ones; humming, mocking birds; bears, coyotes, bobcats, chipmunks; ashen trees, blue, white lupins, wild irises. Desert below like a dead sea. Unfortunately fell off a horse last week, lost consciousness, whisked off to the hospital in town: But O.K. now—what a dumb thing to do!

In November came a long letter from San Francisco, a city she did not at first much like.

. . . Sorry I haven't written before, but things have either moved too quickly, or not moved at all wherein I've found myself completely disoriented. Things have been difficult in the sense of adapting to this country, this city, and have in moments felt like giving up and returning home! Partly the people, partly the apartment, and landlord trouble (he objected to a negro friend who called, and asked me to leave, threatened me with getting his lawyer I reciprocated by saying I would get the Civil Rights onto him—knowing how they would love a case like that! anyway that quietened him down!) anyway things now are a little more settled in the sense that I'm moving over to Sausalito, which is just across from the Golden Gate Bridge, a small boating, fishing town, a bit arty colony, which I can keep out of anyway, but have found a simply lovely apartment, in a crazy yellow old house on a barge, right on the water, large wooden panelled room, with windows overlooking Bay and hills in the distance, where I know I will basically be much happier, and will be able to settle down to some real writing, which up to now has been more or less nil—what with all my wanderings and so on!

Spent ten days in Nassau, the Bahammas, which I loathed, the v. worst rich British, & Americans, only concerned in money & property—ugh! the humidity also knocked me flat, where I couldn't even write a postcard, mind went to marshmallow; it was lovely to get out of there. Spent a long weekend up in Maine, in a palace of a wooden cabin, overlooking a lake, which was nice. Then a couple of weeks out at Tappan, near the Hudson River. Went to a crazy party held on a huge estate out in Connecticut, in honor of a novelist Margarite Young, who's written a colossal novel: eleven hundred and ninety eight pages, took her 18 years to write, would take that long to wade thru—if Edith Sitwell had written a novel, this would have been it—v. baroque, full of angels, trumpets, cherubs, etc. Anyway the party turned out to be full of wall street brokers, and pop painters, and vice versa! Met Anais Nin there, she a very exquisite person, at least seventy, but looks thirty. Also the painter Rothko, who looks like a businessman and is I'm sure! . . .

The State college is full of international politics, especially the Creative Writing Department. I was taken round there and introduced to various members of the staff, I may as well not have been there at all, they just sat around talking amongst themselves about promotion and their own little hangups, it was a relief to get away. Fortunately there is at least one real person who lectures in anthropology there: John Collier Jr., who I had met when I was on the Lawrence Ranch, a very lovely, rare person, with a tremendous knowledge of the Indians, and Indian way of life. Also has that deeper level of contact, which very few people over here have; they all seem so barricaded up, resigned, ingrown, and inevitably v. ugly; also their casualness I think verges onto downright rudeness, which at first numbed me, but now learning to be equally vicious, tho God knows that should never be a need. What is sadly lacking is a sense of spontaneous rhythm between people, which frequently does happen in England—or am I just being romantically nostalgic?! Anyway all this makes people like John Collier even more rare. I went over to his place and stayed with his family in a high tower of a house overlooking the ocean, a place called Muir beach, and walked by the sea, over the cliffs, which brought that stillness, which I haven't had since leaving New

Mexico, and really felt a different person. So now with the fact of moving near the water, and actually being on it what more could a pisces disoriented witch want?! . . .

I have no letters from Ann between 1965 and 1971; some may have been lost or destroyed. In 1970 we corresponded about a story of hers which I printed in the *Antigonish Review*, which I edited during a period of teaching in Nova Scotia. I was mostly in Canada from 1969 to 1972, and during part of this time Ann was ill in Sweden.

In November '71 I was back in England for some months, and received a letter which she had addressed to me in Antigonish, N.S. It was a short letter, written from 22 Lansdowne Road, dated 'After all Souls' [November 1st.] She said that she had been having 'a somewhat bad time' on account of a recurrence of a previous breakdown: '. . . this has meant that I have come to terms at long last with myself—that is I really want to live and have a family.' Because of this breakdown she had lost her secretarial job and run into a bad financial crisis. After I had replied to this letter she wrote again, this time from Narcissus Ward, Springfield Hospital, Upper Tooting. 'Well, things are o.k. but have been pretty bad. . .—still there is peace in my heart though it has been splintered many times at least I have no doubt now that there is a God of many faces, many facets, many visions, many signs.'

I was able to go and see her, and when she left the hospital in December she came to stay at our retreat house, Allington Castle, near Maidstone, until she felt ready to go back to London. This visit went off well, though she was very quiet and kept mostly to herself. Once again she was in need of money, and as soon as she was at home she got a job as a part time waitress at a small café in the Notting Hill Gate area, as she described in her next letter.

> 22 Lansdowne Road
> London W.11
>
> January 2nd '72

Many apologies for not writing sooner to thank you for that lovely time spent at Allington Castle—it was just the right place to stay for those few days after being an inmate at Springfield—it made a kind of harbour before entering this wide ocean of a world—which sometimes I feel I just

cannot face—& recently I have felt I may as well be dead—and that I
guess is because I'm not actually doing a book! I seem to spend most of
my time hibernating—today for instance I didn't wake up till 3 p.m. 14
hours of sleep!

The job is fine & doesn't tire or bore me as secretarial work used to &
I pick up between £4—£5 a day which is nice!

Just reading The Voyage Out by Virginia Woolf—strange but I always
find her books dull except for The Waves which I remember started me
into writing at the age of 14 together with Dostevsky's Crime and
Punishment!

. . . Still it's nice to be back at this flat. Thank God I was able to keep
that on—the thought of looking for a place & possibly ending up in one
room I just could not have faced.

Did you have a good time at Xmas? I actually went to Brighton to stay
with my Mum & of course she was delighted. Ate, slept & watched tele
most of the time—wot a life!

Finding it very difficult to live on my own. . . There is, of course, part
of me that likes being a 'loner' & that often creates difficulties when
living with someone!

Hope you can read this scrawl? Anyway I hope this finds you well & I
wish you all the very best for this New Year.

  Much love
  Ann

In April she wrote to me about the publication party for her
novel *Three*—a party to be held at the offices of her publishers,
Calder and Boyars, and given jointly for herself and Alan Burns.
In this letter she wrote that she would have to leave her flat, that
she was so fond of, by 23rd June, 'partly because the roof has to
be reconstructed. . . .; I'm looking round for a place and it's pretty
depressing, the rents are so grimly high i.e. nothing under £16 a
week it seems; looks as tho I'll end up in a bedsitter again.
Though I am applying for a place at Hillcroft College in Surrey;
have you heard of it I wonder? It's specially for women over 25
without qualifications, and one can get a grant hopefully, and I
hope to study sociology, psychology and literature and perhaps go
on afterwards for a teacher's training course. Alan Burns also
mentioned it might be worth trying for a degree in Eng. lit at East
Anglia, so I'm applying for a place there as well. Don't know if
anything will come of either of these, but I really would like to
have some systematic study etc. for a time and also live out of
London.'

Later Ann won a place at Hillcroft College and completed a

successful course of studies there. Then she was awarded a place at the University of East Anglia, which she would have taken up in October 1973.

Her immediate housing problem was solved without too much difficulty. A letter written from 260 Elgin Avenue, W9, said: 'As you see I've actually moved: a very nice, large room, plus kitchen, and a garden all to myself, and only £4 a week so feeling very relieved and happy about the move. If you are in London next week do please give me a ring and perhaps if it's sunny come and have tea in the garden!' But I did not see her new home, as I had to return to Canada. When I next heard from her it was from

> Hillcroft College
> South Bank
> Surbiton
> Surrey
> 10th February 1973

Good to hear from you—I wondered where you might be, and guessed perhaps you were back in Canada! I didn't unfortunately receive your card/letter at Elgin Ave., unfortunately a rather sordid little scene occurred about that flat: I had sub-let to a girl and she disappeared without telling me, without paying rent, and the Estate Agents went round, found the place had been broken into, and everything covered in cat shit! Didn't care much about rush matting covered in the stuff, but apparently most of my books, manuscripts and notebooks were covered in it so they threw them out and burnt 'em—all that survived it appeared are Messrs Camus and Beckett! Anyway I've given the flat up—too much responsibility and it looks as though I won't be in London for a few years (London University has rejected me!)—not that I fancied being there the course seemed to dwell entirely on Anglo Saxon lit—Beau Wolf etc, which I'm not v. keen on! And I'm also somewhat off London as a place to live in—it might stimulate but it doesn't sustain, and am reminded of what E. M. Forster once said about the place: 'a caricature of the infinite'!

Anyway it looks as tho I might get into Sussex University in September of this year—have been short-listed and have now to do a 2000 words essay by March 14th on Mailer's The Armies of the Night—though I might do an imagined interview with the author about the book! Then I go for an interview on March 23rd—so keep your fingers crossed! Would dearly love to get in there as they seem to have the most interesting course in the English and American School—and of course the countryside around there is absolutely beautiful. Bristol also has rejected me, so that leaves East Anglia and Reading—neither have I heard from as yet.

Am still enjoying my liberal studies course here—tho inevitably at loggerheads with the Eng. lit lecturer! Have just finished off an essay on Middle March—we had to do one on a novel before 1914 that might have inspired the Suffragettes! So I did a dialogue between two suffragettes called Augusta and Emily—certainly had fun with it, sending the whole thing up in the usual Quin fashion—which of course the Tutor won't appreciate! . . .

Yes, I do have a grant to help me thru this year—not very much: about £460—but at least it pays for the residence, food, etc., and allows about £6 a week during term time for pocket money—so it's not bad really. Only thing is it doesn't allow for vacations, and I won't have much by the time summer comes that's why I applied for an Arts Council Grant!

Do hope this finds you well and a wee bit warmer than from the sound of it in your last letter! Hoping v. much I'll see something of you some time this year.

Meanwhile take care and write me again when you can.

The last letter I received in Canada from Ann was written from Brighton on 24th July, 1973. She explained that because her mother had had an accident she would have to remain in Brighton until early in October, when she would be going to the University of East Anglia. In the middle of August I returned to Britain. At Capel-y-ffin, in Breconshire, where I was to stay with friends for a while, I found a letter from Ann, written a day or two before. She was having a difficult time; the house at Brighton in which her mother was living had been sold, and nobody knew to whom. 'Methinks they must be those bloody property developers & if so they will I guess make "life miserable" just to get Mother, who is a "sitting tenant" out!' Ann was clearing out the flat, and trying to get a Council flat for her mother to go to when she came out of hospital. She was expecting to be in Brighton until 3rd October, 'so there's plenty of time in which to arrange for you to come down.'

But in a letter that I received the next day she said she was nearly cracking up under the strain, and asked if she could come to The Monastery, the name of the house where I was staying, and stay for a month. She had forgotten, and I had to explain to her again, that the house where I was staying was in private occupation, a monastery in name only. There had been no monks there since 1924. It was now full of visitors—relations, and friends, with several children sleeping in tents on the lawn, and two more boarded out in a neighbour's caravan. However, I was able to tell her that if she could be patient for a week or two, until the visitors began to thin out, I was hopeful that I could arrange for her to come and stay for a while.

But I was much relieved when she wrote on 18th August:

You must think I am absolutely MAD! Thing is having had Carol and Alan Burns down for the day and discussing the whole situation: in other words 'hearing myself think' I think it would be best if I 'stick it out' here at least for the 1st few weeks after Mother returns [from hospital]—there is, in fact, still a lot to be done in clearing out the 'ghosts' externally and internally in this flat & I think I can be effective enough to see things thru at least until I leave for East Anglia.

So forgive somewhat hectic request of other day—written early a.m. in a wind of dumb panic!

At the same time I would v. much like to see thee, so perhaps you could come here after you leave Wales in September? Either that or I could come to Allington for a few days? I did love it there last winter—no sorry it was 2 years ago—extraordinary how time/space journeys in the mind.

Anyway do get in touch.

Blessings & much love

Ann

Then, one day early in September, someone brought to The Monastery at Capel-y-ffin, which does not normally receive a newspaper, a copy of the day's *Times*. It contained Ann's obituary notice. She had been found drowned, at Brighton. (At the time of her death she was 32 years old.) The same evening, as Frances Horovitz, Oswald Jones, and myself—all of us Ann's friends—were drinking wine together after supper at Mr Jones's bungalow, the telephone rang and someone asked to speak to me. It was Carol Burns, with confirmation of what we already knew. A few days later, on 14th September Carol Burns, Marion Boyars (Ann's publisher), John Carter, Tony Blomfield, of BBC Television, to whom Ann had submitted some plays, her aunt Joan Buitenkamp, and myself met at Victoria Station, and travelled down to Brighton for the funeral. The routine religious service at the crematorium seemed impersonal; a young clergyman who had not known Ann, and had scarcely heard of her, did his best to say a few helpful words, which seemed only to make the occasion bleaker still. Through a muddle, Ann was deprived of the Catholic rites that should have been hers. It was a cold, bright day: warm enough in the sun, and out of the wind, for us to share an alfresco lunch in the tiny courtyard of The Cricketers' Inn, in The Lanes. We drank two bottles of red wine to Ann's memory, which was perhaps a form of ritual salute to her, a tribute to her achievement as a writer, and gesture of farewell, that she would have appreciated.*

NOTE

* Ann's spelling and punctuation in her private letters were always erratic. They have not been changed here.
'Beau Wolf' for *Beowulf* is typical of her fondness for a Joycean play on words.

MONASTIC LIFE TODAY

THERE HAVE BEEN monks and nuns in the Christian church from very early times, and they form an important 'estate' in the Catholic and Orthodox churches today. However, monasticism cannot be said to be an essential element in the Church, for it was not established by Christ; but those who follow this way of life appeal to certain sayings of Christ's for its justification, and as sanction for the three vows of poverty, celibacy, and obedience, which are commonly held to be essential to the monastic state. To these three vows the orders of monks and nuns—in the primary and strict sense of those words[1]—add a vow of stability. The vow of stability attaches the monk or nun permanently to the community in which he or she enters monastic life, even though he or she may perhaps have periods of residence elsewhere.

Present day religious,[2] in spite of the traditional discipline and claustral life in which they have been trained, have been much affected by the prevailing uncertainty and unrest in the Western Church, and in recent years many of them have questioned the validity of their vocation in the modern world. Some have despaired of it in its present form, and have returned to 'the world' to take up other vocations, in which they see the possibility of a more effective Christian service and witness. Among those who have done so are senior men: abbots, provincial superiors, and priors.

There has also been much unrest among the younger members of religious orders and congregations. In 1968 ninety-two student-friars of an Italian province of the Franciscan Order left in a body, in protest against the authoritarian and paternalistic way in which the affairs of their province were conducted. In the United States at about the same time all the members of a large community of teaching nuns returned to civilian life in order to be free as teachers from the interferences of male clerical control.

In the United States in 1968 something like 11,000 members of religious orders and congregations returned to secular life.

In 1981 the torrent of defections has diminished; it is no longer a torrent, but it is a steady trickle, which is gravely damaging. In the 1930s, in England, there were still, on the average, twelve entrants each year into the novitiate of the Dominican Order; the Franciscan level of recruitment would have been much higher. Today three or four entrants would be considered remarkable. Many orders and congregations have none. The recruitment of potential Benedictine and Cistercian monks and nuns is at a similarly low level.

But even before the present crisis, which may be dated from the promulgation of the decrees of the Second Vatican Council, the religious orders were experiencing a falling off in recruitment. It is true that after the war in 1939-1945 there was an upsurge of vocations to the monastic life, but by 1960, at the latest, it had spent itself, and since then there has been a progressive decline. For a while this was attributed to the materialism of the age, but this is now seen to be an insufficient explanation.

In England, as in other countries, if things go on as at present, it will not be long before the monastic scene is much the same as it was at the end of the Middle Ages, when abbeys and priories were more than half empty, inhabited by a few ageing and discouraged religious striving ineffectually to keep up the traditional observances. There are unmistakable signs that this will be so. The English Dominicans, the order by far the most aware of the needs of the times, have been forced by declining numbers to give up the church and priory built for them by André Raffalovich at Pendleton, Manchester, early in the present century. The Dominican novitiate has been removed from the beautiful priory of the Annunciation at Woodchester, in Gloucestershire—which has actually been demolished—and merged with another community. The Dominican novices and student-friars have been removed from Woodchester and Hawkesyard (Staffordshire), to Oxford; while at Hawkesyard a reduced, almost a token community occupies one half of the great building, while the other half has been turned into a retreat house and conference centre for public use. And the Dominicans have closed their two schools, one of which had had a long and distinguished history since its foundation in the Low Countries, by the Dominican cardinal Philip Thomas Howard, in the reign of Charles II.

With the other orders it is much the same story of dwindling or empty novitiates, and the departure of student-religious before reaching ordination. Even the Society of Jesus, a body of much later origin but for long the largest and most flourishing religious order in the country, is in difficulties, and has had to abandon a number of parishes entrusted to its care, and to close its famous public school at Beaumont, Old Windsor.

When one realises that one-third only of any group of novices will eventually reach the priesthood—the others will either leave or be dismissed before ordination—the implications for the future are clear. Some of the secular (i.e., diocesan) clergy openly voice their satisfaction at this state of affairs, and say that in a few years' time all priests will be secular priests. This is a very short-sighted attitude, since even now the seculars are so short of men that in many places they cannot carry on without the help of the regulars. It is an illusion to think that young men who feel drawn to the monastic life are likely to substitute for it the life of the diocesan clergy.

In many Roman Catholic parishes numbers of people would have to go without Mass on Sundays if the parish priest could not rely at weekends on the assistance of some neighbouring religious house. On a Sunday morning there may well be three Masses in the church, and a fourth in the evening. In addition, there may be a hospital or prison chapel to be served, as well as one or more 'Mass centres' in outlying parts of the parish. Few parishes, unless they are served by a religious order, will have enough priests to cope with all this.

So friars, and in lesser degree monks, leave their monasteries on Sunday morning, or even on Saturday afternoon, to give the needed help in the parishes, with the result, all too often, that their own churches and their own community life suffer. Because of lack of numbers the Divine Office is not becomingly celebrated in conventual churches, and often a High Mass, or even a Sung Mass, is not possible on Sunday morning. The sacrifice is in a good cause, no doubt; but the price paid is a considerable impoverishment of the quality of conventual life.

In considering the state of the religious orders today some questions asked by George Gordon Coulton, the great modern medievalist, are relevant. In the opening pages of the first volume of *Five Centuries of Religion*[3] Coulton says:

> The religious orders have been among the main forces of European civilization; at certain times and in certain places they may perhaps have been the greatest of all civilizing forces. Yet every government in Europe gradually followed Henry VIII's example, and herein the State seems to express the mind of the individual, since adult vocations to the cloister are now extremely rare, among men at least . . .
>
> Even in the Middle Ages, Religious must sometimes have doubted not only of final perseverance (as they constantly confess) but also, to some extent, even of wisdom in their choice. They must have asked not only: 'Need I give up so much?' but even: 'Is it right to look upon the abandonment of some of these things as a sacrifice to God?'
>
> The root problem of monasticism is one which every ideal has to face. . . . Can we best serve our higher aim by crystallizing it into a society within Society, and so cutting ourselves off from the contagion of the unideal multitude? Or is it a braver and more effectual choice to keep in full touch with the rest, . . . hoping gradually to leaven the world by constant intercourse?

Coulton's attitude is a little simplistic; half an hour's quiet conversation with his fellow historian and elusive opponent Cardinal Gasquet (a monk of Downside) might have helped him to understand some things better; but his knowledge of monastic history was massive, and the questions that he asks are important. But we can hardly hope to be able to answer them unless we are agreed on the fundamental purpose of monastic life, bearing in mind, however, that the external forms in which it is embodied are capable both of diversity and development. The monks of the Middle Ages lived a life very different from that of the fourth-century Fathers of the Desert; and a medieval religious would be greatly astonished by certain aspects of monastic life in the twentieth century.

It is generally understood that the monk and nun lead a life somewhat apart from, or marginal to, that of society, and that this life is in some special kind of way dedicated to the service of God. But most people seem not very clear as to what this implies. If they view monks and nuns favourably it is usually on account of their visible achievements: for their work as scholars, educators, builders, agriculturists, and so on; perhaps also for the solemnity and splendour of their public worship. These reasons for esteem, though valid in their due degree, are really beside the point; for they have no direct connection with the fundamental purpose of monastic life.

For a short, sound exposition of the meaning of monasticism we cannot do better than to consult *Sancta Sophia*, or *Holy Wisdom*, the classic work of the seventeenth-century English Benedictine, Augustine Baker. In section three of the First Treatise in his book[4] Father Baker says:

What is it, therefore, that a soul truly called by God to enter into religion [i.e., the 'religious' or monastic life] looks for? Surely not corporal labours; nor the use of the sacraments; nor hearing of sermons, &c. For all these she might have enjoyed more plentifully in the world. It is, therefore, only the union of the spirit with God by recollected, constant prayer; to the attaining which divine end all things practised in religion do dispose, and to which alone so great impediments are found in the world.

The best general proof, therefore, of a good call to religion is a love to prayer . . .

It is a state, therefore, of recollectedness and introversion that everyone entering into religion is to aspire unto, which consists in an habitual disposition of soul, whereby she transcends all creatures and their images, which thereby come to have little or no dominion over her, so that she remains apt for immediate co-operation with God, receiving His inspirations, and by a return, and, as it were, a reflux, tending to Him, and operating to His glory.

A little further on Father Baker says:

. . . by the Rule of our holy Father St Benedict, all his disciples are obliged to propose to themselves no other end of their religious profession but only such purity of soul and the operations of it in spiritual prayer; so that how exact so ever they be in outward observances, unless they be referred unto, and efficacious also for the producing of, this internal purity, they shall not be esteemed by God to have complied with their vocation and profession.

This doctrine Baker supports with two quotations from the fourth to fifth century monk John Cassian: (a) 'The end of a monastical profession and the supreme degree of all perfection consists in the perfection of prayer'; (b) 'This is the end of all perfection, that the mind becomes so purified from all carnal defilement that it may be raised up daily to spiritual things, till its whole enjoyment and every motion of the heart may become one uninterrupted prayer.'

This doctrine is the common tradition of monks and nuns of both the Eastern and Western churches. It is the authentic

tradition of the orders of friars and canons regular, no less than of
the monastic order in the more exclusive sense of that term. The
domestic life of the canon regular and the friar is basically a life of
monastic observance. And it is significant that St Dominic always
carried with him on the journeys that took him half over Europe a
copy of Cassian's *Collationes* (or spiritual instructions).

Monastic life, then, within its framework of common life and
regular observance, is a life directed specifically towards seeking
union with God through intensive prayer. In the Holy Rule St
Benedict speaks of the monastery as 'a school of the Lord's
service', and directs that those who seek to enter are to be carefully scrutinised and tested in order that it may be seen whether
or no they are 'truly seeking God' and are fervent in prayer.

In other words, the monastic life is essentially a *contemplative*
life.

This is exactly the teaching of the earliest known Carmelite
writing, a late thirteenth century work known as *The Book of the
First Monks,* which summarises the traditions of the hermits on
Mount Carmel before their migration to Europe. The anonymous
writer says: 'This life has a twofold end. The first end we reach
with the help of grace by our own labour and our continual
striving towards virtue. It is: the offering to God of a pure and
clean heart, a heart free from every stain of sin. The second end is
realised by God's liberality: the possibility that even in this mortal
life we may experience already, in some degree, God's presence
and the joy of heaven.'

The Venerable John of St Samson, a sixteenth-century
Carmelite laybrother, 'the blind mystic of Rennes',[5] expounds the
same doctrine when he says that 'He who strives towards this
contemplation with all his bodily and psychic powers, and so lives
according to his vocation, as far as it is possible, is in some sense
holy enough. And if he does not get very far into this extensive
region, let him do what he can.'

At this point a possible misunderstanding needs to be removed.
From what has been said so far it might seem that the monk's is a
self-centred life. But this is not so. He lives in a community
precisely in order that he may avoid the dangers of an extreme
individualism; and he undertakes his work of self-reformation in
the hope that he may become progressively less self-centred, and

more and more God-centred. The God-centred man or woman sees all other beings somewhat as God sees them, that is, with an intensive love and sympathy. The monk's life is a life for others, in spite of its being lived somewhat apart; as it is even within his own community, where there will be times and places of silence, and where his cell is supposed to be—or at least was until recently—a kind of spiritual fortress, free from invasion. (Recent tendencies in not a few religious houses to abolish times and places for strict silence, to substitute conversation for public reading during meals, to allow the use of lay dress at official community gatherings, and to permit good and harmless monastic customs to fall into desuetude, are greatly to be deplored. Such concessions to the spirit of the age necessarily lower the tone of any religious house; under such conditions the salt quickly loses its savour.)

In the end the monk will be judged on the extent to which he has become a man of prayer, a man of God; not on his degree of success or otherwise as a preacher, scholar, writer, artist, teacher, or administrator.

The monk should be living in the presence of God all the time; but he cannot actually be at prayer all the time. There is work that must be done; the monastery is supposed to be self-supporting as far as possible. He must earn his keep as far as he can. So it is important to know what kinds of work are suitable for monks, and what kinds are not.

St Benedict says in his Rule (ch. xlviii) that 'Idleness is an enemy to the soul; and hence at certain times the brethren ought to occupy themselves in the labour of their hands, and at other times in holy reading . . . And if the needs of the place, or their poverty, oblige them to labour themselves at gathering in the crops, let them not be saddened thereat; because then they are truly monks when they live by the labour of their hands, as did our fathers and the Apostles.' St Albert of Vercelli, who in his Rule for the hermits on Mount Carmel directs that they shall remain in or near their dwellings, meditating on the law of the Lord, unless other just occasions prevent them, devotes a whole chapter to 'Assiduity in Work, for the Avoidance of Idleness'.

From the first, manual labour held an important place in the life of the monks of the West. Some of their time was taken up, as

St Benedict directed, by the *opus Dei*, the daily round of common prayer. At first the chanting of the psalms, hymns, and lessons of the divine office was a relatively short and simple matter; but long before the end of the Middle Ages it had developed into a cycle of lengthy and elaborate church services which took up several hours of the day, so that manual labour began to be left to unordained brethren. For by that time most of the monks were in holy orders.

The monastic life had gradually become clericalised, and for priest-monks literary and scholarly pursuits had largely replaced manual labour. This reorientation of monastic life was largely due to the indirect influence of the canons regular, both the monastic and the canonical orders exercising a strong influence on each other.

In chapter lxii of the Holy Rule, 'Of the Priests in the Monastery', St Benedict says: 'If any Abbot desire to have a priest or deacon ordained for his monastery, let him choose from among his monks one who is worthy to fulfil the priestly office.' And he warns such priests not to 'become forgetful of the obedience and discipline of the Rule', but to 'advance ever more and more in godliness', keeping always to the place due to them, and not claiming any precedence because of their priesthood.

The early monks were nearly all laymen; the canons regular, by contrast, were a specifically clerical body. About the year 360 St Eusebius, bishop of Vercelli, had formed the clergy of his cathedral church into a college or community leading a common life, with profession of celibacy and obedience, in accordance with a Rule drawn up by himself as superior. This canonical way of life, so called from the Greek word *kanon*, meaning a rule, was regarded as in some way related to the common life of the first Christians in Jerusalem. (Cf. *The Acts of the Apostles*, ch. 4, verses 32-35.) Eventually other bodies of clergy besides those attached to cathedrals began to live according to this pattern, and from them eventually developed the various houses and congregations of canons regular.

Following the example of Eusebius and others, St Augustine of Hippo organised his cathedral clergy in this way. Eventually the so-called Rule of St Augustine, a conflation of two letters written for the guidance of a community of women presided over by his sister, superseded the Rules written by Eusebius of Vercelli, Chrodegang of Metz, and others, and those who followed it became known as Canons Regular of St Augustine, or Austin Canons.

The canon regular is always either a priest or a candidate for the priesthood. In his abbey or priory he leads a full monastic life, with which he combines the carrying out of the daily church services with as much solemnity as possible. He is also expected, if so required, to undertake the cure of souls. Most canon regular houses have a number of dependent parishes, sometimes at a considerable distance from the abbey or priory. Thus the small abbey of St Mary and St Petroc at Bodmin, in Cornwall, today supplies the resident parish priests in Bude, Newquay, St Ives, St Austell, and Truro. Also dependent on Bodmin Abbey is the parish of St Edward, King and Martyr, in Swanage, Dorset. If monks find themselves committed to similar activities it is because of special, and temporarily unavoidable circumstances; the cure of souls is no essential part of their vocation.

As we have said, in the course of the centuries the monastic and canonical orders were much influenced by each other. Thus the canons, previously governed in their larger houses by provosts, took over from the monks the office of abbot; and the monks turned their abbots, originally laymen, into prelates lacking little of the outward dignity of bishops. By the end of the Middle Ages nearly all monks were priests, except for novices and students, and so uneducated 'lay brothers' were introduced to take care of the manual work. Conversely, certain houses of canons, such as those of the Windesheim congregation, in the Low Countries—to which Thomas à Kempis belonged—gave up the cure of souls and lived lives of almost Carthusian enclosure and seclusion.

Manual work having been more or less abandoned among the Black monks, it was to a large extent replaced by literary and scholarly pursuits, and by teaching. This was held to be justified, in part, by St Benedict's directions about *lectio divina,* although he clearly envisaged a balanced régime of prayer, manual work, and study. On health grounds alone this was desirable; and in fact the discipline of manual labour has never quite disappeared even from the more sophisticated kind of Benedictine house. David

Knowles recalls in his memoir of Abbot Cuthbert Butler[6] that during part of the time that he was Abbot of Downside Dom Butler was 'in the habit of digging in the garden for an hour or so on two or three days in the week; the spectacle was then to be seen of the abbot president of the English Benedictine Congregation, who was also a scholar of European reputation, issuing from the door of his abbey carrying a spade over his shoulder, rifle fashion, and wearing mud-encrusted boots, ancient trousers and tail coat green with age, with a shapeless green cap on his head, worn back to front.' 'It says much', Knowles continues, 'for the mental power and distinction that was present in every line of Abbot Butler's countenance that even when so clad he would never have passed for an ordinary man.'

In Dr Knowles's opinion it was precisely the lack of satisfying occupation that was one of the greatest difficulties in the monasteries of the late fifteenth century. Agriculture and the manual crafts had come to be considered unsuitable occupations for priests, so that the copying and illuminating of books became the usual employment for priest-monks. But by the middle of the thirteenth century the religious no longer had a virtual monopoly of these clerkly skills, and had to face outside competition. By the end of the fifteenth century these occupations had become 'fossilised and artificial', and no longer gave their practitioners a sense of creative achievement. In any case, by that time the invention of printing had arrived to supplant them.

In some places, as with the great Benedictine Maurist congregation in France, works of pure scholarship became the typical monastic activity. Something of this tradition is still to be found in some English houses of Black monks, notably at Downside, Ampleforth, and Nashdom (the latter being in communion with the see of Canterbury); and for a time it was so at Quarr Abbey, in the Isle of Wight, and at Farnborough Abbey, in Hampshire, during the years when Quarr and Farnborough housed communities of refugee monks from Solesmes, in France. But since the revival of the Venerable English Congregation of the Black monks, its more typical activities have been teaching and parish work; though the latter seems now to be being scaled down. St Benedict expected that there would be some boys in the monastery, who would become future monks. These boys were educated in the monastery, so that teaching has a long and admired history as an occupation for monks. But whether it can be held to justify the ownership and management of large fee-paying public schools, with five or six hundred boys, and a lay staff to help the monks, is another question; though certainly not a few present-day monks seem to find satisfaction in it.

However, it seems unlikely that this kind of school can survive much longer. Economics alone will probably kill them off; and if that fails to do so, the next drab and envious 'socialist' government will probably put paid to them, in the supposed interests of 'democracy'. In any case, the falling-off in monastic recruitment, even if it manages to stabilise at some modest level, will probably make the maintenance of such large-scale institutions impossible before long.

Quite apart from the confusion introduced into the church at every level by the aftermath of the second Vatican Council, a partial explanation of the continuing exodus from religious orders, and their failure in recruitment, may be the fact that these institutions, like their medieval predecessors, are no longer able to offer their members satisfying occupations. (Generally speaking, except in certain rather exceptional houses of monks and friars, learning is no longer much cultivated, and even Cistercians today seem to spend less time in agricultural pursuits.) Training as scoutmasters, youth workers, sociologists, psychoanalysts, social workers, leaders in group dynamics, and so on, as is now becoming fashionable, will be of no help to young monks and friars in their *monastic* life. It may keep them happy for a time, while they are young and able to be a good deal out of the monastery; but eventually, as they get older, they will begin to realise that none of this has anything directly to do with being a monk.

In many religious houses now there is not even an adequate liturgy to support the contemplative life. In the past, the monk, canon, or friar, whatever the trials and difficulties of his life might be, had always the support of the choir. The daily singing of the familiar sacred texts to the familiar ancient plainsong was a constant source of spiritual inspiration and strength which raised his soul to higher things and brought him near to God. Now the liturgy of the Latin Church, which has been in a sense the

backbone of monastic life for at least fifteen hundred years, has
been summarily thrown out, and all that is offered in its stead is a
sorry mess of pottage, a mish-mash of sub-'Basic English' texts,
to be sung, if at all, to the wan melodies of Gelineau and the
insipidities of composers of so-called 'People's Masses'.

Similarly, a high proportion of the venerable customs and
observances which over the centuries had given tone and civility
to claustral life have been jettisoned. It is an old saying that the
vita communis, if the standard of observance is allowed to fall,
quickly degenerates into the *vita vulgaris*.

A prime example, in many religious houses, is the abolition of
reading at meals in favour of conversation. In the Dominican
Order there was always silence in the refectory, apart from the
reading: only the Master-General or a visiting bishop could
dispense from it. With the Carmelites, and many other orders,
silence in the refectory was the general rule, though the Prior
could permit conversation, after a short opening reading from
Scripture, on Sundays and festivals; but his power to do so was
supposed to be exercised sparingly. Anyone whose monastic life
has been passed mostly under the old régime will know how
much he has benefited, over the years, from the many books that
he has heard read in the refectory; by no means all of them works
of 'edification' (saints' lives and the like). Works of church history
and secular as well as religious biography were commonly read in
the refectories of religious houses; and even the occasional work
of fiction. This was an easy, almost painless way of adding to the
sum of one's knowledge, and gaining an appreciation of good
writing, and of turning the callow novice, eventually, into a
clergyman of some modest cultivation. The reading was done,
normally, by novices or students. In a large refectory they had to
speak up if they were to be heard above the unavoidable clatter of
the serving of dishes; and if they were *not* heard they were soon
made aware of it by the prior or subprior. Mispronunciations
were publicly corrected, and the passage read again. Splendid
training for the pulpit. But now even the pulpit is abandoned, in
favour of a microphone on the altar or reading-desk. Even so, the
modern preacher is mostly inaudible; which is just as well, for he
rarely has anything sensible to say, and in any case is frightened
to speak for more than five, at most ten, minutes. (The Roman

Catholic churches of London whose Sunday services are announced in the previous day's *Times* no longer bother to list their preachers; in fact there are none. The sermon has been replaced by something called the homily; too often five minutes of utter banality.)

It is, of course, quite true that over the centuries monastic life had become cluttered up with a whole lumber of outworn and irrelevant practices and conventions, and it was altogether reasonable to put these aside; but to lay rude hands on the most venerable usages just because they are old, and, in the view of philistine reformers, not 'with it', is the way not to repair the crumbling structures of monastic life, but to bring them down in ruins.

One of the justifications for the existence of monasteries and convents must surely be that they house communities in which the Christian life is lived intensively, by men and women wholly dedicated to the service of God and their fellow-men. 'Service' and 'Community' are ideas that have great appeal to the young today; but generally speaking they find them more effectively realisable elsewhere than in the Church's religious orders.

In many religious houses today community life is more like life in a fairly cosy bachelors' club than it is to the common life of the early Christians, who had one heart and one mind in God. But this is nothing new. It was Dr Coulton's judgement, based on his extensive knowledge of history, just as it was Professor Knowles's opinion, also based on history, but confirmed in his case by actual experience of contemporary monastic life, that the life of the medieval monasteries, for all its many saints and its great achievements, fell very far short of an adequate realisation of the monastic ideal. The Orders had too much wealth, too many members, and too many houses. Many monks and nuns had taken up the life as a respectable occupation, and with too little concern for the things of the spirit. Abbots and priors were often immersed in secular offices and ranked as feudal lords. If the religious were idle—and by no means all of them were—it was because there was nothing of interest for them to do; hence their frequent recourse to hunting and hawking. The obligations of the common life were widely evaded—especially among the friars—on one pretext or another, largely by means of privileged exemptions. The whole system was worn out—partly because of the fatal effects on it of the monastic depopulation caused by the Black Death—long before Henry VIII put an end to it for his own far from disinterested reasons.

How, then, do things stand today, one hundred and eighty five years after the beginning of the monastic revival in England in 1796, when French Cistercian monks, exiles from the Revolution, founded St Susan's monastery at Lulworth?

Even today a few Orders seem to have too many members for spiritual health; many have an excess of external commitments—schools, parishes, etc.—which have often been assumed in order to win the favour of local bishops. This has led in some instances to a lowering of the standards of recruitment in a desperate attempt to keep the numbers up. And there are too many men in the Orders who have entered as an easy way to the priesthood rather than out of any real understanding of, and devotion to, the monastic state. Superiors today are not likely to be engaged in secular employments—at court or elsewhere—but they are sometimes unduly attached to office. In Orders where the superiors are not all elected, but are appointed by some kind of governing body, a kind of 'old boys' network' sees to it that when their terms of office expire they are simply translated to new positions of authority elsewhere: a process which is liable to continue until old age sets in, or even beyond.

The common life is reasonably well kept; but the notion that the religious lead a life of 'holy poverty', except in an academic sense of the term, is somewhat chimeric. It is doubtful if any religious order in England today could be described as wealthy; some are even in debt. But Chaucer and Langland would recognise in some modern superiors the old unhealthy interest in legacies and benefactions which they satirised. All *ad majorem Dei gloriam*, no doubt; but open to misinterpretation.

Where renewal and adaptation are concerned—and the need for a proper and reasonable *adjournment* is undeniable—the monks have a considerable advantage over the friars, and over most canons regular. Within a loose federation, for purposes of mutual aid, each house of monks is an autonomous unit, or at least may hope to become so eventually. Within the wide limits of the Rule each community is free to determine its own way of life and its own kinds of work and apostolic activity. Friars have no such freedom; or, at best, very little. All the houses in each province of the order are subject to a common higher superior, the Provincial Prior or Minister, and his council. The provinces are dependent on the General of the Order, in Rome, and *his* council. Consequently, every major alteration and improvement in the way of life has to be fought for over long years before it can take effect. The outlook for such unwieldy and highly centralised bodies as the orders of friars is not hopeful. The canons regular are mostly in the same plight. With a few exceptions, their houses are now grouped into congregations, each of which has an Abbot General—a being of whom both St Benedict and St Augustine would have been much astonished to hear—in Rome or elsewhere.

Also, an autonomous house of monks will choose and test its recruits with great care, and as they will, if accepted, belong to that community for life there is a good prospect of a strong community spirit being built up and continued, with a definite *esprit de corps*. But the community in a friary is continually changing, the men being moved from one house to another at not infrequent intervals, there usually being a whole crop of such changes after each six-yearly provincial chapter. This lack of continuity in personnel makes it much more difficult to create a real spirit of fraternity. Voltaire is supposed to have said that religious 'are people who come together without knowing each other, live together without loving each other, and die without regretting each other.' Things are rarely as bad as that; but the fact is, while a religious ought, if he is living his life properly, to experience a good deal of solitude, his existence ought not to be one of *loneliness*; and it is to be feared that the life of a good number of religious in their communities is fundamentally a lonely life, and that this loneliness has in the past accounted for many defections: as it still does today.

A report issued in May 1969 by the Carmelite friars of the Province of Rio de Janeiro says that it was agreed by those taking part that the main reason why so many religious do not arrive at a fully human development as persons must be attributed to the fact that in their training the centre of gravity was that of chastity rather than love. It was candidly admitted that some members of the Province had given up and left, without at the time having any intention of marrying. But often a woman came along and filled the already existing emptiness, with marriage as the natural result. It is good to find Carmelites discussing the crisis of their Order with such candour and discernment; the spirit behind such discussions affords hope for the future.

All religious orders in the Western Church—except for purely local foundations (diocesan institutes)—are now directly subject to the authority of the Holy See: that is to the Sacred Congregation for Religious, at the Vatican. There seems to be no real reason, except for historical causes, why this should be so; any more than there is for the Holy See's claim to the right of appointment of all bishops in the Western Church, a claim that has only been universally admitted within the last hundred years. However, in 1968 the Holy See issued an *Instruction on Renewal of Religious Formation* which sought to open up a way of renewal by means of certain ideas which were put forward on an experimental basis since 'it is evident that no clear and definite legislation can be formulated except on the basis of experiments carried out on a sufficiently large scale and over a sufficiently long period of time.' The principal point made in the *Instruction*, a wholly sound one, was that much greater attention should be paid to the stages in religious life previous to the taking of final vows. The age of admission to novitiates should be raised, and there must be a preliminary period of testing and formation, lasting up to two years, before candidates are admitted as novices. Except in purely contemplative orders the novitiate is no longer to be a period of absolute seclusion from normal contact with the world. Instead, there is to be 'a proper balance of periods set aside for solitude with God, and others devoted to various activities and to the human contacts which these involve'.

These instructions have been fairly generally followed, and the raising of the age of entry and the extra period of preliminary testing have been found beneficial. The abolition of the year's novitiate as a period of seclusion, except in the case of purely contemplative orders, is more questionable. But what is meant by 'purely contemplative orders'? Presumably the semi-eremitical orders, such as Carthusians and Camaldolese, Cistercian monks, certain strict observance Benedictines, and, among women, cloistered nuns such as Benedictines, Cistercians, Carthusians, Second Order Dominicans, Carmelites, and Poor Clares. But why are the masculine orders of 'mixed' life; i.e. those who to a contemplative life in their monasteries subjoin a certain active apostolate, to be equiparated with post-medieval congregations of active life, whose spirit is totally different: Jesuits, Passionists, Redemptorists, etc.? The mission of the Dominicans (Blackfriars) is 'to give to others the fruits of contemplation', and until recently the Constitutions of the Carmelite Order (Whitefriars) have affirmed specifically that the Carmelite vocation is twofold: to the contemplative life, overflowing into a modest pastoral activity. And of these two elements the contemplative has always been affirmed by the Constitutions to be the *pars principalior*. The new Constitutions promulgated in 1971 affirm the same, although, unfortunately, in much less clear and telling language: a symptom, it would seem, of a dangerous tendency within the Order to make a life of almost frenzied activity the *pars principalior*. (This is sometimes caused by lack of sufficient men to cope with all the work that has to be done.)

The traditional doctrine is clear; but it seems unlikely that the end which it proposes can be reached by turning the quiet and seclusion of the traditional novitiate into something between a boy-scout camp and a summer school. The scheme can hardly succeed; perhaps in the end the old ways, in this particular context, will be seen to be best.

The temporary vows, binding for three years only, made at the end of the novitiate may now be replaced by some form of less stringent promise, made not to God but to the community. The *Instruction* of the Sacred Congregation recognises that 'a certain number of young candidates come to the end of their novitiate without having acquired the religious maturity sufficient to bind themselves immediately by religious vows, even temporarily.' The new promises can be dispensed from by the appropriate monastic authority, without recourse to the Holy See, which was required for release from the old temporary vows. These are wise provisions; but it is not likely that they will do much to arrest the general decline from which the religious orders are suffering, since, as with the priesthood, celibacy is no longer an ideal that has much attraction for the young.

The monastic way of life, as we have inherited it, comes down from a time when the idea that celibacy was a higher state than marriage was universally accepted in the Christian church. Behind this view, not to trace it back any further, lies the powerful influence of St Augustine, which still bears heavily on Catholic teaching about sex. His treatise *On Marriage and Concupiscence* teaches that every sexual act, even within marriage, contains an element of sin. 'Although', he affirms, 'conjugal copulation for the generation of offspring is not in itself a sin (because the good will of the mind controls the pleasure of the body instead of following pleasure's lead, and the human judgement is not subjected to sin), yet in the use of the generative act the wound of sin is justly present.' Anyone who believed this would naturally think that celibacy was a higher state than marriage. No one, I imagine, thinks in this way now, so that celibacy must be embraced, if it is, from quite different motives.

Present-day novices usually have the monastic ideal of celibacy presented to them as part of the *sacrificial* aspect of the life, with emphasis on the monk's free surrender to God, from a super-natural motive, of one of the best of God's gifts: the possibility of marriage and family life. This is a sound approach; but it does not carry quite the conviction that it might, since, however attractive an idea in itself, it is part of a general ascetical ethos which is today not widely understood.

There is no need to stress here the difficulty of the celibate ideal, which in itself is a noble one. But it is hardly a vocation to be suggested to the average man; and religious orders are full of average men and women, so that the number of failed, or seemingly failed, vocations is not surprising. (But even so, what is average by nature can be raised to above average by grace.)

From this point of view the decline in the number of vocations to the religious life is to be welcomed. Nothing could be more misguided than the feverish efforts now being made by many religious orders and congregations to drum up recruits by means of advertisements in newspapers,—even in papers like *Private Eye* and *Time Magazine*—talks to children in Catholic schools (a captive audience indeed), 'Vocations Exhibitions', holiday camps, retreats conducted according to the latest secular psychological methods—some of which come very near to brain-washing—etc.

But to say this, and it requires to be said, is not to deny that even very young children may not sometimes be conscious of a call to the religious life or the priesthood. One thinks of outstanding religious such as Father Bede Jarrett and Father Vincent McNabb whose vocations developed very early. With the average age of entry now nearer twenty-five than the previous sixteen or seventeen, many potential vocations of this calibre seem likely to be lost. On the other hand, we shall perhaps be spared histories like that of Joseph McCabe, author of that entertaining yet sad book *Twelve Years in a Monastery*, who when little more than a child was more or less pushed into the Franciscan Order by his mother.

The complaint that it is the practice of the friars to attract into their orders boys who are far too young to know their own minds is a very old one.[7] It forms part of the indictment levelled against the friars, especially the Franciscans, by Richard FitzRalph, archbishop of Armagh, in a sermon on the text 'Judge not according to the appearance, but judge righteous judgements', preached at a papal consistory at Avignon on 8th November, 1357. St John Capistran was once heard to say, when discussing with Pope Eugenius IV the affairs of the Observant Franciscans: 'If you should wish, Holy Father, to carry out a proper reform of our Order, there are three P's that you must get rid of.' The three P's were *Pecunia*, *Pueri*, and *Petulantia*; that is, money, young boys, and irresponsibility in office-holders. The saint's advice is not entirely irrelevant today.

Another disturbing factor in the lives of many present-day religious is the question of holy poverty. Religious make public profession, which they confirm by vow, of following Christ in his life of poverty. Yet all too often there is nothing noticeably poor about the way we live. True, we have no individual possessions, and our earnings, of one kind and another, all go into the common fund. But we do not seem to lack for much. We have a roof over our head, a room of our own, possibly three good meals a day, and no worries about what will become of us in old age. Of course, it is possible for the individual religious to lead an effectively poor life. Father Vincent McNabb must have saved his Order considerable sums of money by his practice of walking everywhere in London, where he lived, and not using public transport; also by writing his letters on the back of printer's proofs or on the inside of the dust-jackets of books; and by re-using the envelopes of letters that he had received. And since he always wore his religious habit, he never had to have a suit of clothes made; and as his habits were made of handwoven cloth they lasted three or four times longer than ordinary ones.

The religious who is prepared to go to such lengths, and to cut out altogether the use of tobacco and alcohol, shows a certain heroism; but perhaps he does not really accomplish so very much as he is still living off a system which professes poverty but in practice negates it.

This indeed is nothing new. The medieval monk lived an incredibly austere life by modern standards; yet even so, he was better off materially than most of the people outside his monastery. The problem is perennial, and perhaps insoluble within the inherited monastic structures. The days of the large monastery may be nearly over. The new phenomenon of friars, Franciscans mainly, forming small communities, or fraternities, of from three to six men, living and working among the poor in ordinary working-class accommodation, may be the beginning of a reorientation. Among the Carmelites a growing enthusiasm for work in and for the Third World is another good sign.

The fact is, the monastic revival of the last one hundred and fifty or so years got off to a wrong start. All over Europe the Orders that had survived the Reformation upheavals were virtually swept away in the aftermath of the French Revolution. When the time came, the small bands of survivors had a wonderful opportunity to make a new beginning. But no one seemed to realise that the world had changed, and that the 'feudal' pattern of religious life was not relevant to the new conditions. Far from that, the medieval monastery was regarded as the classic, all-time example to be followed; and so, thanks largely to Dom Guéranger, who entertained a highly romantic notion of monastic life in the Middle Ages, Solesmes arose somewhat on the pattern of Cluny, and the liturgical worship of the monks took on a medieval splendour. Liturgy became a spectacle, and monasteries centres of tourism. This pattern still survives, but under increasing strain. Presumably it is nearing its end. It seems certain that never again will monasticism occupy the dominant position in society which it had in the Middle Ages. That we need not regret. The fact of the matter is, the religious orders were already finished long before the Revolution; when the time came for the revival, they were revived on partly mistaken lines.

The romantic, Wagnerian notion of the religious life was stimulated by the cult of the crack-pot, who seems to be almost the typical figure in the Church at times of general indifference to religion, just as the martyr is the typical figure in times of hostility and persecution, and the confessor in times when the Church is approved by Society. The personality-cult of eccentric near-geniuses has flourished in the religious world during the past century or so; one has only to think of such spellbinding figures as the Reverend Joseph Leycester Lyne (Father Ignatius) at Llanthony, Abbot Aelred Carlyle at Caldey, Father Hope-Patten at Walsingham, and Father Malachy Lynch at Aylesford. These men, and others like them, in order to fulfil their need for self-realisation and for the fulfilment of their dreams, propagated a romantic, visionary, and folk-loric brand of religion and of monasticism that had immense appeal and brought in the funds needed for the realisation of their grandiose projects. These men were absolutely sincere, and had real piety; unfortunately, they tended to leave behind them a collection of white elephants and financial embarrassments. In their fantastic efforts to restore the monastic life they were in fact assuring its rapid decay.

Yet, for all its shortcomings, there is a great deal that is admirable about the life that is lived in the monasteries today. The brethren are faithful to their duties, and live together surprisingly harmoniously considering their different origins and temperaments. Sick and aged brethren are carefully looked after; the occasional erring brother who has 'gone off the rails' in one way or another is treated with understanding and indulgence. The religious are sincere, hard-working men; but with the contemplative element in their vocation falling into increasing disesteem, and with the lack of anything really creative to replace it, it is not surprising that many of them are now asking themselves exactly where the 'relevance' of their life is to be found. Few of them with any length of claustral experience can fail to recognise the truth, and applicability to themselves personally, of the words in which Professor Knowles summed up the story of the pre-Reformation religious orders in England.

At the end of this long review of monastic history [he says] a monk
cannot but ask what message for himself and for his brethren the long
story may carry. It is the old and simple one; only in fidelity to the Rule
can a monk or a monastery find security. A Rule, given by a founder
with an acknowledged fullness of spiritual wisdom, approved by the
Church and tested by the experience of saints, is a safe path, and it is for
the religious the only safe path . . . When once a religious house or a
religious order ceases to direct its sons to the abandonment of all that is
not God, and ceases to show them the rigours of the narrow way that
leads to the imitation of Christ in his love, it sinks to the level of a purely
human institution, and whatever its works may be, they are the works of
time and not of eternity.[8]

'It sinks to the level of a purely human institution . . .' This is
the ever-present threat to monasticism. If monasteries cease to be
true schools of the Lord's service, where eternal wisdom is both
taught and learned, this is what must happen.

It is not likely that the monastic life will disappear. There will
always be men and women drawn to a community life of
contemplative service, whose generous dispositions find their
fulfilment under the discipline of the vows. The pattern of life
sketched out by the great legislators, St Benedict, St Augustine,
St Francis, and St Albert in their Rules has an appropriate
timelessness, and will always attract followers. Monasteries will
always be needed. Those of the future will probably be fewer than
in the past, smaller, and—with the necessary safeguards to ensure
their contemplative basis—more open to the world that
surrounds them. Their quiet sapiential presence is more
necessary than ever in the cold, impersonal climate of the world
of technology. As technology advances, man's thirst for 'wisdom'
seems to become stronger, springing as it does from the human
desire for the direct intuition of reality, the *simplex intuitus
veritatis*. This is the wisdom, or gnosis, that all the major
religious traditions of mankind seek to impart; and where will it
be found if not in the monasteries, whether of men or women, or
those 'double' monasteries, of the Gilbertine and Brigittine
traditions that now seem to be reviving?

NOTES

1. The principal orders of monks are the Benedictines (Black Monks), Cistercians (White Monks), Carthusians, and Camaldolese.

    In common parlance canons regular and friars are often spoken of as 'monks', but this usage is inaccurate. Since the monastic element in the life of canons and friars is so important, and since their 'spirituality' is almost identical with that of the monks, any general discussion of monasticism will include friars and canons within its terms of reference.

2. *Religious*: a handy contraction of the technical term 'religious person'; meaning men and women in general who live a community life under vows, in a form approved by the church.

3. Cambridge, 1923.

4. *Sancta Sophia. Or Directions for the Prayer of Contemplation &c. Extracted out of more than XL Treatises written by the late Ven. Father F. Augustine Baker . . . and Methodically digested by the R. F. Serenus Cressy, Of the Same Order and Congregation*. Douai, 1657.

    The quotations here given are from the edition edited by Abbot Norbert Sweeney: London, 1876; pp. 151 ff. The latest edition is that of Dom Gerard Sitwell: London 1964.

5. For John of St Samson *see* Suzanne-Marie Bouchereaux, *La Réforme des Carmes en France et Jean de Saint-Samson*: Paris, 1950.

6. Reprinted in David Knowles, *The Historian and Character*: Cambridge, 1963.

7. Cf. *passim*, John Moorman, *A History of the Franciscan Order from its Origins to the year 1517*: Oxford, 1968.

8. David Knowles, *The Religious Orders in England*, vol. iv, p. 462.

CATHOLIC SPIRITUALITY,
ANGLICAN AND ROMAN

THE WORD 'CATHOLIC' in common usage has more than one connotation. In the present context I use it in the sense given to it by E. G. Selwyn in his Preface to the third edition, 1929, of a once-famous book, *Essays Catholic and Critical*. The Preface says: 'By Catholicism we mean . . . a presentation of Christian thought, worship, and life to which no church—Anglican, Roman, or Eastern—has any exclusive title; and yet which does permeate all those bodies with a thoroughness and tenacity sufficiently marked to distinguish them from all those bodies which call themselves, and are known to history as, Protestant.' To go a little further, we can perhaps agree with Baron von Hügel that it is a characteristic of Catholicism that it 'gives to the institutional element in Christianity a place not less fundamental than that given to its mystical and intellectual elements.'

The word 'spirituality' originally meant the clergy; as in the estates of the realm: the Spirituality, the Nobility, and the Commons. But here I use it, in its more usual sense, as meaning 'a man's personal and communal commerce with God through Christ, as it is created and developed by the Holy Spirit and as it leads him to seek and do God's will'.[1]

The Anglican repudiation of papal authority in the 16th century did not mean the breaking of *all* links with the historic Western or Latin church. Nor did the Act of Supremacy of 1559 and the Acts of Uniformity of 1559 and 1662 destroy all continuity of the Church of England by law established with the medieval *Ecclesia Anglicana*. As the Gothic Revival architect Augustus Welby Pugin, himself a convert from Canterbury to Rome, put it in 1851: 'It is impossible to peruse certain Anglican writings [on Catholic antiquities] and, indeed, many of the most celebrated of the old authors of the English church, without being impressed by the fact that they never considered themselves as a newly created body detached from the ancient church, but as a

217

strictly continuous succession of the ancient men, deprived of much of the ancient dignity of religion, differing in discipline, and hampered by the state articles,[2] but still the representatives of the old system.'[3]

Roman Catholic spirituality and Anglican spirituality are both rooted in the Bible and the Liturgy. The ancient liturgical offices, as set out in the missal and the breviary, consisted largely of passages taken from the sacred scriptures; this pattern was preserved, and even extended, in the Book of Common Prayer. In the days of the old Latin service books it was natural that liturgical prayer should remain to some extent the special province of the clergy; but in course of time vernacular prayer books, Primers and Manuals, came to be provided for the use of the laity. The *Book of Common Prayer* was intended as a book of liturgical prayer that could be used by both clergy and laity.

From early times the writings of the Church Fathers had been held in high regard and used for both devotional and theological purposes, and this tradition also was continued in the post-Reformation Church of England. Behind this long tradition there stand, in particular, St Augustine of Hippo and St Benedict of Nursia, the two Fathers whose thought, more than any others', has influenced the spirituality of the Western Church.

In his writings Augustine lays great stress on the doctrine of original sin; the belief that the natural man is 'very far gone from original righteousness'. The sacrament of Baptism destroys this state of alienation from God, but it does not of itself destroy man's innate weakness and proneness to evil-doing. Man has to combat this through self-discipline (asceticism) undertaken in response to God's love, and through the grace won by Christ's passion and death and mediated to us by the sacraments of the eucharist and of penance. In St Augustine's thought our Christian life is built up and sustained by the eucharist, the divine office (public liturgical prayer), and private devotion, which constitute the three basic elements of a sound spirituality.

The way of life which St Benedict charted for his monks in the Holy Rule is based on this same triple scheme: Mass, divine office (the *opus Dei*, or work of God), and private prayer. This 'Benedictine' plan of the *opus Dei*—that is, Benedict's disposition of the liturgical 'Hours' throughout the day and night—provided

the basis for the arrangement of the service books known later as
breviaries, and is the remote origin of the Prayer Book arrangement for the recitation of the psalter.

Augustine's thought strongly influenced St Anselm and other
Benedictines; and, of course, those spiritual writers who were
Augustinian Canons; notably the Victorines—twelfth century
spiritual writers of the abbey of St Victor, in Paris—and in
England the Austin canon Walter Hilton, author of *The Scale of
Perfection*. The thought of St Augustine can also be traced in
other English mystical writers of the fourteenth century, such as
Richard Rolle, Dame Julian of Norwich, and the anonymous
author of *The Cloud of Unknowing*.

Thus the Bible, the Fathers of the Church (especially
Augustine and Benedict), the Liturgy, and the medieval English
mystical writers are the common heritage of both Anglicans and
Roman Catholics.

After the disturbances and changes of the times of Henry VIII,
Edward VI, and Queen Mary came the Elizabethan Settlement in
matters of religion. But the so-called Settlement settled nothing.
Puritans and Papists stood out against it, and England remains to
this day a religiously fragmented nation. The attempt to enforce
the settlement was harsh to the point of savagery, and those who
held by the old ways were soon reduced to a state of spiritual near-
destitution. Under these conditions it became imperative to
supply the oppressed English Catholics with suitable books of
devotion, to help them to maintain their spiritual life at a time
when access to the sacraments became more and more difficult
and hazardous. One of the first such books to be printed was *A
Catechisme, or a Christian Doctrine, necessarie for children and
ignorant people*. This little book was written by Laurence Vaux,
former headmaster of Manchester College, and an Augustinian
canon. It was printed and published at Antwerp in 1573. Vaux's
Catechism was based on Scripture, the General Councils of the
church, the Fathers, and Counter-Reformation writers such as
Peter de Soto and St Peter Canisius. Appended to the Catechism
is an account of a number of church ceremonies, followed by the
full text of the devotion known as the Jesus Psalter. This popular
devotion seems to have been composed in the time of Henry VIII
by Richard Whitford, a Brigittine monk of Syon Abbey, on the

Thames, near London. It was intended to supply the unlettered with a substitute for the Psalter. There are 150 psalms of David; the Jesus Psalter consists of 150 petitions, based on a ninefold invocation of the name of Jesus. Thus:

Certaine devout and Godly Petitions commonly called
IESVS PSALTER

'There is none other name under heaven given
unto men, in which we must be saved.' Act. 4.

The fyrst petition

Jesu. Jesu. Jesu. mercy
,,   ,,   ,,   ,,
,,   ,,   ,,   ,,

Jesu have mercy on me, and forgive me ye great offences which I have donne in the syght of thee.

Grant me grace, Jesu, for the love of thee, to despise synne and all worldly vanitie.

Have mercy on all synners, Jesu, I beseech thee: turn theyr vices into vertues, and make them true observers of thy law and lovers of thee, bring them to blisse in everlasting glory.

Have mercy also on the souls in Purgatory for thy bitter Passion, I beseche thee, and for thy glorious name Jesu.

The holy Trinitie, one very God, have mercie on me.
PÁTER   AVE

The Jesus Psalter derives from that devotion to the Holy Name of Jesus that is so characteristic of Richard Rolle and others of the earlier English mystical writers. It remained an extremely popular devotion among English Catholics until very recently. It was included in the official *Manual of Prayers* for use in churches right down to its last edition, of seventeen or so years ago, which was suppressed, for reasons that remain obscure, by the Roman Catholic bishops, and has not been reprinted since. A section or sections of the Jesus Psalter was commonly used as a Sunday evening devotion, before the service of Benediction of the Blessed Sacrament.

Another early recusant work of long-lasting popularity was *A Christian Directory*, or, more correctly, the first part of the never-completed directory, *The Book of Resolution*, written by the famous Jesuit Robert Persons.[4] The *Directory* demonstrates, in

an admirably clear, energetic prose, 'That there is a God', offers
evidences for the truth of Christianity, and discusses, 'Who is a
true Christian'. A Jesuit scholar of our own day, the late Father
Herbert Thurston, has said that 'Father Persons's *Resolution* was
the most popular book of devotion known to Englishmen not only
of that day, but almost down to the publication of Baxter's *Saints'
Everlasting Rest* and Jeremy Taylor's *Holy Dying*. Moreover,
there was no disguise about the authorship!'[5] In Persons's own
day, and much to his annoyance, an Anglican Puritan divine put
out an edition of the *Resolution*, with 'corrections' and excisions,
which went through many printings over the years. The last
edition, a Catholic one, was published in Dublin in 1820.

In its early days the Elizabethan Anglican church had
necessarily to look to 'Roman' sources for works of devotion.
Hooker, in his *Treatise on the Laws of Ecclesiastical Polity*
(1594) expressly says: 'Where Rome keepeth that which is
auncienter and better; others whom we much more affect leaving
it for newer and changing it for worse, we had rather follow the
perfections of them whom we like not, than in defects resemble
them whom we love' (*Laws*, v, 28.)

In 1611 the Authorized Version of the Bible was published, by
authority of King James I: a capital event in the history of English
spirituality. In many of their renderings the translators owed a
considerable debt—which they chose not to acknowledge—to the
scholarship and originality of Dr Gregory Martin and his
collaborators in the slightly earlier Rheims-Douai version of
the Scriptures. Conversely, when Bishop Challoner, in the
eighteenth century, made his revision of Rheims-Douai he did
not hesitate to take over many readings from the AV. This is an
excellent example of the kind of cross-fertilisation that has always
gone on between the two churches.

One of the translators of the Authorized Version was Lancelot
Andrewes (1555-1626), bishop of Winchester, whose *Preces
Privatae* (not published until 1642) is one of the most celebrated
Anglican devotional works. A few manuscript copies seem to
have been in circulation during Andrewes's lifetime; one was in
the possession of Archbishop Laud. In his essay 'For Lancelot
Andrewes' T. S. Eliot says that Andrewes has 'a place second to
none in the history of the formation of the English Church'. In

these devotions the bishop draws on the Fathers, and on medieval writers, Greek liturgies, and the breviary and the missal. *Preces Privatae* contains forms for morning and evening prayers, prayers for the days of the week, devotions for holy communion, a form of preparation for confession, etc. The book was originally written in Latin; in Oxford Movement days it was translated anew by John Henry Newman and James Mason Neale.

Here is a brief extract from the section headed 'Praise' from Andrewes's prayers for Sunday. It will be recognised at once that it derives from the Preface to the Canon of the Mass in the *Missale Romanum*, and from the Order of Holy Communion in the Prayer Book.

> Up with your hearts;
> we lift them up unto the Lord
> As it is meet, and right, and fitting and due,
>   in all things and for all things.
> At all times, in all places, by all means
>   in every season, every spot,
>   every, everywhere, everyway
> To make mention of Thee, to worship Thee . . .
>   to give thanks to Thee
> Who art the Maker, Nourisher, Preserver,
> Governor,
> Protector, Author, Finisher of all . . .

In 1625 (temp. Charles I) Nicholas Ferrar, who had travelled much on the Continent, formed that remarkable, devout family-community at Little Gidding, which inspired T. S. Eliot's poem of that name, as earlier it had inspired J. H. Shorthouse's novel *John Inglesant*. The rule of corporate prayer and worship at Little Gidding, based on the Bible and the Prayer Book, and influenced by the Benedictine-monastic tradition, owed something to the Counter-Reformation also. In his travels on the continent Ferrar had encountered the Brothers of the Common Life and the Oratories of St Philip Neri. In Spain he had read the works of St Teresa, and among the books bound by the ladies of Little Gidding is a copy of St Francis of Sales's *Introduction to the Devout Life*.

In 1627 was published the *Collection of Private Devotions* by John Cosin, Master of Peterhouse and, from 1660, bishop of Durham. Cosin told the diarist John Evelyn that King Charles I had suggested to him the writing of this book since the Queen, Henrietta Maria, had remarked on the lack in the English church of books of devotion similar to the 'hours' of the breviary. The *Collection of Private Devotions* was written partly in the hope of preventing further secessions to Rome from among the Queen's ladies. (Cosin's own son was to go overseas to seek ordination in the Roman church.) To a large extent the *Devotions* are an adaptation of the old Primers—vernacular prayer books for the laity that had been authorised by Henry VIII, Edward VI, Queen Mary, and Queen Elizabeth in order to propagate and protect varying theological positions. Cosin's Preface to the *Devotions* states:

For the good and welfare of our souls, there is not in Christian Religion any thing of like continuall use and force throughout every Houre of our lives, as is the ghostly Exercise of *Prayer* and *Devotion*.

An Exercise it was, which the holy Apostles had often observed their Lord and Master to use, *Ever and anon to be still at his PRAYERS*; in the *MORNING* before day, in the *Evening* before night, and Otherwhiles to go out and spend the *whole Night* in Prayer . . .

A part of . . . ancient Pietie are THESE DAILY DEVOTIONS AND PRAYERS that hereafter follow . . .

1. . . . to continue and preserve the authority of the ancient Lawes, and the old godly *Canons* of the Church . . .

2. . . . to let the world understand that they who give it out, and accuse us here in ENGLAND to have set up a *New Church*, and a *New Faith*, to have abandoned All the *Ancient Formes of Piety and Devotion*, to have taken *away all the Religious Exercises and Prayers of our Forefathers*, to have despised *all the old Ceremonies*, and cast behind us the *Blessed Sacrament of Christe's Catholicke Church*: that these men doe little else but betray their owne infirmities, and have more violence and will, than reason or judgement for what they say . . .

3. . . . That they who are this way already religiously given. . . might have here a Daily and Devoute order of Private Prayer, wherein to exercise themselves, and to spend *some houres* of the day at least . . .

Cosin's book contains Tables of Fasting Days (thirteen in the year in addition to Lent, the Ember Days and Rogation Days, and all Fridays except within the octave of Christmas). The Precepts of the Church are listed: these include Holy Communion three times a year, preceded by confession and absolution if the need is felt. The Spiritual and Corporal Works of Mercy follow; then the Eight Beatitudes, Seven Deadly Sins (with contrary virtues), and the Four Last Things: Death, Judgement, Hell, and Heaven. The

morning prayers include the *Venite* (psalm 94), a translation of
the hymn from the breviary office of Prime ('Now that the Day-
Star doth arise': *Jam lucis orto sidere*), three psalms, a lesson from
the Book of Proverbs, and the Te Deum. The book also contains
the Seven Penitential Psalms, the Prayer Book Litany, the collects
for all Sundays and Holy Days, prayers for before and after holy
communion, and for confession, prayers for the King, for the sick
and dying, etc. Cosin also draws on texts from later Roman
Catholic theologians, and from the old Sarum missal and
breviary, and from the Elizabethan *Manual of Prayers* published
on the Queen's authority in 1583.

Cosin's *Collection of Private Devotions* was, not surprisingly,
heavily assailed by William Prynne, the Puritan, who said of it:
'That book . . . is altogether Popish.'

In even a cursory consideration of Caroline spirituality something must be said of George Herbert's manual of pastoral
theology *The Country Parson,* which was not published until
1652, nearly thirty years after Herbert's death. In this book he
achieved a neat balance between traditional Catholic theory and
practice and the insights of the Reformers. Thus in his chapter on
'The Parson's state of Life' he says: 'The Country Parson
considering that virginity is a higher state than Matrimony, and
that the Ministry requires the best and highest things, is rather
unmarryed than married. But yet as the temper of his body may
be, or as the temper of his Parish may be . . ., he is rather married
than unmarried.' In the following passage from the tenth chapter,
'The Parson in the Sacraments', he affirms the Real Presence of
Christ in the eucharist, though in language a good deal less
satisfactory than Aquinas's *non confractus, non concisus* (from
his Corpus Christi hymn *Lauda Sion*). Herbert's view concerning the admission of children to holy communion anticipates
that of St Pius X:

The Country Parson being to administer the Sacraments, is at a stand
with himself, how or what behaviour to assume for so holy things.
Especially at Communion time is he in great confusion, as being not only
to receive God, but to break, and administer him . . .

The time of everyones first receiving is not so much by yeers, as by
understanding: particularly, the rule may be this: When any one can
distinguish the Sacramental form from common bread, knowing the
Institution, and the difference, he ought to receive, of what age soever.

Two years previously, in 1650, there had appeared another famous work, Jeremy Taylor's *Holy Living*, to be followed by *Holy Dying*. Together these two books constitute a spiritual and literary classic, a work of moral theology that aims at supplying the devotional and ascetical needs of Anglicans. Taylor knew the works of St Ignatius of Loyola and St John of the Cross, and the *Devout Life* of St Francis of Sales. He frequently alludes to or borrows from the *Imitation of Christ*, which had first been done into English by Richard Whitford, 'the poor wretch of Syon', who had composed the Jesus Psalter. But Taylor does not follow the *Imitation*—which was originally written for the Augustinian Canons of the austere Windesheim Congregation in the Low Countries—in its spirit of rather severe monastic asceticism. Jeremy Taylor made use of Roman Catholic books with some reserve, saying: '. . . but yet our needs remain, and we cannot be well supplied out of the Roman storehouse; for though there the staple is, and very many excellent things exposed to view; yet we have found . . . the wares too often falsified.'

On the Roman side, the year 1657 saw the publication of *Sancta Sophia*, or *Holy Wisdom*, 'methodically digested' from the literary remains of Dom Augustine Baker, the Welsh Benedictine (1575-1641) by his confrère Dom Serenus (Hugh Paulinus) Cressy, a former Anglican dean of Windsor. *Sancta Sophia* is the last classic work of spirituality in direct succession from the 14th century school of English mysticism. Written primarily, though not exclusively, for monks and nuns, it has always had readers among the laity, both Anglican and Catholic. Thus in a letter of January 1909 Evelyn Underhill, the Anglican writer on mysticism, says: 'I am so glad you like *Holy Wisdom*. I think it very solid and trustworthy.' And in a letter of November 1930 she speaks of 'that wise old saint Augustine Baker'. Father Baker was steeped in the teaching of the 6th century mystical theologian known as Dionysius, or Denis, the Pseudo-Areopagite, which had been extensively drawn on by Walter Hilton and the author of *The Cloud of Unknowing*, whose works Baker possessed. Father Baker's commentary on the *Cloud* is very much in the spirit of Hilton. For Baker 'A spiritual life consists in following the Divine light and impulses, in humbling and subjecting the soul to God and to all creatures according to his will in loving God above all things, in pursuing prayer and performing it according to Divine guidance—all qualities proceeding from the Divine operation, a state into which none but the Holy Spirit could bring the soul' (Baker, *The Inner Life of Dame Gertrude More*). Writing here chiefly for nuns—the English Benedictine Dames in Cambrai—he teaches that faithfulness to the ordinary round of monastic life makes much self-examination and formal methods of prayer unnecessary. Ordinary faults and failings are best dealt with by entrusting them to the purifying action of God's love—which is what St John of the Cross teaches also.

On the Anglican side a book that was to be a popular companion to the Bible and the Prayer Book for over 150 years was *The Whole Duty of Man*. This work, of uncertain authorship, appeared round about 1658 and is a set of discourses, intended for lay people, on Christian morals. Its standards are exacting. Instructions are given for the careful reception of holy communion; confession is taken for granted. Prayer is taught as being easy if only people will give their mind to it. 'Prayer is a pleasant duty . . .'

Let us pass on to the eighteenth century, so commonly thought of, not without some justification, as a spiritually barren century. In 1728 was published one of the most delightful of all works of Anglican spirituality, William Law's *A Serious Call to a Devout and Holy Life*. Modelled somewhat on the *Devout Life* of St Francis of Sales, it possesses something of the same kind of charm. Like Jeremy Taylor, William Law was a Non-Juror. In 1737 he defended the doctrine of the Real Presence against Benjamin Hoadly, the Latitudinarian bishop of Bangor. Here is a pleasing specimen of Law's manner, taken from chapter xv of the *Serious Call*, 'Of chanting or singing of psalms in our private devotions'.

You have seen . . . what means . . . you are to use, to raise and improve your devotion . . .
There is one thing still remaining . . . and that is to begin all your prayers with a psalm . . .
I do not mean, that you should ever read over a psalm, but that you should chant or sing one of those psalms, which we commonly call the reading psalms. For singing is as much the proper use of a psalm as devout supplication is the proper use of a form of prayer; and a psalm only read is very much like a prayer that is only looked over.

Now the method of chanting a psalm, such as is used in the colleges, in the universities, and in some churches, is such as all persons are capable of . . .

For there is nothing that so clears a way for your prayers, nothing that so disperses dullness of heart, nothing that so purifies the soul from poor and little passions, nothing that so opens heaven, or carries your heart so near it, as these songs of praise.

Law was influenced by the teachings of the Rhineland mystics of the 14th century, notably the Dominican John Tauler and the Augustinian canons John Ruysbroeck and Thomas à Kempis. (Later he came under the spell of the Protestant mystic Jakob Boehme.) Law's contemporary Samuel Johnson thought very highly of the *Serious Call*. He told Boswell that when at Oxford he had taken up this book expecting to find it dull, and perhaps laughable. 'But I found Law quite an overmatch for me; and this was the first occasion of my thinking in earnest of religion, after I became capable of rational enquiry.' And on another occasion he recommended Law's book as 'the finest piece of hortatory theology in the language'. Johnson had a tenderness for the Roman church, and numbered many Catholics among his friends. He lived within a quarter of a mile of the lodgings of Dr Richard Challenor, titular bishop of Debra *in partibus infidelium* and vicar-apostolic of the London District, but they never met. Challenor was obliged to court obscurity, and to live to some extent in hiding, to avoid the notice of informers who might, for monetary gain, invoke the penal laws against him.

Challenor's task was to hold together the oppressed adherents of the 'Old Religion' in their darkest hour. It has been estimated that by the mid-eighteenth century there were barely 100,000 Roman Catholics left in the country; but the holy bishop one day said to his chaplain, Mr Barnard: 'There will be a new people.' Challenor gave the English Catholics a new and more readable version of the Bible, and translations of St Augustine's *Confessions*, the *Imitation of Christ*, St Francis of Sales' *The Devout Life*, and St Teresa's autobiography. He provided them with a revised Catechism, which remained in general use at least down to 1945, and which is still in print. His popular prayer book *The Garden of the Soul* has enjoyed a similar span of life, as has his famous *Meditations for Every Day in the Year*, first published in 1753. These three-point meditations aim, he says, to set forth the great truths of the Christian religion 'in their plain native colours'. They 'are not designed to be a matter of barren study, or speculation of the brain; but to be the seeds of pious affections in the heart; which affections are looked upon by spiritual writers as the principal part of mental prayer, as tending directly to bring the soul to her God, and to unite her to him by divine love . . . Mental prayer, by the way of meditation, is very easy, even to the meanest capacities; it requires nothing but a good will, a sincere desire of conversing with God, by thinking of him and loving him . . .; and who is there that can even live without *thinking* and *loving*?'

Robert Wilson, Warden of Keble College, Oxford, in its early days, says that the plan of his book of devotions *Before the Altar*, and many of the prayers in it, are taken from Challenor's *Garden of the Soul*. Lord Halifax, one of the Anglican representatives at the Malines Conversations, used Challenor's *Meditations* on the recommendation of Canon Liddon. Probably it was on Lord Halifax's recommendation that in 1915 the Society of SS. Peter and Paul, Anglo-Catholic publishers, issued an elegant india-paper edition of Challenor's *Meditations*, printed at the Oxford University Press in the typeface designed by Bishop Fell, one of the possible authors of *The Whole Duty of Man*.

Dr Johnson's prayers and meditations have often been reprinted. He was a very exact and observant churchman, always most careful in his preparations for holy communion, and in keeping the fast days enjoined by the Prayer Book. In his diary for 17th April, 1778, Good Friday, he says: 'When we came home from church in the afternoon we had tea, and I ate two buns, being somewhat uneasy with fasting, and not being alone. If I had not been observed I should probably have fasted.' Johnson had an attraction to the monastic life; something that had been lacking in the English church since the Dissolution of the Monasteries under Henry VIII. It was not until 1870 that Father Ignatius of Llanthony (Joseph Leycester Lyne) established his Benedictine monastery at Capel-y-ffin; in the Roman communion, of course, monks and friars had continued an underground existence in England, in small numbers; missionaries, like Father Augustine Baker, ministering to the oppressed Catholic minority, mostly living in hired lodgings, frequently changed, and with no possibility of regular community life. Dr Johnson doubted the wisdom of vows, but it was a saying of his that 'I never read of a monastery but I could fall on my knees to kiss the pavement.'

By the end of the 18th century the Church of England was spiritually at a low ebb. John Wesley had found the churches closed to him, and so had had to begin his field-preaching. The Clapham Sect (Venn, Wilberforce, Zachary Macaulay, and others) had begun to promote the Evangelical Revival. Then came the Oxford Movement, which in spite of the secession to Rome of John Henry Newman, Robert Wilberforce, Henry Edward Manning, and others, kept up the endeavour to restore to the English church a consciousness of its Catholic heritage. Initially the concern of the Tractarians was the recovery of Catholic dogma, especially in respect of the Sacraments and the Apostolic Succession. The next step was the restoration of Catholic worship. Only when these were secured was it possible for the restoration of Catholic devotion to follow. In this context the greatest name is that of Edward Bouverie Pusey, who was by no means the dry-as-dust theologian that he has sometimes been taken for. Dr Owen Chadwick, in his introduction to his anthology *The Mind of the Oxford Movement,* says that 'If we think of the Catholic Movement in the Church of England as consisting in a doctrine of authority, a pastoral concern for worship, sacraments, and new modes of sanctification, derived from wider sources than those common within Protestantism (priestly ideals, retreats, confession, devotional books, ways of private prayer, and the like), then Pusey should be principally associated with this last. He it was who in the years after 1841 and 1842 translated and adapted continental books of devotion for English usage. He did more than anyone to encourage the revival of the monastic life, and was in the closest touch with the new foundations of nuns.' Pusey has been called the *doctor mysticus* of the Oxford Movement, for his emphasis on the Church as the mystical body of Christ, on the union of the Christian soul with its redeemer, and the eucharist as the vehicle of the divine indwelling.

The Roman church seems to have been more successful than the English in providing forms of popular worship that can appeal to simple and sophisticated people alike. In theory the Prayer

Book had got rid of the 'twofold office'; that is, one form of worship for the clerks in the choir of the parish, collegiate, or monastery church; another for the people in the nave. But beyond a vernacular communion office and morning and evening prayer it had relatively little to offer, even though hymn singing had been introduced into the Prayer Book rites. By contrast, Roman Catholics had a wealth of para-liturgical services: Benediction of the Blessed Sacrament, Stations of the Cross, the Forty Hours' Prayer, Novenas etc.; but these have now largely fallen into desuetude, as a result of the current puritanism and iconoclasm affecting the Roman church. Some of these devotions were taken up in Anglo-Catholic churches, where they still survive. Pilgrimages to sacred shrines and sites, however, seem to be still popular in both communions. The pilgrimage to Walsingham, first revived by Anglicans, is now a major Catholic event as well; and both communions now have regular pilgrimages to Glastonbury and other ancient sanctuaries. Popular with both communions, largely because of its ease of access from London, is the Roman Catholic shrine of St Simon Stock at Aylesford, in spite of its having had no special significance in medieval times.

    Retreats, a Roman Catholic post-Reformation phenomenon which can be traced to the Spiritual Exercises of St Ignatius of Loyola, have long enjoyed great popularity in the Anglican communion. As in the Roman church, the conducting of retreats has become in a special, though not exclusive, way the province of the regular clergy: monks, friars, and clerks regular. Two of the most admired and loved retreat conductors of our own day were the Dominican Father Vincent McNabb and the Anglican Franciscan Father Andrew, of the Society of the Divine Compassion. Here are two short passages taken from the printed text of their retreat conferences. First, Father McNabb, speaking on verse three of the second chapter of St Matthew's gospel.

There was no room for them in the inn . . . No room for God! . . . In a sense our failure to go on to perfection is our denying God the right to come into all the rooms of our soul, putting Him perhaps with the cattle in the stable, and not with our chosen friends in the banquet-room. Looking back on a year, some of us on a life-time, we can begin to ask ourselves, does this phrase mean anything to us? Is there any way in which there was no room for Him in our soul? . . .

    I don't think anyone turns God out of the soul. God isn't turned out.

He is crowded out . . .

To add anything to the Gospel phrases seems to insult their perfect simplicity. I just want to go to our Lord and say Imagine my crowding you out! What a tomfool I have been! I have made room for this, that or the other, some human desires, and imagined my soul widened, when I was denying a place to you, the Infinite![6]

And now Father Andrew.

I must be detached with relation to past and future. I must not look back to, and sigh for, things that are taken from me, or persons I have had to leave, in such a way that I want to possess them again for myself. I must not fret if I cannot finish the things I set out to do. That must be left wholly in God's hands, or I have not yet learnt detachment. If I have, then I, my past, my present, my future, are wholly in God's hands, and in his hands are perfectly safe.

Three things must pass completely out of my life if I am to attain to true detachment: (1) the passionate desire to possess; (2) all sense of resentment and discontent with regard to people and things; (3) all fear and ambition for the future. 'The Lord gave, and the Lord hath taken away. Blessed be the Name of the Lord.'

Someone who did much to help many in both churches as a counsellor and guide in their life of prayer was the Roman Catholic Baron Friedrich von Hügel, who died in 1935. In his book *The Life of Prayer* the Baron tells us that:

The decisive preparation for prayer lies not in the prayer itself, but in the life prior to the prayer. That is, distractions and dryness, indeed even the real fruitlessness in and of our prayer, spring largely from our faulty dispositions, doings, and driftings when out of prayer. The cure for such faults committed out of prayer, and for their effects upon and within prayer, lies in the very wise ordering, and in the very faithful execution of such ordering, of our active life . . .

After practising a daily 3-point meditation for some 25 years, the new Helper sent to me by God advised me that my prayer should now be mainly informal—more of the prayer of quiet type; but that there should always remain short vocal prayers morning and night, Mass and Holy Communion twice a week, with Confession once a week or once a fortnight; and (perhaps most characteristic point of all) one decade of the rosary every day—this especially to help prevent my interior life from losing touch with the devotion of the people. After over thirty years of this mixed régime, I am properly convinced of the penetrating sagacity of this advice.

Here we must bring this survey to an end. In recent years the writings on prayer of the Anglican C. S. Lewis have won for themselves many Catholic readers, while many Anglicans have been attracted to the spiritual writings of the Cistercian monk Thomas Merton and the Jesuit Pierre Teilhard de Chardin. Whether these writers will hold the field in the way that Jeremy Taylor, William Law, Augustine Baker, and Richard Challenor have done it is impossible to say. The spirit breathes where it will. But certainly this scriptural, sacramental, incarnational tradition of prayer, or spirituality, which may rightly be called Catholic, is the common heritage of the two churches, English and Roman. And behind this common life of prayer lies a common faith that subsists in the two communions, notwithstanding the issues that divide them.

NOTES

1. Rupert Davies, 'The Spirituality of Ecumenism', in *Christian Spirituality: Essays in honour of Gordon Rupp*, edited by Peter Brooks: London, SCM, 1975.

2. The Thirty-nine Articles of Religion, appended to the Book of Common Prayer.

3. A. Welby Pugin, *An Earnest Address on the Establishment of the Hierarchy*: London, Charles Dolman, 1851.

4. His name is usually spelled Persons, but it is to be pronounced 'Parsons'.

5. H. Thurston, 'Catholic Writers and Elizabethan Readers', in *The Month*, December, 1894. Many of Persons's books, mostly works of religious controversy, were published either anonymously or pseudonymously, for reasons of security. This was a usual proceeding among Catholic recusant writers.

6. Vincent McNabb, O.P., 'Room for God', in *In Our Valley*: London, Burns Oates and Washbourne, 1938.

7. Father Andrew, S.D.C., 'Detachment', in *In the Silence: Four Retreats*: London, Mowbray, 1947.